MASTERS OF THE KEYBOARD

I. PADEREWSKI

MASTERS
of
THE KEYBOARD

by

DONALD BROOK

GREENWOOD PRESS, PUBLISHERS
WESTPORT, CONNECTICUT

Originally published in 1946
by Rockliff, London

Reprinted from an original copy in the collections
of the Brooklyn Public Library

First Greenwood Reprinting 1971

Library of Congress Catalogue Card Number 75-114479

SBN 8371-4768-9

Printed in the United States of America

CONTENTS

CONTENTS

PART II
SOME PROMINENT PIANISTS IN BRITAIN TO-DAY

ILLUSTRATIONS

ILLUSTRATIONS

INTRODUCTORY NOTE

THESE sketches are mainly biographical, but most of them also contain information concerning the technique and methods of the artists concerned, which will, I hope, be of some help to those who wish to trace the development of the pianistic art. This is not, however, intended to be a musical text-book.

The length of each sketch has been determined solely by the amount of biographical and other material that in my opinion would interest the reader, and does not in any way reflect the status of the biographee.

DONALD BROOK.

London,
Summer, 1945

PART I

GREAT VIRTUOSI OF THE PAST

Dr. John Bull

IT is appropriate that this book should open with a sketch of a representative of the glorious Tudor period—the Golden Age of both English music and literature, and it is fortunate that the greatest executant of this age was an unusually interesting character : Dr. John Bull, whose name since the beginning of the eighteenth century has been used to describe some of the best characteristics of the Briton, and who is still regarded by millions as the composer of the National Anthem, for he wrote a piece of music for the clavier that closely resembles the tune adopted for our national hymn.

He was born of good yeoman stock at Wellow, Somerset, in 1562. His father's house was frequented by the famous merchant adventurers of the West country, and as a boy he would listen enthralled to their tales of high seas and strange distant lands when after supper they gathered around the huge open fireplace and recalled their experiences. Contact with men of this type played an important part in the shaping of his character, for he was no effeminate musician of the *salon*. At the same time, he was profoundly moved by the folksongs he heard in the quiet little Somerset villages in the vicinity of his home.

That he was a remarkably intelligent, accomplished boy is proved by the fact that he was only ten years old when he was chosen as one of the Children of the Chapel Royal, and came under the influence of William Blitheman, the Organist and Master of Song, who perceived that he had " a natural genie to the faculty " and who " spared neither time nor labour to advance it to the utmost." Blitheman was an extremely good teacher, a reputable composer and a brilliant organist :

> " Whom all took greate delighte to heare
> Him on the Organs playe."

Under the guidance of this able musician the boy acquired a wide knowledge of his art and became highly proficient on all the keyboard instruments. It is not surprising, therefore, to find that he was barely twenty when he was appointed organist of Hereford Cathedral, and shortly afterwards, Master of the Choristers.

While he was at Hereford his fame as a performer on the virginals began to spread all over the country, and he was also esteemed as one of the greatest composers for that instrument. One of his best friends in those days was Nathaniel Giles, the organist of Worcester Cathedral ; a gifted musician famous for his " Descant of thirtie-eighte Proportions of sundrie

13

kindes," in whose house he met Elway Bevin (a pupil of Thomas Tallis) who was later to become the organist of Bristol Cathedral, author of *A Briefe and Short Introduction to the Art of Musicke*, and composer of some excellent cathedral music[1]. He also wrote for the virginals, notably a little piece called *Bevin, His Fancy*, and for viols.

Various disputes between Bull and the Custos and Vicars of the College at Hereford caused his friend Blitheman to recommend him for appointment as a Gentleman of the Chapel Royal, and he was sworn in during January, 1585. Queen Elizabeth, who remembered him as one of the Children of the Chapel, took an interest in him and made him one of her chamber musicians. A contemporary recorded an incident that occurred one day when the Queen was playing a few of his compositions on the virginals : " The queenes will beinge to knowe the sayd musicke, her Grace was at that tyme at the virginalls : whereupon, hee, beinge in attendaunce, Master Bull did come by stealthe to heare without, and by mischaunce did sprawle intoe the queenes Maiesties Presence, to the queenes great disturbance. Shee demaunding incontinent the wherefore of such presumption, Master Bull with greate skill sayd that wheresoever Maiesty and Musicke so well combyned, no man mighte abase himself too deeplie ; whereupon the queenes Maiesty was mollifyde and sayd that so rayre a Bull hath songe as sweet as Byrd. So by Gods will and greate fortune it came to pass that distresse was turned to mirthe."

Political activities for the Queen were combined with the study of music at this time. In 1586 he acquired a degree of bachelor of music at Oxford, being recognized by the University as a " Person who had a most prodigious hand on the Organ " and who was " famous throughout the religious world for his Church music." He appears to have toured extensively as a virtuoso, for there is no lack of reports extolling him as " the first performer in the world," and suchlike, though it has been suggested that he gave recitals in various places as a cloak for espionage activities undertaken for the Court to augment his income. He was certainly very extravagant, and had no qualms about appealing to the Queen for financial assistance.

After the death of Blitheman in 1590, Bull became the Organist and Master of Song at the Chapel Royal. He was then honoured by Cambridge University with a doctor's degree, and a similar distinction was conferred by Oxford University shortly afterwards.

Bull's salary at the Chapel Royal was but forty pounds a year—equivalent to about three hundred to-day—and on April 20th, 1591, he was obliged to petition for a lease in reversion worth thirty pounds a year " to relieve his greate povertie, which altogether hindereth his studies."

It was the Queen's influence that secured Dr. Bull the first professorship in music at the newly-founded Gresham College in 1597 despite his inability

---

[1] His fine service in D is still in use at many cathedrals to-day.

14

DR. JOHN BULL

(or unwillingness) to read the first part of his lectures in Latin as prescribed by the will of the founder. For his special benefit, the terms of his tenure were amended—probably at the Queen's command—so that the clause concerned ran :

" The solemn Musicke lecture, to be read twice every weeke, in manner following, *viz.*, the theorique part for one half houre, or thereabouts, and the practique, by consort of voice or instrument for the reste of the houre ; whereof the first lecture to be in the Latine tongue and the seconde in the English. . . . But because at this time Mr. Dr. Bull, who is recommended to the place by the Queenes Moste Excellent Maiestie, beinge not able to speak Latin, his lectures are permitted to be altogether in English, so long as hee shall continue in the place of musicke lecturer there."

In addition to this appointment, which carried a salary greater than that of Organist of the Chapel Royal, the Queen gave him an annuity in 1597 totalling over ten pounds a year drawn from certain land in the counties of York, Surrey, Lancashire, Derby and Anglesey : a sure indication of the favour he enjoyed.

Dr. Bull's hasty departure from this country in 1601 has been attributed to trouble at Court by some, and to a mission of espionage for Elizabeth by others, but the fact remains that he proceeded to Calais, and then spent a great deal of time travelling in France, Belgium, Germany and the Netherlands. For what it is worth, I will quote Anthony à Wood's record of his visit to St. Omer :

"At length, hearing of a famous musician belonging to a certain cathedral (St. Omer's, as I have heard) he applied himself as a novice to him, to learn something of his faculty and to see and admire his works. This musician, after some discourse had passed between them, conducted Bull to a vestry or musick school joyning to the cathedral and shew'd him a lesson or song of forty parts, and then made a vaunting challenge to any person in the world to add one more part to them ; supposing it to be so compleat and full, that it was impossible for any mortal man to correct, or add to t. Bull thereupon desiring the use of ink and rul'd paper (such as we call musick paper) prayed the musician to lock him up in the said school for two or three hours ; which being done, not without great disdain by the musician, Bull in that time, or less, added forty more parts to the said lesson or song. The musician thereupon being called in, he viewed it, try'd it, and retry'd it. At length he burst out into a great ecstasy, and swore by the great God that he that added those forty parts must either be the Devil or Dr. John Bull, etc. Whereupon Bull making himself known, the musician fell down and ador'd him.[1]"

[1] A story something like this concerning Liszt's genius as a pianist will be found later in this book. Such tales are not without interest but their degree of accuracy often leaves much to be desired.

It is almost certain that Bull was received by Henry IV, King of France, for the monarch was keenly interested in music, and it is said that he played at the French court, making a sensation by producing a work of his own that could not only be played backwards with equal effect, but upside down as well !

In Germany he was the guest of the Duke and Duchess of Brunswick. As evidence of this we have two pieces for the virginals, *Almayn, the Duke of Brunswickes Toye* and *The Dutchess of Brunswickes Delighte.*

At Amsterdam, Bull met the eminent Dutch composer, J. P. Sweelinck, who was also a brilliant executant. They found much in common and soon became great friends ; each influencing the other's style of composition.

Bull was back in London for the funeral of Queen Elizabeth in 1603, and retained his offices when James I came to the throne. At first, the changed circumstances at Court were very distasteful to him, but in time he adapted himself, and on December 31st, 1606, " the Kinges Docktor of Musicke," as he was known, was one of the favoured servants to receive " gold chaines, plates and medales."

In December, 1606, Bull was admitted to membership of the famous Merchant Taylors' Company, and was called upon to play an important part in the great ceremony of July 1607, when the Company entertained the King and Prince of Wales. The magnificent banquet was described in detail by Stowe, who informs us that the King dined in an apartment adjacent to the great hall " in which chamber was placed a very rich paier of Organs whereupon Mr. John Bull, Doctor of Musique and a Brother of this company, did play all the dynner time and Mr. Nathaniel Giles, Master of the Children of the Kynges Chappell, together with diuers singing men and children of the said Chappell, did sing melodious songs at the said dynner."

The " moste excellent melodie " composed by Bull for the occasion won him the highest esteem of his fellow members of the Company, whose records tell us that " Dr. Bull was admitted into the Lyvery of the Worshipfull the Merchant Taylor Company, and the Lyvery hoodes put upon his shoulders but not sworne ; this fauor was done him for havinge composed the Musique which was performed at their Hall by the Gentlemen and Children of the Kynges Chappell when his Maiesty King James the first, Prince Henry and many Honourable Persons dined there on Thursdaie July 16, 1607."

In the same year Bull was obliged to resign his professorship at Gresham College because on December 22nd he applied for a licence to marry " Elizabeth Walter, of the Strand, maiden, aged about twentie-foure . . ." and no married men were allowed to hold office at the College. That so virile, handsome and witty a man should have waited until he reached the age of forty-five to get married is rather curious, but he was a restless

AN ÆTAT

II. DR. JOHN BULL

III. J. S. BACH

IV.   DOMENICO SCARLATTI

V.   J. S. BACH

VI.   THE DEATH OF MOZART, after O'Neill

VII.   (Below) MORNING PRAYER WITH J. S. BACH

VIII. MOZART AS A CHILD

IX. MOZART

X.   IGNATZ MOSCHELES, from a painting by Felix Moscheles

XI. CHOPIN, after Scheffer

XII.   CHOPIN, from the painting by Delacroix

XIII.   LISZT

Rischgitz

XIV. LISZT

ischgitz

XV. CLARA SCHUMANN (Clara Wieck)

XVI.   CLARA SCHUMANN

XVII.   RUBINSTEIN, from the painting by Felix Moscheles

Photo by H. S. Mendelssohn

XVIII. LESCHETIZKY

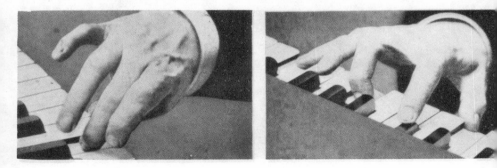

By courtesy of Messrs. Schott & C

XIX. LESCHETIZKY'S HANDS

XX. BUSONI

Elliott & F

XXI. PADEREWSKI

XXII. RACHMANINOFF

XXIII. RACHMANINOFF'S HANDS

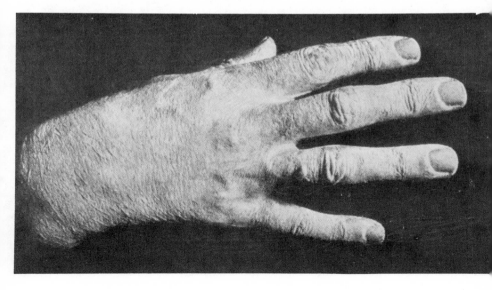

XXIV. LISZT'S HANDS from a Plaster Cast at Weimer

character, and holding a somewhat glamorous position at Court, he probably enjoyed so many *affaires* that while the wild oats lasted they were to be preferred to the more sedate pleasures of matrimony. Elizabeth, twenty-one years his junior, was probably something of a prize, for she inspired him to write a piece for virginals, *Moste Sweete and Fayre*. Moreover, by making her his wife, Bull had to renounce the handsome income from the College.

His sacrifice was duly rewarded, however. Prince Henry heard of his resignation from the College and immediately invited him to become one of his household musicians at a salary not very much less than the income attached to his professorship.

A lullaby for virginals called *Bull's Goodnighte* was inspired by the son that arrived in due course, but within the following year a tragedy smashed his happiness : Elizabeth died giving birth to a second child, stillborn.

In 1611 Dr. Bull shared with William Byrd and Orlando Gibbons the honour of having compositions published in the first volume of music printed from engraved plates, the famous *Parthenia* " or The Maydenhead of the first musicke that euer was printed for the Virginalls Composed By three famous Masters, William Byrd, Dr. John Bull and Orlando Gibbons, Gentilmen of his Maiesties most illustrious Chappell. Ingrauen by William Hole."

Soon after the death of Prince Henry in November, 1613, Dr. Bull suddenly left his post, went to Brussels, and accepted an appointment as organist at the archducal Chapel Royal. The Cheque Book of our own Chapel Royal recorded his departure thus : " John Bull, doctor of Musicke, went beyond the seas without licence and was admitted into the Archdukes service and entered into paie there about Michaelmas, and Peter Hopkins a Base from Poules[1] was sworne in his place the 27 of December followinge : his wages from Michaelmas unto the daie of the swearinge of the sayd Peter Hopkins was disposed of by the Deanne of his Maiesties sayd Chappell."

King James's annoyance at Bull's precipitate action may be judged by the demand for his extradition made by Sir William Trumbull, the English Ambassador at Brussels, who described his interview with the Archduke in a letter to James dated May 30th, 1614, which ran : " . . . I tolde him that I had charge from your Maiestie to acquaint him that your Maiestie upon knowledge of his receiuing Dr. Bull . . . without your Maiesties permission or consent . . . that your Maiestie did justly find it strange as you were his friend and ally, and had neuer used the like proceedinge either towardes him or any other foraign prince, addinge that the like course was not practysed among priuate persons, much less among these of greater place and dignity, and I tolde him plainly that it was notorious to all the worlde that the sayd Bull did not leaue your Maiesties service for any wrong done unto him or

---

[1] A bass singer from St. Paul's.

for matter of religion, under which fained pretext he now sought to wrong the reputation of your Maiesties justice, but did in that dishonest manner steale out of England through the guilte of a corrupte conscience, to escape the punishment, which notoriously he had deserued, and was designed to haue been inflicted on him by the hande of justice for his incontinence, fornication, adultery and other grieuous crimes."

This slanderous attempt to injure Dr. Bull convinced the Archduke of nothing, for he was as well acquainted with Trumbull's fabrications as with Bull's integrity. However, Bull did not stay in his service for long because in 1617 he succeeded Romold Waelrent as organist of Antwerp Cathedral, although he remained on very friendly terms with the Archduke, who had a palace in that city.

The restless musician seemed settled at last, for in that charming Flemish city he met Rubens, the great painter, and also enjoyed the friendship of that brilliant English composer, Peter Philips, who spent most of his later life in Brussels and Antwerp. He was also able to keep in close touch with his friend Sweelinck of Amsterdam, with whom he is considered to have inaugurated the wonderful period of contrapuntal keyboard music which culminated in the supreme genius of the immortal J. S. Bach. He died at Antwerp in March, 1628, and was buried in the Cathedral he had served in his closing years.

J. S. Bach

THERE are already so many excellent biographies of J. S. Bach in existence that an attempt to tell the whole story of his life in this modest volume would be superfluous. Instead, I will concentrate upon those of his activities that had a significant effect upon the development of the pianistic art. Unlike Mozart and other executants in this book, Bach was not a " public " virtuoso, and as the pianoforte was in his time still in its infancy, he always preferred to use the clavichord, yet his contribution to the art was too important to be overlooked by anybody concerned with the evolution of keyboard technique.

Johann Sebastian Bach, the supreme genius of that wonderful family of Thuringian musicians, was born at Eisenach on March 21st, 1685, and was left an orphan before he was ten years old. His eldest brother, Johann Christoph, a church organist, became his guardian and taught him to play the harpsichord. He received his general education at the Ohrdruf Lyceum, and distinguished himself there as a chorister. At fifteen he went as a salaried descantist to the convent of St. Michael, Lüneberg, but soon after his arrival his voice broke, and he might have been compelled to leave had not his unusual skill as an instrumentalist been noticed by the Cantor. Bach was therefore appointed accompanist for the rehearsals, and was also expected to play the violin. He was allowed plenty of time for study, and did not waste a minute of it. The convent possessed an exceptionally fine music library which was of the utmost value to him, and he worked with prodigious energy. He also came under the influence of two organists : Böhm of St. John's Church, and Loewe of St. Nicholas's, and by making occasional journeys to Hamburg, thirty miles distant, became acquainted with Reinken, another distinguished organist, who encouraged his early efforts at composition. Bach was also sufficiently enlightened to appreciate the value of French music in his time, and there is evidence that he would travel as far as sixty miles to hear the band attached to the ducal court at Celle.

When he was eighteen, Bach received an invitation from Johann Ernst, the younger brother of Duke Wilhelm Ernst, to become one of the court musicians at Weimar : he was given the title *Hofmusikus* and was expected to play the violin in the orchestra. Soon after his arrival at Weimar he visited Arnstadt to try the new organ in the church of St. Boniface. While he was playing, various members of the Consistory entered the building and could not fail to compare the glorious strains produced by this talented youth with the poor, clumsy playing of their own organist. They came to a decision quickly, and making immediate arrangements for their present organist to do other duties, they offered Bach the post.

The pleasure derived by the young organist from this appointment was further enhanced when he was allowed to take over the instruction of the small choir-school and to play occasionally in the band employed by Count Anton Günther at Neideck Castle nearby. This nobleman also had a private theatre in which operettas were performed from time to time, and there is little doubt that Bach found scope for his remarkable talents here as well. It was while he was at Arnstadt that Bach's pre-eminence as an organist became generally recognized : he soon found that there was nobody in that part of the country who could compete with him, much less teach him anything. Moreover, he began to find scope for his compositions.

But self-satisfaction was not one of Bach's qualities, and towards the end of 1705 we find him applying for a month's leave of absence so that he could make the two-hundred mile journey to Lübeck *on foot* in order to study the technique of Buxtehude, who was then one of the greatest organists in the world. The musical life of Lübeck was so agreeable to him that he overstayed his leave by three months, and when he returned to Arnstadt he had some difficulty in explaining his conduct. This strained his relations with the Consistory, and as he found it almost impossible to conceal his impatience with the somewhat stupid members of his choir, he applied for the important post of organist at the church of St. Blasius, Mühlhausen. He was successful and took up his duties there in September, 1707. A month later he returned to Arnstadt to marry his cousin Maria Barbara Bach.

Disappointment was soon to come in his new work, however. There arose a religious dispute between the Pietists and the Old Lutherans, and Bach, of course, sided with the latter, because the former regarded all art as " worldly " and therefore something to be discouraged. The situation soon became intolerable, and he decided to return to Weimar as court organist and chamber musician to Duke Wilhelm Ernst. Here, the environment was almost ideal, for his employer was a man of culture, and the organ at the palace was a good instrument, though small.

Bach's chamber duties included the playing of the harpsichord and violin in the company of the other court musicians : about twenty in all. He had by that time become so accomplished an executant on the clavier that he once boasted to his friend Johann Walther that he could play absolutely anything correctly at first sight. This induced Walther to compose a piece that was almost impossible to play at all. When it was finished he left it casually on his harpsichord and invited Bach to breakfast. While the meal was being prepared, Bach noticed the piece and sat down to play it.

J. S. BACH

He got through about a dozen bars and then had to give up, solemnly informing his friend that of course no man on earth could guarantee to play *everything* at first sight !

While he was at Weimar, Bach became interested in Italian instrumental music, and this afterwards influenced him when he wrote some of his clavier concertos, suites for violin, and so forth. He also arranged sixteen of Vivaldi's violin concertos for the harpsichord.

Although Bach was composing assiduously, it was as an organist that his fame spread throughout north and central Germany, for he frequently made tours to try different organs. In 1713 he visited Halle and gave such a magnificent performance upon the large sixty-three-stop organ in the Liebfrauenkirche that he was offered the position of organist, and he might have accepted it if the salary had not been inadequate. An expedition to Cassel in the following year gave him an opportunity to play before Prince Friedrich (subsequently King of Sweden) who withdrew one of his most precious rings and gave it to the young organist.

Three years later, Bach happened to be in Dresden for the opera season when Jean Louis Marchand, the eminent French organist arrived. Marchand was the organist at Versailles and was tremendously popular in Paris ; an unusually vain creature. It was not long before the Dresden musicians began to argue whether Bach was not greater than this distinguished visitor, and eventually a musical contest was arranged. In great excitement a brilliant company of musicians assembled on the appointed day, and Bach arrived punctually only to find that Marchand was not present. About an hour later it was discovered that the French organist had left the town in great haste just after dawn !

In the summer of 1717 Bach accepted a musical directorship offered by Prince Leopold of Anhalt-Cöthen, an old enemy of Duke Wilhelm Ernst, chiefly because he had been passed over when a new director of music was required at Weimar. The Duke was furious, and in an attempt to prevent Bach from leaving his service, arrested him and sent him to prison. The great musician was an extremely obstinate fellow, however, and refused to submit to the Duke's will, so in the following December he was released.

At Cöthen Bach was required to perform not upon the organ but upon the clavichord, and he made his great contribution to the art of the clavichordist by revolutionizing the system of fingering. This is where Bach becomes of special importance in the evolution of keyboard technique. At the beginning of the seventeenth century there was no definite method of playing on keyed instruments, in fact Michael Prætorius declared that if a note were produced clearly and agreeably to the ear, it was a matter of indifference how it was done, even if the performer played it with his nose.

21

It was not until the eighteenth century that any sort of system became general : up to that time the thumb was almost entirely excluded from use— although Purcell timidly suggested that it should be employed in his *Choice Collection of Lessons for the Harpsichord*—and the little finger was but rarely brought into operation. The reason, of course, was due to the difference in length between the three middle fingers and the thumb and little finger. The early keyboard players had to acquire considerable skill in passing one finger over another, and the frequency with which they did so has often puzzled those who have made a study of the music written for the virginals, spinet and harpsichord. It must be remembered, however, that the " fall " of the keys of these instruments was little more than half the depth to which we are accustomed on the modern piano, and therefore it was much easier to pass the fingers one over another. Nevertheless, the neglect of the thumb and little finger necessitated frequent twisting of the hands, and here and there in the early keyboard music we find phrasing that was obviously dictated by the old system of fingering. Bach saw the absurdity of this tradition, and began to make full use of the thumb and little finger. This necessitated the bending of the fingers so that their tips rested perpendicularly upon the keys, thus superseding the old rigidity and giving the fingers a comfortable position that promoted elasticity. It also brought the hand forward and raised the wrists, so that it became possible to give the keys a sharp blow instead of heavy pressure, a matter of the utmost importance when the harpsichord was superseded by the pianoforte, that is, when " touch " became an art in itself.

Bach was one of the first to acquire equality of touch by all the fingers and to make either hand completely independent of the other. He could perform trills with the fourth and little finger just as evenly as with the second and third. The natural tendency of the thumb to bend towards the hollow of the hand was cleverly exploited in passing under the other fingers, and he established the rule that the thumb of the right hand must fall immediately after the two semitones in the ascending scale, and before them in the descending scale. This, of course, applies *vice versa* to the left hand. When releasing notes, Bach withdrew his fingers inward rather than lifted them and thus acquired his famous *cantabile* effect while at the same time assuring the clearness and smoothness of rapid passages.

When he was playing, his hands scarcely seemed to move at all, except of course, up and down the keyboard ; his fingers hardly seemed to touch the keys, and his body was motionless.

It should be noted here that Bach's most brilliant son, Carl Philipp Emanuel, who was also responsible for the development of keyboard technique, considerably modified his father's rules. He was the author of *The True Manner of Keyboard Performance*.

J. S. BACH

J. S. Bach was also a pioneer in that he tuned his instruments in equal temperament, as we do at the present time, although experiments in this method of tuning had, it is true, been made by Werckmeister (1644-1706). Philipp Spitta[1] records : " It is expressly stated that he took all the major thirds a little sharp—that is to say, slightly augmented—which is indispensable for the equalisation of the diesis. But as it is impossible that he should have tuned from nothing but major thirds, he must have proceeded as we still do at the present day—that is to say, by four successive fifths, each slightly flattened, so that the last note forms a major third with the key-note, and with the aid of the first fifth, a common chord on it. Of the various artifices which are used to facilitate the application of this method, he must have known, at any rate, that which consists in testing the deviation of the fifth by striking it, together with its octave, the fourth below the key-note, and taking the fifth up again from thence. That he evolved all this by his own study and reflection, and not from reading theoretical treatises, would be very certain, even if we had not the testimony of his contemporaries ; and he carried out his method with such rapidity and certainty that it never took him more than a quarter of an hour to tune a harpsichord or a clavichord."

Bach regarded the *cantabile* style as the foundation of good clavier-playing. Because he possessed a particularly charming touch he preferred the clavichord to the harpsichord, for the latter, though susceptible to a variety of expression, had not sufficient " soul " for him. Yet even that did not satisfy him entirely : for the performance of his Suites, Inventions and Sinfonias he desired an instrument that could produce the volume of the organ together with the expressive qualities of the clavichord—in fact he was seeking an instrument not unlike our modern concert grand pianoforte. The earliest pianofortes were then being made : Cristofori had in 1709 exhibited harpsichords with hammer action capable of producing *piano* and *forte* effects, and a few years later one or two of his instruments found their way into Germany, but as far as we know, it was not until about 1740 that Bach was able to try one. When he did he spoke enthusiastically of the instrument's tone and possibilities, but criticized its heavy touch and the feebleness of its upper notes. Gottfried Silbermann, who had constructed it, was at first disappointed in the great composer's judgment of the instrument, but he continued to make improvements to its action, and eventually earned Bach's unqualified praise.

It seems that Bach never acquired one of these early pianofortes, and we may safely presume that their mechanism was not sufficiently accommodating to his exacting technique. Noteworthy also is the fact that in 1740 he devised a lute-harpsichord, which Zacharias Hildebrand, an organ builder,

[1] *Johann Sebastian Bach* (1880).

constructed for him. This instrument had gut strings, two to each key, and a set of octave metal strings. There was a cloth damper which could check the ringing tone so that the instrument sounded like a lute, or which could be raised to make it sound more like a theorbo.

By this time, Bach had gathered around him a distinguished circle of pupils. Spitta gives us some idea of his method of instruction : " In the first instance he gave only exercises in touch, in fingering and in the equal and independent action of every finger of both hands. To this he kept the pupil for at least a month, but would sweeten the bitter dose by giving him graceful little pieces, in each of which some special technical difficulty was dealt with. Even embellishments and *maniers*, as they were called, had to be practised persistently in both hands from the very first. When a certain proficiency had been attained in these elements he went on at once to the root of the matter in difficult compositions, by preference in his own. Before the pupil began to study one, he played it to him, thus rousing his zeal and a desire not to fail of a happy result. He set the highest value on industry, and set himself up as an example to them in this alone. ' I have to be diligent,' he would say, ' and any one who is equally so will get on equally well.' He never seemed to be aware of his wonderful gifts."

When his eldest son was nine, Bach decided to cultivate his obvious musical talent, and prepared his *Clavier-Büchlein* (Little Clavier-book) for the lad. In this, he introduced compositions that started with the simplest elements and became progressively more difficult.

To return to a purely biographical narrative for a while : Bach made a prolonged visit to Carlsbad with six members of the Cöthen court ensemble in 1720, and on his return was greeted with the news that his wife had died and been buried during his absence. It was probably this tragic loss that made him apply for the post of organist at St. Jacob's Church, Hamburg. It was offered to him, but for some reason unknown to us, he declined it.

On December 3rd, 1721, he married Anna Magdalena Wilcken, a singer at the court of Anhalt-Zerbst, aged twenty-one. Two years later he was appointed Cantor of St. Thomas's, Leipzig. The authorities there never recognized his great genius, however, and he was soon to encounter troubles and irritations, yet this move to Leipzig led to the most glorious period of his creative life. His immortal *St. Matthew Passion* was first performed on Good Friday, 1729, at St. Thomas's Church. Bach was at that time trying to enlist the sympathy of the authorities for his efforts to improve his choir, and he hoped that the great music of the *Passion* would make them accede to his request for the institution of nine choral scholarships. They ignored the request, and the music made little impression upon them ![1]

[1] They might almost have been the Chapter of an Anglican Cathedral.

J. S. BACH

Petty grievances and quarrels such as one encounters in dozens of English churches to-day blighted Bach's artistic life year after year, yet he continued to produce his masterly work for the edification of a pathetically small-minded community.

But at home and in musical circles Bach's amiable character endeared him to all. His modesty contrasted vividly with the conceit of the average virtuoso : when a colleague once spoke of his amazing skill at the keyboard he waved it all aside with the remark : " There is nothing very wonderful about it ; you have only to hit the right notes at the right moment, and the instrument does the rest." He was a man entirely without affectation, and he would never refuse to play even to the most humble of listeners.

Although Bach was a master of extemporization, he would rarely begin by playing anything of his own. This was not due to modesty, but to the fact that he generally required the impetus of somebody else's work to stimulate his own inventive genius. He would often play quite a short, simple piece by some other composer and then develop it into a masterly impromptu. He always took a genuine interest in the work of his contemporaries.

Bach was a well-built man, broad and stalwart. He had inherited a deep religious conviction, and frequently read devotional books. His life at home was one of contented happiness : he had seven children by his first wife and thirteen by his second, several of whom distinguished themselves in the world of music. His sense of hospitality was such that his house was never without visitors ; he was always ready to extend a hearty welcome to all who felt disposed to call upon him, and even the most casual caller was invited to partake of the family meals. It is not surprising, then, to learn that the household expenses absorbed the greater part of Bach's income and that throughout his life he was compelled to exercise the strictest economy. Music was made upon the slightest provocation and when concerted, Bach would generally choose to play the viola so that he could be " in the midst of the harmony " both literally and metaphorically.

Thus in a home that represented German family life at its best—and what a different place the world would have been if all German homes had reflected the culture and contentment of this lovable man's household—Bach spent the closing years of his life.

In 1733 he dedicated the *Kyrie* and *Gloria* of his B minor Mass to King Augustus III, and went to Dresden to present the work personally. Three years later, after persistent applications, he obtained the coveted title of Composer to the Saxon Court (*Hofcomponist*), but even this failed to make any impression upon the Consistory at Leipzig. Bach's genius was deliberately ignored, and he still had to endure petty irritations.

His sight began to fail after 1740, seriously restricting his work and ability to travel. In that year Carl Philipp Emanuel Bach became director of music to Frederick the Great and aroused the King's interest in his illustrious father. Frederick expressed a desire to hear him and eventually became so insistent that in 1747 Bach, though disinclined to travel, was obliged to visit Potsdam with his son Wilhelm Friedemann. His reception can best be described in his son's own words :

" When Frederick II had just prepared his flute, in the presence of the whole orchestra, for the evening's concert, the list of strangers who had arrived was brought to him. Holding his flute in his hand, he glanced through the list. Then he turned round with excitement to the assembled musicians and, laying down his flute, said ' Gentlemen, old Bach is come.' Bach, who was at his son's house, was immediately invited to the palace. He had not even time allowed him to take off his travelling clothes and put on his black court dress. He appeared, with many apologies for the state of his dress before the great prince, who received him with marked attention and threw a deprecating look towards the court gentlemen, who were laughing at the discomposure and numerous complements of the old man. The flute concerto was given up for this evening ; the king led his famous visitor into all the rooms of the palace and begged him to try the Silbermann pianos, of which he (the king) thought very highly, and of which he possessed seven. The musicians accompanied the king and Bach from one room to another ; and after the latter had tried all the pianos, he begged the king to give him a subject for a fugue, upon which he could extemporize. Frederick thereupon wrote out the subject and Bach developed this in the most learned and interesting manner, to the great astonishment of the king, who, on his side, asked to hear a fugue in six parts. But since every subject is not adapted to so full a working-out, Bach chose one for himself, and astounded those present by his performance. The king, who was not easily astonished, was taken completely by surprise at the unapproachable mastery of the old cantor. Several times he cried : ' There is only one Bach.' On the following day Bach played on all the organs in the churches of Potsdam, and again in the evening on the Silbermann pianos. From here he paid a visit to Berlin, where he was shown the opera house."

Bach's sight had by that time become so poor that his work on *The Art of Fugue* was causing him great distress. In 1750 his friends persuaded him to allow the eminent English oculist, John Taylor, to perform an operation, but as a result he became totally blind and never left his house again. He continued to work, however, and dictated his chorale, *When we are in the greatest need*, to his son-in-law, Altnikol.

He woke up one morning and discovered that he could see again, but a few hours later suffered an apoplectic stroke which was followed by a violent fever, and he died on July 28th, 1750. He was buried in the St. John's churchyard, but his grave was soon forgotten ; indeed, the majority of the citizens of Leipzig took no notice of his passing. His widow supported the younger children as well as she could, but eventually her dwindling means reduced her to the status of an almswoman : she died in poverty and was buried in a pauper's grave. For many years after his death, Bach's music passed into oblivion and his name was almost forgotten. Yet, as Robert Schumann said, he was a genius " to whom music owes almost as much as a religion does to its founder."

Domenico Scarlatti

THE next of these miniature biographies must, of course, be of Domenico Scarlatti, "the father of modern piano-playing." He was probably the greatest virtuoso of the clavier that Italy ever had, and he was certainly the most famous executant of his time. His influence on the technique of playing continued for centuries after his death, in fact it is doubtful whether any single virtuoso contributed so much to his art until Chopin rose to fame.

What a pity it is that we have so little authentic information concerning his life. The few facts that are available can be stated in quite short a space. He was born in Naples on October 26th, 1685, son of Alessandro Scarlatti, the great composer of opera and the founder of the Neapolitan school. Domenico learnt his art from his father in the first instance, and then from Gasparini. Some historians assert that he also received instruction from Pasquini and Gaetano Greco.

When he was nineteen he was given the task of revising Polaroli's opera *Irene* for production in his native city, and in the following year he went to his father in Rome, who sent him with the great singer Nicolini (Nicolino Grimaldi) to Florence, giving him a letter[1] addressed to Ferdinand de' Medici which ran : " His talent found scope indeed, but it was not the sort of talent for that place. I send him away from Rome also, since Rome has no roof to shelter music that lives here in beggary. This son of mine is an eagle whose wings are grown ; he ought not to stay idle in the nest, and I ought not to hinder his flight. Since the virtuoso Nicolino, of Naples, is passing through Rome on his way to Venice, I have thought fit to send Domenico with him ; and under the sole escort of his own artistic ability (which has made great progress since he was able to be with me and enjoy the honour of obeying your Royal Highness's commands in person, three years ago), he sets forth to meet whatever opportunities may present themselves for making himself known—opportunities for which it is hopeless to wait in Rome nowadays."

In 1708 Domenico Scarlatti was studying with Gasparini in Venice, where in the following year he met Handel, and became so attached to the great composer that he followed him to Rome. Here Handel was warmly welcomed by Cardinal Ottoboni, a great patron of music, who on hearing of Scarlatti's genius as a player of the harpsichord, arranged a contest

[1] Preserved now in the Medici archives at Florence.

between the two musicians. This resulted in a general agreement that on the harpsichord they were of equal skill, but when the test was made on the organ, Handel was obviously the superior performer, a fact so readily and cheerfully acknowledged by Scarlatti that the two remained friends for the rest of their lives.

Scarlatti became quite obsessed with Handel's genius. Mainwaring, in his *Memoirs*, tells us that he revered the composer to such an extent that whenever the name of Handel was mentioned he would reverently cross himself. The admiration was evidently mutual, for another authority assures us that Handel would speak of Scarlatti's skill with tears in his eyes.

For the next ten years—until 1719—Scarlatti was in the service of Queen Marie Casimir of Poland (widow of Sobieski) who was then living in Rome and was so passionately fond of drama that she maintained a private theatre of her own. Scarlatti's chief task was to compose operas for her company, but although he produced a number of such works, he must have realised that he did not possess his father's creative genius. While he held this appointment he also succeeded Tommaso Bai as *maestro da cappella* of St. Peter's, and was obliged to write numerous masses and other forms of liturgical music.

Scarlatti came to England in 1719 and was engaged to play the harpsichord at the Italian Opera, London. He stayed for about two years, but alas ! nothing is known of his first sojourn in this country except that his opera *Narciso* was performed in London on May 30th, 1720, although Handel was in London at that time, and there must have been frequent meetings between the two friends.[1]

In 1721 Scarlatti went to Lisbon to become the Court cembalist (harpsichordist) to the King of Portugal and music teacher to the princesses. He became a great favourite there, but does not appear to have been very happy, for, in 1725, he returned to Naples, where he stayed for four years before accepting an appointment at Madrid as teacher to the Princess of the Asturias. His fame had, by that time, spread all over Europe, yet there is extremely little biographical detail upon which the story of his life can be completed.

The next twenty-five years were spent at Madrid. He received high honours at the Court : he was made a knight of St. James, and enjoyed special privileges when the Princess became Queen and appointed him as her chamber-player. His first published works were dedicated to her.

During those years he travelled to some extent, for he visited Dublin in 1740 to visit his friend Roseingrave, and was in London in the ensuing

---

[1] The association of Handel, Nicolini, Cuzzoni, and others with the Italian opera at the Haymarket is described in my book *The Romance of the English Theatre*, chapter iv., but the Scarlatti mentioned in the text was, of course, Alessandro Scarlatti.

year. Visits to Naples were undoubtedly made occasionally. Antonio Soler, a monk at the Escurial was one of his pupils in later life, so the Queen evidently permitted him to work outside the Court circles if he wished.

According to Dr. Luise Bauer, of Cologne, an eminent musicologist, Domenico Scarlatti's death in 1757 took place in Madrid at his own house in the Calle de Leganitos, and he was buried in the Convent of the Mostenses. He had been an inveterate gambler and left his family so destitute that Farinelli, the famous castrato soprano, who had been his friend for years, was obliged to support them.

Some valuable information concerning Domenico Scarlatti and his work is contained in Dr. Charles Burney's book, *The Present State of Music in Germany* (1773), in which he describes his meeting with M. L'Augier, who was intimately acquainted with Domenico Scarlatti in Spain. When the great virtuoso was seventy-one years of age[1] he composed for L'Augier ". . . a great number of harpsichord lessons which he now possesses, and of which he favoured me with copies. The book in which they are transcribed contains forty-two pieces, among which are several slow movements, and of all these, I, who have been a collector of Scarlatti's compositions all my life, had never seen more than three or four. They were composed in 1756 when Scarlatti was too fat to cross his hands as he used to do, so that these are not so difficult as his more juvenile works, which were made for his scholar and patroness, the late Queen of Spain, when Princess of Asturias. Scarlatti frequently told M. L'Augier that he was sensible he had broke through all the rules of composition in his lessons ; but asked if his deviation from these rules offended the ear and, upon being answered in the negative, he said that he thought there was scarce any other rule worth the attention of a man of genius than of not displeasing the only sense of which music is the object.[2] There are many passages in Scarlatti's pieces in which he imitated the melody of tunes sung by carriers, muleteers and common people. He used to say that the music of Alberti, and of several other modern composers, did not, in the execution, want a harpsichord, as it might be equally well, or perhaps better, expressed by any other instrument ; but as nature had given him ten fingers and as his instrument had employment for them all, he saw no reason why he should not use them."

It was Domenico Scarlatti's brilliance as a virtuoso that freed the harpsichord from the restricted polyphonic style preserved by the composers

[1] Burney gives this as seventy-three years of age, but this is an error.

[2] Burney adds the following footnote here : " Scarlatti was the first who dared to give way to fancy in his compositions by breaking through the contracted prohibitions of rules drawn from dull compositions produced in the infancy of the art, and which seemed calculated merely to keep it still in that state. Before his time, the *eye* was made the sovereign judge of music, but Scarlatt' swore allegiance only to the ear."

for the organ. He wrote a large number of pieces for the harpsichord, introducing quite revolutionary arpeggios, double-note passages and rapidly-repeated notes. Many of his best effects were obtained by the crossing of the hands—a practice in which he personally excelled until, as Burney has told us, great corpulence made it almost impossible ! There are about six hundred of his pieces altogether, all of them being quite short.

There can be no doubt that the music he heard in Spain and Portugal influenced him, for many passages in his works suggest scraps of guitar rhythms. He published only one book of compositions himself : a collection of thirty pieces entitled *Esercizi per Gravicembalo*, which appeared sometime before 1746. These pieces are called " Sonatas," but are not, of course, in the modern sonata form, and the last of them is the delightful " Cat's Fugue," based on a theme which, we are told, was suggested to the composer by a cat walking over the keys of his harpsichord.

As we play his wonderfully vivacious music on our pianos to-day and marvel at his remarkable gaiety, humour and love of the grotesque, we cannot help wishing that we knew more about his personality. He must have been a wonderful character. When we consider the stodgy periods that English music passed through after the death of Purcell (1695), we find it all the more amazing that this dazzling Italian virtuoso should have written such daring music early in the eighteenth century. Needless to say, in some of the editions of his works published during the nineteenth century his consecutive fifths and other " ungrammatical horrors " were carefully removed by stupid editors.

Scarlatti did not strive to portray any great depth of emotion in his compositions. " Amateur or professor, whoever thou art," he wrote in a preface to a collection of his works, " seek not in these sonatas for any deep feeling. They are only a frolic in art, intended to increase thy confidence on the clavier."

Mozart

This great composer-virtuoso was one of the first to establish the piano-forte, although he was trained at the harpsichord, and did not readily adapt himself to the pianistic style. In his day the harpsichord was still in general use, and the piano was not fully developed, yet he was the greatest concerto composer of the latter part of the eighteenth century.

In relation to the general theme of this book, he is of special importance because he may be said to have laid the foundations of the Viennese " school " of playing. Hummel was his pupil, and carried on the tradition when he in turn taught Thalberg, Henselt, Czerny and Hiller. This " school " was famous for its warmth of expression ; then something of a novelty.

Wolfgang Amadeus Mozart was born at Salzburg on January 27th, 1756, son of Leopold Mozart, violinist and composer at the Court chapel of Archbishop Sigismund of Salzburg. There were seven children, but only two survived—Wolfgang and his sister Maria Anna (called Nannerl or Marianne at home), who was five years his senior.

When he was only three years old, the boy would watch his sister being taught the clavier by her father, and when she had finished, would sit at the instrument and spend hours amusing himself by playing thirds and other simple chords. A year later he began to learn properly, and in a few weeks could play minuets and other little pieces with amazing accuracy. Another few months and he was composing !

Some idea of his precocity may be gained from a letter written many years later by Andreas Schachtner, Court trumpeter at Salzburg, to Mozart's sister, which tells how he and Leopold Mozart came home one afternoon and found the four-year-old Wolfgang busy with a pen. His father enquired what he was doing. " Writing a concerto for the clavier. The first part is almost done " the lad replied.

" Your father took it from him and showed me a daub of notes for the most part written over dried ink-blots." Schachtner wrote " We laughed at first at this apparent nonsense, but then your father began to note the theme, the notes, the composition, and his study of the sheet became more intent until at last tears of wonder and delight fell from his eyes. ' Look, Herr Schachtner ' he said, ' how correct and orderly it is ; only it is of no use because it is so very difficult that nobody could play it.' Then Wolfgang exclaimed : ' That is why it is a concerto, one must practise it until one can do it ; look ! this is how it goes.' He played but could only bring out enough to show us what he intended. He had then the notion that playing concertos and working miracles were the same thing."

In 1762, when Mozart was six, his father decided to take him with his eleven-year-old sister on an experimental journey to Munich, for both of the children were showing prodigious skill at the clavier. They spent three weeks there, and played before the Elector, but little is known about this first journey. However, it was evidently successful, for in September of the same year they went to Vienna by way of Passau, where they played to the Bishop, and Linz where they appeared at a concert given by Count Schlick.

Writing to a friend from Vienna on October 16th, Mozart's father related : " When I was alone in the Opera on the 10th I heard the Archduke Leopold saying from his box that there was a boy in Vienna who played the clavier wonderfully, etc. The very same evening at about eleven I received a command to go to Schönbrunn. . . . I had the firm intention to let you know as soon as we came from Schönbrunn, but we had to go direct to the Prince von Hildburghhausen . . . there is only time to tell you that we were so graciously received that as I tell it, it will be reckoned a fairy tale. Let it suffice that Wolferl[1] sprang upon the lap of the Empress, put his arms around her neck and vigorously kissed her. We were with her from three till six."

Another letter three days later states " . . . the Treasurer paid me one hundred ducats with the statement that Her Majesty would send for us again . . . Would you like to know what Wolferl's dress looks like ? It is of the finest cloth, lilac-coloured ; the vest of silk of the same colour, the coat and waistcoat embroidered with broad gold braid. It was made for the Archduke Maximilian. Nannerl has the Court dress of a Princess of white embroidered and hand-trimmed taffeta."

While they were in Vienna, Wolfgang was taken ill with scarlet fever, and many of the nobility sent their doctors to his bedside. The attack delayed them four weeks, and after a visit to Pressburg, they did not return to Salzburg until January, 1763.

Within six months they were on the road again, this time to make a much more ambitious tour of the German courts, and finally to visit Paris. At Wasserburg, *en route*, Mozart was shown an organ, and amazed his father by playing the instrument as if he had been using it for months. His skill as a violinist, too, was displayed when they reached Munich, for here he played a violin concerto before the Elector of Bavaria and the Archduke Clemens. At Schwetzingen the Court assembled and listened enraptured

---

[1] Short for Wolfgangerl.

from five until nine o'clock, but one of their greatest successes on this tour was at Frankfurt, for a local newspaper dated August 20th, 1763, tells us : " The general astonishment awakened in all hearers by the . . . two children of Herr Leopold Mozart, Kapellmeister at the Court of Salzburg, has necessitated the threefold repetition of the single concert originally intended. . . . The little girl who is in her twelfth and the boy who is in his seventh year will not only play concertos on the clavecin or harpsichord, and concertos by the greatest masters, but the boy will also play a violin concerto, will accompany symphonies on the clavier—the manual or keyboard being covered with a cloth—with as much facility as if he could see the keys ; further, he will name exactly all tones singly or in chords given on the clavier or on any other instrument, bells, glasses, clocks, etc. Finally, he will improvise from his head on the harpsichord or organ in the most difficult keys as requested for as long as desired in order to show that he understands how to play the organ as thoroughly as the harpsichord, though it is quite a different matter."

At one of these concerts Goethe was present—he was then only a boy, of course, for he told Eckermann many years afterwards : " I saw him as a seven-year-old boy when he gave a concert. . . . I was about fourteen years old and I remember still quite distinctly the little fellow with his powdered wig and sword."

Princess Amalie, a sister of Frederick the Great, heard them at Aachen, but according to Mozart's father, her enthusiasm was expressed in the wrong manner, for in a letter dated October 17th, 1763, he complains : " If the kisses which she bestowed on my children, especially on Master Wolfgang, had been *louis d'or*, all would have been well, but neither the hotel nor the post-horses can be paid with kisses. . . ."

Arriving in Paris on November 18th, they were invited to stay with the Bavarian Ambassador, Count von Eyck. The two children appeared before Louis XV and the Court at Versailles. ". . . you can imagine what a sensation it must have aroused among the French when the King's daughter, not only in her apartment but also in public, on seeing my children let them kiss her hands and returned their kisses," Leopold Mozart wrote in a letter on February 1st 1764. He also added " Four sonatas by Monsieur Wolfgang Mozart are now at the engravers. Imagine the sensation these sonatas[1] will make in the world when one sees on the title page that they are the work of a seven-year-old child, and how when a proof is wanted of this incredible capacity, as has already happened, he will put a bass immediately to any minuet without touching the clavier, and also, if desired, a second violin

---

[1] These were the first printed works of Mozart, and appeared under the title : *Sonatas pour le Clavecin qui peuvent se jouer avec l'accompagnement de Violin, dediées à Mme Victoire de France par J. G. Wolfgang Mozart de Salzburg âgé de sept ans. Œuvre première, à Paris aux addresses ordinaires.*

part!   . . . God daily performs new miracles with this child. . . . He accompanies and transposes at sight and reads any piece, French or Italian, that is put before him."

After a tremendous success in Paris they came to London on April 23rd, and four days later played before King George III and Queen Charlotte at St. James's Palace. Some idea of the reception they got may be judged from the fact that a week later they were walking in the Park, dressed in ordinary clothes, when the King and Queen drove past, and his Majesty recognized them, lowered the window of his carriage, and greeted them with great enthusiasm. On May 19th they were at Court again, and the King was so fascinated by Mozart's skill that he fetched a pile of music himself and placed pieces by Handel, J. Christian Bach and Wagenseil before the lad one by one and watched him play them at sight. Mozart then played the organ and accompanied the Queen when she sang a song. Finally, he astonished everybody by a brilliant extemporization.

The summer was spent at Chelsea, but in October they took apartments in Frith Street, Soho, from which on January 18th, 1765, another set of sonatas was published, dedicated to the Queen. There was another Court performance, and one or two other concerts in " The Little Theatre in the Haymarket." If we exclude royalty, Mozart's most interesting acquaintance in London was J. C. Bach (the youngest son of J. S. Bach) the music-master to the Queen. He used to persuade Mozart to sit on his knee at the clavier and play sonatas, each taking a bar in turn. This became almost a parlour trick, for they played so smoothly that nobody would have suspected that they were " sharing " the music.

Mozart left London with his father and sister on July 24th, 1765, and after a short stay at Canterbury proceeded to The Hague at the request of Princess Caroline of Nassau-Weilburg. Unfortunately, as soon as they arrived in Holland, illness once again upset their plans.

This great European tour was concluded by another stay in Paris, a visit to Biberach, and finally to Munich. They arrived home in Salzburg in November, having been away for over three years.

Their next tour started in the autumn of 1767, when they went to Vienna. All Mozart got here during the first month or two was an attack of small-pox, but he recovered in the house of Count Leopold von Podstatsky at Olmütz, and was able to return to Vienna early in January to be received at Court by the Empress Maria Theresa. This was gratifying, of course, but they received only a medal of no particular value for their services. They found that the majority of the nobility at that time had little taste for good music, and Mozart's father wrote in a slightly bitter tone about the fine gentlemen who would enthusiastically applaud burlesques, harlequinades, and so forth, but would pay no attention to serious drama or music, and worse still, would chatter noisily when it was being presented. But that was not their only trouble, for Leopold Mozart also complained : ". . . I found that all the clavier-players and composers in Vienna were opposed to us with the single exception of Wagenseil, who being ill, however, could be of little use to us. The tactics these people used were to avoid carefully any opportunity of seeing us and of learning the extent of Wolfgang's capacity. And for what reason ? In order that when asked whether they had heard the boy and what they thought of him they might be able to reply that they had not heard him, and that what was said of him could not be true, but must be an imposture or humbug, and that what he was given to play was prepared, and it was ridiculous to suppose that he could compose."

Leopold Mozart was not easily beaten, however. He continues : " But I set a trap for one of these gentry. I persuaded someone to give us private notice of when he would be present, and to induce him to bring an exceptionally difficult Concerto which should be put before Wolfgang. We arrived and he had the opportunity of hearing his Concerto played by Wolfgang as if he knew it by heart. The astonishment of this clavier-player and composer, his expression and his exclamations in his amazement made us all realize the truth of what I have already told you. In the end he said : 'As an honest man I can only say that this boy is the greatest musician in our time in the world. I could not have believed it.'

"And so to convince the public of what it has before it I determined on something quite exceptional, to wit, that Wolfgàng should compose an opera. Can you imagine the outcry that arose among the composers ? ' What ! shall we hear Gluck to-day, and to-morrow see a boy of twelve years of age sit at the harpsichord and conduct his own opera ? ' Yes, and in spite of all braying idiots ! I have even brought Gluck on to our side. . . ."

A libretto was supplied by Marco Coltellini, and Mozart set to work. The opera—*La Finta Semplice*—was finished by Easter 1768 : a score of no less than five hundred and fifty-eight pages. But getting it produced was another matter. Affligio, the impresario, raised every possible objection ; the principals all pronounced the arias to be unsuitable ; and the orchestra refused to be conducted by a mere boy. It seemed hopeless, so they returned to Salzburg early in 1769.

The Archbishop of Salzburg, Sigismund, Count of Schrattenbach, was indignant when they told him of their difficulties with the opera in Vienna, and forthwith arranged for it to be performed at his palace. It led to Wolfgang's appointment as *Concertmeister* in the following year.

Shortly before his fourteenth birthday, Mozart and his father made their first Italian tour. After having given many performances on the way they arrived in Florence on March 30th, 1770, and met Count Rosenberg, the Austrian Ambassador at the Tuscan court. At their first concert on

April 2nd, according to Mozart's father, " the admiration was all the greater since the musical director, the Marquis Ligniville, is one of the first contrapuntists in Italy and put before Wolfgang the most difficult fugues and gave him the hardest subjects which he developed and played as one eats a piece of bread. Nardini accompanied. To-day we see Manzuoli. The castrato Nicolini is also here. . . ."

At Rome, a few days later, they heard the celebrated *Miserere* of Allegri in the Sistine Chapel : a setting so treasured that the musicians were forbidden under threat of excommunication to allow a single part of it to be taken out of the chapel, or to copy any part of it. Mozart heard it on the Wednesday in Holy Week, went straight back to the inn, wrote it all out from memory, and returned to the Chapel on Good Friday to hear it again, taking the manuscript inside his hat so that he could make corrections !

When they proceeded to Naples in May, monks of the Augustian monastery accompanied them because the roads were infested with robbers. Their first concert in that city, as in every other Italian centre of music, was a tremendous success. In the audience were the English ambassador, Sir William Hamilton, and his wife.

Back in Rome later in the summer, Wolfgang went to the Vatican to receive the Order of the Golden Spur from the Pope, which carried with it the title *Ritter* or *Cavaliere*. For some time afterwards Leopold made his son use this title, but Mozart himself was never keen to do so, and in later years dropped it entirely.

Later in the year they were in Milan, where at Christmas, Mozart's recently-completed opera *Mitridate, Re di Ponto* was performed many times with great success. It is interesting to note that an orchestra of sixty players was used : fourteen first violins, fourteen second, six violas, two 'cellos, six contrabasses, two bassoons, six oboes, two flutes, four French horns, two trumpets, and two claviers.

Writing about the first performance on December 26th, Leopold Mozart declared : " Never in living memory was there such a desire to see the first opera of the season in Milan as on this occasion. Patronage cannot help the success of an opera since everybody who goes in will talk, cry out and judge for himself what he gets for his money. Patronage serves only and necessarily to prevent the composition of the work being hindered and to protect the composer at the rehearsals from any malice on the part of the orchestra." A week or so later he writes again : " Our son's opera continues its success. . . ."

In the early spring they went to Venice for the carnival season, where Mozàrt gave another brilliant concert, and then returned to Salzburg by way of Padua, Vicenza, Verona and Innsbruck, having been away from home nearly two years.

Mozart's next two Italian tours need not be described here in detail, for there were no events of outstanding importance as far as we are concerned. So now we find him back in Salzburg again, an astonishingly intelligent youth of seventeen giving more time to composition than to public performances. But for a short visit to Vienna and another to Munich, he spent the whole of the next four years—1773 to 1777—at home, and unfortunately we have not a great deal of authentic biographical information upon which to draw for this period, for there is little correspondence available. Mention should, however, be made of the first performance of another opera, *La Finta Giardiniera*, at Munich, on January 13th, 1775. It was so enthusiastically supported that Mozart wrote home to his mother : " God be praised ! My opera was produced yesterday and succeeded so well that I cannot possibly describe the reception . . . the theatre was so full that many were turned away. After every aria there was a terrific uproar with clapping and cries of ' Viva Maestro ' . . . Afterwards, Papa and I went into a room where the Elector and Electress and the whole Court were gathered, and kissed their hands. They were very agreeable . . . and congratulated me that the opera had so exceptionally pleased everybody. . . ."

Mozart's father had been hoping for some time that his son would be offered a position at one of the Courts, for his prospects in Salzburg were not bright. Archbishop Sigismund had died and been succeeded by Hieronymous, Count of Colloredo, an extremely parsimonious creature, who disliked Leopold Mozart and cared nothing about his brilliant son. Wolfgang's official appointment as Concertmeister was very poorly paid, so he decided to resign and seek his fortune elsewhere.

Twenty-one years of age, Mozart then set out on another long tour, this time with his mother. Everything was disappointing until they reached Mannheim, where Elector Carl Theodor granted him an audience and described his playing as " incomparable." Mozart was desperately in need of money to meet his heavy expenses, and he was delighted when on several occasions he was allowed to play at court. In due course, after indirect requests for payment, he received—a gold watch ! He already possessed five. His chief desire, of course, was to obtain an appointment at court, and when the Elector said that he would consider the matter, Mozart decided to stay in Mannheim until the matter was settled. With his mother he lived in a very poor apartment, and they had to economise to such an extent that despite the severe cold they could have a fire only for about an hour each day. They waited patiently for several weeks and then heard that the Elector had resolved not to make the appointment.

At Paris, Mozart spent money freely in driving here and there to the houses of influential people in the hope that they would help him. They generally heard him play and gave him nothing but empty compliments.

MOZART

The maturity of his musicianship lacked the novel attraction of his musical precocity as a child. While they were in the French capital his mother died, and financial difficulties compelled him to go from house to house giving lessons like the most ordinary of rank and file musicians. Yet he knew that the music he was writing was good, and would someday find recognition. Some of his compositions were being performed and applauded, but their creator received barely sufficient to pay for life's necessities.

On leaving Paris, Mozart made his way to Munich where he hoped to marry Aloysia Weber, an attractive girl to whom he had given lessons gratuitously owing to her father's lack of means. She had made a brilliant career for herself and was holding a well-paid appointment at the Munich Opera. Alas ! success had turned her heart and she refused him with a jeer at his clothes.

He arrived back in Salzburg on January 16th, 1779, and on the following day was appointed organist at the Court of the Archbishop : the prelate he had hoped never to set eyes on again. This post had been secured for him by his father so that he could pay off the heavy debts that had accumulated during his absence. The unpleasantness of having to serve the objectionable Archbishop was relieved shortly afterwards when he received a commission from Munich to write the *opera seria* for the Carnival of 1781. *Idomeneo* was the result, and six weeks leave of absence was granted so that he could go to Munich for its production. This leave, incidentally, was prolonged by his father's intervention. The opera was a great success : the Elector declared "I was quite astonished. No music has ever so impressed me ; it is *magnifique.*" Yet within a little while it was entirely forgotten.

The Archbishop and his retinue were then staying in Vienna, and Mozart received a peremptory order to proceed immediately to that city. He arrived to find that he was expected to live as a lackey in the palace and to eat with the servants. Two valets took precedence over him. Why this miserable ecclesiastic should have treated Mozart so badly is difficult to understand, but the matter culminated in an interview at which His Grace lost his temper and called Mozart a vile wretch, a scamp, rogue and other insulting names, and finally discharged him. A day or two later, the loss of such a fine musician evidently made him regret his outburst, for he instructed the Court Marshal to send for Mozart and to act as mediator, believing that the " vile wretch " would come cringing and begging to be reinstated. But Mozart stood upon his dignity and refused to return ; whereupon the Marshal also became abusive and kicked him out of the room.

His father's displeasure at the loss of this regular employment made Mozart stay in Vienna, and he took a room at the house of Madame Weber, the mother of the girl he had hoped to marry. Aloysia had married Joseph

Lange, the actor, but she had several sisters, one of whom, Constanze, a woman quite unworthy of such a cultured husband, succeeded in ensnaring him.

Vienna was, of course, an ideal centre for Mozart, and it was not long before he was receiving commissions. The Emperor thought highly of his skill as a pianist and invited him to play in competition with the celebrated Clementi. Substantial bets were made : the Emperor backed Mozart, and the Archduchess favoured Clementi. Mozart won and received a gift of fifty ducats. It is worth recording that Clementi was charmed by Mozart's playing, but Mozart described his opponent's skill thus : " He has a brilliant right hand, but in other respects not a farthing's worth of taste or feeling : he is a mere mechanic."

He married Constanze Weber on August 4th, 1782, and settled down to a moderately comfortable life, though his income was never adequate and his wife must have numbered among his greatest disappointments. During this period his finest operas were produced. *Figaro* appeared in 1786 but its success brought him little reward, and he was still obliged to take pupils in order to pay his way. He was still teaching four years later, because Dr. Frank went to him in 1790 and described him thus : " I found Mozart to be a small man with a large head and fleshy hands, who received me somewhat coldly. . . . I played him a fantasia of his own. ' Not bad,' he said, to my great astonishment, ' now I shall make you listen to it.' Beneath his fingers the piano became a completely different instrument. He had reinforced it with a second instrument, which served him as a pedal." Hummel, as I have already mentioned, was one of Mozart's pupils, and lived with him for two years in Vienna.

At Christmas 1786 *Figaro* was produced in Prague, and Mozart spent several happy weeks in that city enjoying the wonderful enthusiasm with which his great opera was received. He also gave a concert that brought him no less than three thousand florins and another contract for a new opera. We are told that at the conclusion of the concert " Mozart improvised for a full half-hour on the piano. His features glowed with satisfaction at the enthusiastic reception accorded him by the public. He was beginning for the third time with heightened zest and performing miraculously when someone suddenly called out ' Play us something from *Figaro*.' Whereupon he began with the theme of the favourite air, *Non piu andrai*, and extemporized a dozen wonderful variations upon it, finishing amidst deafening applause."

Returning to Vienna he found a public still apathetic, and when his *Don Giovanni* was finished there was no great desire to hear it performed. But for an Imperial Command, its *première* might have been postponed indefinitely. A fairly successful revival of *Figaro* induced the Emperor

Joseph to commission another opera for an honorarium of two hundred ducats, and *Così fan Tutte* came into being. It had a short-lived success in 1790, but it soon became apparent that Vienna cared little for Mozart, for his operas or for his three greatest symphonies which he had written in 1788. The Court neglected him, he got heavily into debt and pawned his silver table service. At Mannheim he went to the dress rehearsal of *Figaro* but looked so shabby that one of the actors mistook him for a " journeyman tailor " and told him to get out. What humiliation for the great musician who had once been one of the most elegant artists that ever moved in Court circles !

The year 1791 found him in poverty : almost everything of value in his home had been sent to the pawnbrokers. There was a slight improvement in his circumstances in the spring, when he was asked to write a German " magic " opera. He spent the summer in writing *The Magic Flute*. It was produced in the following October and was a great success, but very little of the profit found its way into the composer's pocket. If we were considering Mozart's activities as a composer in this book there would be much to be recorded of the last few years of his life. His health had been failing for some months owing to kidney trouble, and by the autumn he was in a state of collapse, yet as soon as he finished *The Magic Flute* he set to work on his *Requiem*. On December 4th, 1791, he was sinking, but he insisted upon his unfinished *Requiem* being brought to his bed, and with a few singers tried to rehearse part of it. He broke down during the *Lacrimosa*, and later in the day instructed his favourite pupil Süssmayr to complete the score. His death occurred just before one o'clock on the following morning.

Count Deyn, the Director of the Cabinet of Arts made a plaster cast of Mozart's features before his burial, but unfortunately the mask was afterwards allowed to disintegrate. The great musician had the poorest of funerals ; a storm turned back the mourners, and without ceremony, Mozart was buried in what was little more than a pauper's grave. His wife did not even bother to mark its position : she was so busy collecting up the money that her husband's work was belatedly producing that not once during the following sixteen years did she visit the cemetery. It is said that until some time after Mozart's death, only one person ever tried to find the grave— Josef Deiner, a janitor. Constanze was in later years rebuked by King Ludwig I of Bavaria for the neglect of her husband's grave. She left a fortune of two hundred and fifty thousand florins.

There has been a great deal of speculation about the personality of Mozart. He was certainly not the naïve character portrayed by some of his early biographers. A kindly soul, yes, and quite unspoilt by his early successes, but he was never lacking in self-assurance. A musician who died in 1851 left this record of his skill as an executant : " As a young man I admired many a virtuoso . . . but imagine my amazement when I was privileged to hear the immortal W. A. Mozart not only play variations but also improvise on the piano before a vast audience. To me his playing was creation of quite another character from any that I had hitherto been accustomed to hear. Even the most accomplished master of music could not sufficiently admire and marvel at the way his fantasy soared up to the heights and then swooped down again into the depths. I can still, now that I am an old man, hear those heavenly, incomparable harmonies resounding in my ears, and shall go to my grave in the fullest conviction that there has been but one Mozart." Another contemporary tells us : " When he improvised on the fortepiano, how easy it was for him to work up a theme, to make it emerge, peep forth or work itself out, now so boldly and crisply, now so supplicatingly and dolefully, here so drolly, there so solemnly, that he could do what he wished with his audience—even had an unkind fate saddled him with the veriest crosspatches, so long as they had *some* musical education."

The outstanding qualities of Mozart's playing were its gracefulness and lucidity, which combined with good expression and amazing dexterity to make him the greatest artist of his day. His *staccato* is said to have possessed a peculiarly fascinating and brilliant charm.

Moscheles

I GNATZ MOSCHELES was born in Prague on May 30th, 1794, son of a cloth
merchant who was a keen amateur musician and whose greatest ambition
was that one of his children should find fame in the art he loved.

Prague was famous for its military bands when Moscheles was a boy,
and his greatest delight was to be allowed to hold a bandsman's music. He
started to learn to play the piano from a local teacher when he was very
small, but although he was determined to become a musician, he had little
patience with the laborious exercises that the piano student of those times
had to endure for the first couple of years. He used to borrow music from a
circulating library and scramble with wild delight through the Beethoven
Sonatas, caring nothing about accuracy and even less about expression,
except perhaps in the more dramatic passages, which were hacked out with
gusto. When he reached the age of seven his father took him to Dionys
Weber to enquire whether he had real talent or not. The pianist listened
patiently but with obvious discomfort as the boy tore through a sonata, and
then remarked " Probably, yes, but he is upon entirely the wrong road. He
must not be allowed to make a hash of Beethoven. I will take him for
three years on condition that he plays only the music I prescribe. During
the first year he will play nothing but Mozart, Clementi during the
second, and Bach during the third. He must not touch Beethoven,
who, clever though he is, writes a lot of hare-brained stuff and leads
pupils astray."

The course with Dionys Weber evidently helped the lad to make excellent progress, for in 1808, shortly after the death of his father, he was sent
to continue his studies in Vienna, though only at the cost of great personal
sacrifice on the part of his mother. He studied harmony, counterpoint and
composition under Kapellmeister Albrechtsberger, and in due course was
able to indulge in the music of Beethoven, for which he had the deepest
veneration.

By the time he was twenty, he was recognized as one of the most promising pianists of the day, and was refusing all but the most brilliant pupils.
Moreover, he had found his way into the highest social circles, and had
become well acquainted with Beethoven, who suggested that he might like
to undertake the task of arranging *Fidelio* for the piano. He became one of
Meyerbeer's personal friends, and was regarded by many Viennese musicians

as the rival of Hummel, whose soft touch and precise running passages contrasted with Moscheles' dashing bravura, though the two pianists were always on good terms of mutual respect.

In the autumn of 1816 Moscheles made his first long tour, visiting Leipzig by way of Prague, then proceeding to Dresden, Munich, Augsburg and Amsterdam, finding favour with the nobility and commonalty alike. Then he went on to The Hague, Brussels and Paris, and in the French capital met Spohr at the residence of Baron Poiféré de Cère, where the artistic *élite* were accustomed to gather. On May 28th of the following year he arrived in London, little thinking that it was to become his second home, as he always called it in later years.

One of the first musicians he met in London was J. B. Cramer, whose long, thin, aristocratic hands, he observed, were horribly stained by snuff. Moscheles recorded in his diary that even the keys of his piano were clogged with it. The same diary also tells us of his great delight on hearing Braham, the famous tenor, singing at Drury Lane, and the brilliant assembly in the boxes at His Majesty's Theatre (Haymarket). " This galaxy of charming and beautiful women, with their elegant toilettes and jewels, and the house brilliantly illuminated, formed a splendid scene.[1]"

On June 11th, Moscheles played his own E-flat Concerto at a Philharmonic Concert with great success, and on the following July 4th held a concert of his own at the Argyll Rooms. A week later, according to his diary, he attended " a grand evening musical party at the Rothschilds', at their country house on Stamford Hill, given to the foreign Ministers present in England on account of the approaching coronation of George IV. I was introduced to most of the Ministers, who, with the old Prince Esterhazy, expressed themselves greatly pleased with my playing."

Moscheles made his second visit to London in 1822, when he appeared on one occasion with Cramer in a work for two pianos, and incidentally, made the acquaintance of Mrs. Siddons. " I feel more and more at home in England, for people here evidently wish to show me respect and friendship ; I feel deeply grateful for this."

In January of the following year he was in England again, visiting Bath, Bristol and other provincial cities, and would have returned again in 1824 but for a serious illness which kept him at his mother's house in Prague for over four months. A concert given before the Austrian Royal family in May of that year led to his presentation to the Emperor a few weeks later. His Majesty received Moscheles with the words " You pleased me when you were merely a boy, and since that time it has always given me new pleasure to hear you."

---

[1] This and subsequent quotations from the diary of Moscheles, are quoted from the *Life of Moscheles*, by his wife (1873).

A visit to Hamburg in 1825 resulted in his meeting a young lady pianist, Charlotte Embden, whom he married within a couple of months. After a short tour through Bremen, Aix-la-Chapelle and Paris, the young couple arrived in London on May 2nd for another series of concerts.

Some idea of the trials of touring in those days may be gained from Moscheles' account of his journey to Ireland in the following year. It started from Liverpool, where he had concluded another long tour of provincial towns, and entailed first a wearisome journey to Holyhead by coach, which included the crossing of a turbulent river in an open boat in the middle of the night. Then after a long wait at Holyhead for the Chester mail, they were told that there was no steamboat available because the violent gales of the past few days had kept all the steamers on the other side of the Irish Sea. Eventually a sailing vessel was made available for the mail, and Moscheles and a few other passengers were asked if they would care to make the crossing in it. The story can now be continued in an extract from his diary. " We agreed, and embarked shortly after seven o'clock. It rained in torrents, and the sea was so high that we soon betook ourselves to our berths. I suffered so violently that after a few hours I was completely prostrate. The gale meanwhile increased. I counted the passing hours. It grew dark but we did not land. The steward, on being asked when we should be released, whispered ' Who knows ? We are doing badly ! '—words too clearly verified by the lurching of the boat. Although I lay smothered in blankets and clothes, my feet were perished with cold. It cost me no slight effort to shake off my drowsiness, and, groping about, to discover that the sea-water had got into my berth : the ship had become leaky. There was no longer any mystery about that, for the water came hissing into the cabin. The storm howled fiercely ; it was pitch-dark. The captain could offer no other comfort than the assurance that we were not far from shore. Of course, not near enough to land. We were surrounded by rocks and sandbanks, and yet not near enough for a distress signal to be perceptible from the coast. At last, after a long battle and the most fearful shocks from the waves, which knocked our vessel about like a plaything, we were able to throw out anchors, and there we poor victims lay till daybreak. . . . At last, in the afternoon, the welcome tidings came ' We are all right, a boat has reached our ship, and will take us up.' Whereupon, after getting together our goods and chattels, we were thrown, so to speak, with them into the reeling boat, and after a short fight with the foaming surf, landed in Howth Harbour."

Moscheles had by that time established a home in London for his wife and child. Those were the days when Kemble's acting, and the voices of Pasta, Madame Vestris and Braham were filling the theatres. Carl Maria von Weber was conducting his own operas at Covent Garden, and Sir George Smart was leading the capital's musical life in the concert halls.

Early in 1827 Moscheles was profoundly shocked to receive a letter from Beethoven asking him to approach Sir George Smart and the London Philharmonic Society to arrange a concert on his behalf, for he was suffering from dropsy, and was in grave financial difficulties. While the Society were meeting, another letter from the great composer arrived :

". . . On the 27th February I was operated on for the fourth time, and now the return of certain symptoms makes it plain that soon I must expect a fifth operation. What will come of it ? What will become of me if this state of things continues ? Truly my lot is a very hard one, but I bow to the decree of fate. . . .

Your friend,

Beethoven."

The Philharmonic Society made immediate arrangements for the concert and gave Moscheles a hundred pounds to send on to Beethoven as an advance of the proceeds. It is perhaps worth while to quote the concluding sentences of the letter of acknowledgement that Beethoven wrote from Vienna on March 18th, 1827 :

". . . May Heaven only soon restore me to health, and I will prove to the noble-hearted English how highly I appreciate their sympathy with my sad fate. I shall never forget your noble conduct, and hope soon to send a special letter of thanks to Sir Smart and to Herr Stumpff. Farewell, with sentiments of true friendship, I remain, with the greatest esteem,

Your friend,

Ludwig van Beethoven."

Ten days later, Moscheles received a letter from his friend Rau which ran " Beethoven is no more ; he expired on the evening of the 26th of March, between five and six o'clock, after a painful struggle and terrible suffering. . . ."

As most people are aware, the Viennese musical circles tried to hide their shame when Beethoven's request to the London Philharmonic Society became known, by reprimanding Moscheles for approaching the Society, and by asserting that the great composer had not been in need of English charity.

In the same year Moscheles played before the Court circle assembled at the Duchess of Kent's Kensington Palace. " The little Princess Victoria was present, and the Duchess begged me to play *at once*, so that the Princess, who was obliged to go to bed early, might hear me. . . . The Royal party took a very friendly interest in my performance, but what I think pleased them more than all was my improvisation on some Tyrolese melodies."

At Edinburgh early in 1828 the Moscheles family met Sir Walter Scott, but the Scottish way of spending a pleasant Sunday—three dry church services, more prayers at home, thumb-twiddling and a ban upon the reading of any book but the Bible—made them thankful when the time came for their return to London.

Moscheles came to the height of his powers as a pianist within the next two years, and his many compositions were by no means neglected. Much of the credit for his great achievements at the keyboard he generously gave to the fine Erard instruments he generally used. He loved their resonant, organ-like tone. Always very sparing in the use of the pedals, he would say "A good player must only rarely use the assistance of either pedal, otherwise he misuses it." His chief criticism of many of the other pianists enjoying popularity at that time centred round the use of the pedals. " I wish he had not his feet so perpetually upon the pedals " he would say, "All effects now, it seems, must be produced by the feet—what is the good of people having hands ? It is just as if a good rider wanted for ever to use the spurs." He was one of the advocates of the " peaceful wrist " theory : he believed that the wrist should be kept flat and so steady while playing that one should be able to balance a glass of water on it.

In passing, I cannot resist the temptation to quote from Moscheles' diary his impression of his first railway journey in February, 1831 : " On the 18th I went by rail from Manchester to Liverpool ; the fare was five shillings. At 1.30 I mounted one of the omnibuses which carried all passengers gratis to the great building called the ' station.' Eight to ten carriages, each about as long as an omnibus, are joined closely to one another ; each carriage contains twelve places, with seats like comfortable armchairs ; at a given signal every traveller takes his place, which is marked with the number of his ticket, and the railway guards lock the carriages. Then, and not before, the engine is attached to the foremost carriage ; the motion, although one seems to fly, is hardly perceptible, and the traveller is amazed when he looks out of the window and observes at what incredible speed the train approaches the distant object and suddenly whirls by it. Words cannot describe the impression made on me by this steam excursion. . . ."

Moscheles became a Director of the Philharmonic Society in 1832, the year in which his friend Mendelssohn arrived in London. On the evening of April 24th, the day after the great composer's arrival, Moscheles heard him play for the first time his *Instrumental Lieder für Clavier*, which afterwards became famous as *Lieder ohne Worte*, and the Capriccio in B-minor.

Apart from his public appearances with Mendelssohn, Moscheles enjoyed the composer's company on many quiet evenings at home, when they played over a great number of their compositions before sending them to the publishers. Similarly, when Moscheles visited Berlin he was a constant guest at Mendelssohn's house. An entry in his diary during one of these visits reads : " I practise daily on Felix's magnificent Erard, and he is going to lend it to me for the concert ; we often extemporize together, each of us trying to dart as quick as lightning on the suggestions implied by each other's harmonies, and to construct others upon them. Then Felix, whenever I introduce any motive out of his own works, breaks in and cuts me short by playing a subject from one of my compositions, on which I retort, and then he, and so on *ad infinitum*."

Moschele's recital before the Royal family in the Brighton Pavilion in December, 1832, was chilled by the condescending attitude of Sir Andrew Barnard, to whom were entrusted the arrangements of the evening. King William IV, Queen Adelaide and their suite formed a dazzling array at one end of the room, and the pianist with the King's band sat right at the other end, Sir Andrew having provided as much space between them as possible so that no member of the Royal Party could conveniently approach Moscheles. During the performance the King came quite near to the pianist, and seemed to be listening, " he bowed condescendingly when I arose, but did not say a syllable ; the company talked loudly," Moscheles recorded in his diary. " Sir Andrew asked me to play on the organ, and later in the evening I had to accompany eight imperfectly trained performers in some selections from Haydn's *Creation*. Only the Princess Augusta and the Marchioness of Cornwallis took any interest in my *Alexander Variations* and extempore playing, and that in spite of the general buzz of conversation. . . . The Court withdrew after Sir Andrew had handed to the Queen a copy of my *English Fantasia*, an honour I myself had solicited, but been refused. Sir Andrew dismissed me as before with a few polite courtly phrases about the satisfaction felt by their Majesties, but none of the company exchanged a word with me." This, and the fact that he had been obliged to play with the King's band without rehearsal and on a piano that had been standing in a cold room for about six months, left Moscheles in a bad humour.

He was at that time making acquaintance with the works of Chopin, and it is rather interesting to note his first impressions : " I gladly pass some of my leisure hours of an evening in cultivating an acquaintance with Chopin's Studies and his other compositions. I am charmed with their originality, and the national colouring of his subjects. My thoughts, however, and through them my fingers, stumble at certain hard, inartistic, and to me inconceivable modulations. On the whole I find his music often too sweet, not manly enough, and hardly the work of a profound musician." One cannot help wondering what Moscheles would have thought of the " inconceivable modulations " that we, a century later, have to swallow ! And what would he have thought of modern valuations of Chopin as compared with the works of his illustrious friend Mendelssohn ?

Moscheles was, of course, present at the great musical festival held in Westminster Abbey in June, 1834, when the Royal family and nearly three thousand other people gathered to hear a choir of over six hundred accompanied by an orchestra of two hundred and twenty-three and a magnificent organ built for the occasion by Gray. The diary reads : " On the 20th of June, at twelve o'clock in the forenoon, Sir George Smart for the first time raised his baton, and Handel's Coronation Anthem, performed by such a host, in such a place, was so grand that none present are likely to forget it ; the newspapers talked of several ladies weeping, and some actually fainting. I was deeply moved by these sounds, and must confess I never heard such an effect produced before. We had the whole of the *Creation* and a part of *Samson*. The solo singers were old Bellamy, who had sung in 1784, E. Seguin, a young pupil of the Royal Academy of Music, and the admirable Phillips ; the tenors were represented by Hobbs and the inimitable Braham ; Miss Stevens and Madame Caradori Allan, both excellent, sang the soprano parts. The chorus and orchestra were first-rate, and the first day might deserve to be called a perfect success."

The second day of the festival opened with another Coronation anthem by Handel, the *Hallelujah Chorus*, and Handel's *Israel in Egypt*, of which Moscheles recorded : " My own impression far exceeded all that I ever dreamt of realizing, and I believe my feelings were in unison with nearly all of those who were present." A miscellaneous programme took up all the third day, but on the fourth, the *Messiah* caused such a wild scramble for seats that wealthy people were offering fantastic sums to gain admission to the Abbey. The King and Queen had been present on all four days.

Thalberg, one of Moscheles' most brilliant pupils, had by 1836 established a reputation almost as great as that of his master. Referring to one of his compositions, Moscheles wrote in his diary : " I find his introduction of harp effects on the piano quite original. His theme, which lies in the middle part, is brought out clearly in relief with an accompaniment of complicated arpeggios which remind me of a harp. The audience is amazed. He himself remains immovably calm ; his whole bearing, as he sits at the piano, is soldier-like ; his lips are tightly compressed, and his coat buttoned closely. He told me that he acquired this attitude of self-control by smoking a Turkish pipe while practising his pianoforte exercises ; the length of the tube was so calculated as to keep him erect and motionless."

At about the same time Herz introduced his seven-octave piano, but because of its thin tone, very few concert pianists cared to use it. Another innovation was Broadwood's first bichord (semi-grand) piano, which gave a powerful tone with only two strings to a note ; an instrument that found favour with Moscheles on many occasions.

He was then busy preparing the English edition of Mendelssohn's oratorio *St. Paul*, which was to receive a triumphant *première* at Liverpool.

The great event of 1838 was, of course, the Coronation of Queen Victoria. Moscheles was unable to obtain a ticket for the ceremony, but Sir George Smart solved the problem by dressing him up in a cassock and surplice and putting him in the choir as a bass singer. The splendour of the occasion was duly reflected in his diary : " What an imposing sight, the gorgeously decorated Abbey crowded with splendidly dressed women ; and what an impression was created by the sight of the youthful Queen in her robes, surrounded by all the nobility of her realm ! Everything was imposing, but most of all Handel's chorus, *Zadock the Priest* and his *Hallelujah*, which moved one almost to tears."

In the same year Hummel died, and Moscheles was offered his place in the establishment of the Grand-Ducal family at Weimar, but he preferred to stay and enjoy the comparatively free life of concert-giving and teaching in London.

Two months in Paris during 1839 enabled Moscheles to meet Chopin and to discover how much his personality resembled his music. " He played to me . . . and I now for the first time understand his music ; all the raptures of the feminine world become intelligible. The *ad libitum* playing, which in the hands of other interpreters of his music degenerates into a constant uncertainty of rhythm, is with him an element of exquisite originality ; the hard inartistic modulations, so like those of a dilettante—which I never can manage when playing Chopin's music—cease to shock me, for he glides over them almost imperceptibly with his elfish fingers. His soft playing being a mere breath, he requires no powerful *forte* to produce the desired contrasts ; the consequence is that one never misses the orchestral effects that the German school demands of a pianoforte player, but is carried away as by some singer who troubles himself very little about the accompaniment, and follows his own impulses . . . he is perfectly unique in the world of pianoforte-players."

While they were staying in Paris in 1839 Moscheles and Chopin were commanded by King Louis Philippe to play before the Royal family at St. Cloud. " We passed through some splendid apartments to a ' salon carré ' where only the Royal family was assembled ; the Queen . . . Madame Adélaïde, the Duchess of Orleans, and the ladies of the Court. They one and all treated us kindly as if we were old acquaintances. The Queen . . . declared that they still remembered with gratitude the delight I gave them at the Tuileries. The King came up to me to say the same thing. . . . The Queen asked if the instrument—a Pleyel—was placed as we liked it ; was the lighting what we wanted ? First of all Chopin played a ' melangé of Nocturnes and Etudes,' and was extolled and admired as an old Court favourite. I followed with some old and new ' Studies,' and was honoured with similar applause. . . . The small audience now listened intently to my E-flat major Sonata, which was interrupted by such exclamations as 'divin! délicieux!' After the *Andante* the Queen whispered to one of her suite : ' Ne serait-il pas indiscret de le leur redemander ? ' which was tantamount to a command ; so we played it again with increased *abandon*, and in the *Finale* gave ourselves up to a ' musical delirium.' Chopin's enthusiasm throughout the whole performance of the piece must, I think, have kindled that of his hearers, who overwhelmed us both with compliments. . . . Better than all the words of praise . . . was the King's close attention during the entire evening. Chopin and I revelled like brothers in the triumph. . . ."

A year later Moscheles was appointed pianist to Prince Albert, but his services were not demanded very frequently. He was then accepting only occasional engagements to play in public, and these were chiefly at the Philharmonic Concerts. His growing fame as a conductor as well as pianist was reflected in a report of a Philharmonic Concert in *The Times* of May 4th, 1841 : "Artists and amateurs now are glad to own that Beethoven's Ninth Symphony is as much remarkable for majesty and grandeur as for simplicity. For this recognition we are in a great measure indebted to Moscheles, who conducted the work with great care and conscientiousness. As a conductor he surpasses almost all our musicians, for whenever he swings his baton he leads the orchestra, whereas others are led by it. Nothing would so much tend to elevate the character of these concerts as the permanent appointment of Moscheles as a conductor ; he is one who inspires the orchestra with a respect due to him, and would always lead it onwards to new successes."

Liszt was at that time a constant visitor at the house of Moscheles in London, and they frequently played duets together. ". . . he plays with the most perfect execution," Moscheles tells us, " storming occasionally like a Titan, but still, in the main, free from extravagance ; for the distinguishing mark of Liszt's mind and genius is that he knows perfectly the locality, the audience, and the style of music he brings before that audience, and uses his powers, which are equal to everything, merely as a means of eliciting the most varied kind of effects."

A command performance before the King of Prussia at Berlin was one of Moscheles' earliest engagements in 1842, a year that brought to London a swarm of foreign artists, among them the young Anton Rubinstein. " This Russian boy has fingers as light as feathers, and with them the strength of a man " we are told in the diary. In May of that year the news of the great fire at Hamburg caused Moscheles to give a concert in aid of the many thousands left homeless in that city. Mendelssohn arrived in London at the last moment and joined in, with the result that well over six hundred pounds was raised.

A return visit to Vienna in 1844, when he again played at Court, produced one or two interesting entries in his diary. We find, for instance : " Instead of Beethoven, Donizetti is now the sun of the music world. That sun does not warm me, not does it light me forward on my path . . ." ; and " My patience has been sorely tried at a performance of Mendelssohn's *Lobgesang*. You may imagine how I delighted in hearing that music . . . while the public sat listening in stolid indifference."

Mendelssohn had, in 1843, accepted the post of director of the new Leipzig Conservatoire, and for some time had been pressing Moscheles to give up his work in London—chiefly teaching—and to accept an appointment at that institution. Early in 1846 he wrote " On the day that you accept, I intend drinking my best wine and a glass or two of champagne into the bargain," adding that " the universal wish of the people in Leipzig, and their joy at the prospect of your coming . . . are in no way commensurate with the honour you would confer on them by your settling amongst them. . . . In a word, I wish you would come ! " Disregarding the great financial sacrifice involved, for the salary of the Leipzig professorship was but eight hundred thalers a year, Moscheles accepted, and one of his last engagements in this country while he was a resident here was at the great Birmingham Festival of 1846, where he conducted everything except the *Elijah*, which Mendelssohn directed himself and thereby won a tremendous ovation.

He arrived in Leipzig with his family on October 21st. " Felix Mendelssohn and his wife received us most affectionately . . . we found every arrangement made for our comfort. . . . I have probably now arrived at the final chapter in my art-career."

A visit to London in the following year made him remark upon the number of foreign musicians who dominated the musical circles of our capital. " Musical matters are in no way changed here," he recorded, " Besides Lablache and Madame Castellan, there are heaps of ' inis ' and ' ettis ' with their shakes and quavers ; but nowhere a full room."

On the 4th of November he was back in Leipzig beside the death-bed of his greatest friend. Mendelssohn died at twenty-four minutes past nine that evening. " I knelt down at the bedside, my prayers followed heavenwards the soul of the departed, and I pressed one last kiss on that noble forehead before it grew cold in the damp dew of death."

In the years that followed this tragic loss, Moscheles devoted himself to his duties at the Conservatoire, and although they were by no means uneventful, there is little of outstanding interest to record, except perhaps a visit to Liszt at Weimar, when he heard that great composer's Fantasia on the letters B-A-C-H for the first time ; " a piece full of extraordinary combinations, and stupendously played." Another meeting with Liszt was at Leipzig shortly afterwards, when the two played duets together. " It was a genuine treat to draw sparks from the piano as we dashed along together. Liszt's genius seemed to culminate when he played my old *Variations*, and finally my *Sonate Mélancholique*."

At Paris in the summer of 1860 Moscheles met Rossini. " In the course of our conversation he was full of hard-hitting truths, and brilliant satire on the present study and method of vocalization. ' I don't want to hear any more of it,' he said, ' they scream ! All that I want is a resonant, full-toned, not a screeching voice. I care not whether it be for speaking or singing ; everything ought to sound melodious.' He then spoke of the pleasure he felt in studying the piano. . . . He complains that the piano is now-a-days only maltreated. ' They not only thump the piano, but the armchair and even the floor.' When we talked of the Leipzig Conservatoire he was delighted to hear that encouragement was given to the serious study of organ-playing, and he complained of the decay of Church music in Italy. He was quite enthusiastic on the subject of Marcello's and Palestrina's sublime creations."

In 1861 Moscheles once again visited London and played at a Philharmonic concert " as a friend and not as a professional." Although he had not played in London for fifteen years a storm of cheers broke out from the audience as soon as he stepped upon the platform. His last visit to England was made five years later, when he attended the great Handel Festival at Crystal Palace : ". . . the effect at times of the double choruses was so thrilling that I thought to myself, ' Fancy old Handel standing and conducting his gigantic works in this gigantic place ! ' "

On March 1st, 1870, the forty-fifth anniversary of his wedding, he played an arrangement of the overture to *Der Freischütz* for four performers, with his daughter and two friends, at a little party given at his home ; and on the following day, though very weak, he insisted on attending the Gewandhaus rehearsal, but this was his last effort. He died on March 10th.

Chopin

THE little village of Zelazowa Wola, not far from Warsaw, provides the opening scene of this sketch : "a clump of trees surrounding the *dwór*, or nobleman's house ; the barns, cow-houses and stables form a spacious square court-yard, in the middle of which a well has been sunk, to which the red-turbaned girls go to fill their pails ; roads planted with poplars and fringed with thatched huts ; then fields of rye and wheat, stirred by the wind as with rippling waves, gilded and gleaming in the sun ; fields of yellow-blossomed colza, lucerne and silvery clover ; then forests which, in proportion as they are more or less remote, either stand out in dark masses against the horizon, or stretch out like a girdle of blue, or shimmer in a gauzy vapour. A few feet away from the castle . . . a little slate-roofed house, flanked with a small flight of wooden steps. Nothing has changed for nearly a hundred years. It is crossed by a gloomy vestibule. On the left, in a room lit by the ruddy flame of slowly burning logs, or by the flickering light of two candles placed one at each end of a long table, the serving maids spin as in olden days, relating to each other a thousand wondrous legends."

There, in the words of the poetic Count Wodzinski,[1] is a perfect description of the house in which Frédéric Chopin was born on February 22nd, 1810. He was the son of a private tutor in the employ of the Countess Skarbek, and had three sisters, Louise, Isabelle, and Emilienne. His mother came of a noble family in sadly reduced circumstances.

Eight months after Chopin's birth his father was appointed professor of French at the Warsaw Lyceum, so the family had to move into the city. Two years later Nicholas Chopin took a similar post at the School of Artillery and Military Engineering, but his salary was so inadequate that he was compelled to run a small private boarding school to supplement his income.

According to Karasowski, Frédéric Chopin was so sensitive to music in his early days that any emotional melody would make him burst into tears. He showed such interest in the piano that when he reached the age of six his parents sent him to the Czech pianist Adalbert Zywny for lessons. This able teacher—a great admirer of J. S. Bach—found in him a brilliant pupil who, according to Frederick Niecks, "played the piano as the birds sing : with unconscious art."

[1] *Les trois romans de Frédéric Chopin:* Paris 1886.

CHOPIN

At the age of eight the little pianist was a great favourite in the homes of the Polish aristocracy, and had actually made his first public performance by playing a concerto by Gyrowetz at a charity concert. Two years later he had written a march, dedicated it to the stern Grand Duke Constantine, and had the satisfaction of hearing it played by a military band in the Saxon Square.

His remarkable ability to extemporize greatly intrigued his fashionable audiences, though he preferred to play in this manner when he was at home and could have the room in complete darkness.

In 1824 he was sent to Elsner, the director of the Conservatoire, for lessons in harmony and counterpoint, and also to the Warsaw Lyceum. He was a delicate, intelligent boy, sensitive and temperamental, subject to alternating fits of high-spirited gaiety and melancholy yearning. He read the poetry of his native land with the same passionate love that he felt towards its countryside. Above all, he delighted in mixing freely with the peasants to hear their folksongs and to watch them doing their traditional dances. The rhythms of these melodies—and even the tunes themselves— found their way into many of his compositions : the mazurka, Krakowiak and the polonaise. Liszt tells us how Chopin would accompany the dances of the lovely Polish peasant women at the piano : " There he saw displayed the chaste graces of his captivating fellow-countrywomen, who left in him an indelible memory of the spell cast by their enthusiasm, so spirited and yet so controlled, when the major key once again introduced one of those figures which none but the spirit of a chivalrous people could create and make a national possession."[1]

It should perhaps be noted here that Chopin's love of the countryside waned in later life when he became enamoured with the musical life of fashionable Paris. At least, that is the view of M. Elie Poirée, who says in his own book on Chopin that " In him the impressions of nature did not go beyond either the early years of his youth or the frontiers of his native land ; it is these memories to which he goes back later, when he goes on writing polonaises or mazurkas. The countryside of Berry, the landscapes of the Balearics, do not seem to have awakened any artistic sensations in him." Liszt, on the other hand, would never accept this point of view.

Chopin's career as a virtuoso started when he was fifteen, for in the summer of 1825 he played at two concerts given by one of the professors of the Conservatoire. His first composition of any importance, the Rondo in C-minor dedicated to Madame von Linde, wife of the rector of the Warsaw Lyceum, appeared almost simultaneously. This was published by Brzezina of Warsaw.

[1] *F. Chopin:* Leipzig, 1852.

Although we are not, of course, studying Chopin's compositions in this sketch, mention should be made of the Rondo in the Style of a Mazurka (Opus 5) which he wrote in 1827, the year in which he completed his studies at the Lyceum, for in this work, Frederick Niecks declares, " Chopin's personality and nationality begin to be plain beyond a doubt. Who could fail to recognize him in the peculiar sweet and persuasive flows of sound, and the serpent-like winding of the melodic outline, the widespread chords, the chromatic progressions, the dissolving of the harmonies, and the linking of their constituent parts ? "

His concert engagements now became more frequent, and an ever-recurring item in his programmes were the Variations on *La ci darem la mano* (Opus 2), for piano and orchestra, which eventually found their way to the desk of Robert Schumann, who wrote of them in the *Allgemeine Musikalische Zeitung* thus : " I turned over the pages mechanically : the mysterious joy of music without sound has something enchanting about it. Besides, it appears to me that every composer's manuscript presents to our eyes a peculiar physiognomy of its own : Beethoven has a different look from Mozart on paper. . . . But now I imagined that eyes quite unknown, the eyes of flowers, of basilisks, of peacocks, the eyes of young girls, were gazing at me in wondering wise. In many places it began to seem plainer : I thought I perceived Mozart's *La ci darem la mano* entwined with a hundred chords : Leporello seemed actually to wink at me, and Don Giovanni flitted before me in a white cloak."

Very nearly as good is Schumann's analysis : " The first variation might be considered a little too full of distinction and coquetry : the grandee of Spain flirting charmingly with a peasant girl. This rights itself of its own accord in the second, which is already much more intimate, more comic and more teasing, like two lovers pursuing each other, laughing at their own play. What a difference in the third ! Moonlight in February ; Mazetto standing aside, and swearing, quite distinctly ; but Don Giovanni is not stopped by such a trifle." He then reviews the fourth, and concludes with a reference to the Adagio (in B-flat minor) and the Finale : " Leporello, hiding behind a bush, defies his master ; the clarinet and oboe charm us with wooing strains ; suddenly the key of D-flat major is introduced to indicate the first kiss. . . . But all this is nothing to the finale. Corks pop, bottles are smashed. Then follow the voice of Leporello, the apparition of the spirits, the flight of Don Giovanni, and lastly, a few closing bars of calm and farewell."[1]

With these variations Chopin made his début in Vienna in 1829 at a concert given at the Imperial Theatre. He had also arranged to play the Krakowiak, but in this the orchestra made so many mistakes at the rehearsal

[1] Quoted by Henri Bidou in *Chopin* (Knopf.).

that is had to be abandoned. Chopin was furious, for he was obliged to replace it by two improvisations, one on a theme from *La dame blanche*, and the other on the Polish song *Chmiel*. " I was in despair," he wrote to his friend Titus Woyciechowski on September 12th, " and yet the Variations made such an impression that I was recalled several times. All I know about my improvisation is that it was followed by a thunder of applause and several recalls."

Let us now see what the critics had to say about the young pianist. The *Allgemeine Musikalische Zeitung* declared without hesitation " The exquisite delicacy of his touch, the indescribable dexterity of his technique the subtle finish of his gradations of tone, reflecting a profoundly sensitive nature, the clearness of his interpretation . . . reveal a virtuoso richly endowed by nature, who is appearing on the horizon . . . as one of its most brilliant meteors." The *Wiener Theaterzeitung* was more restrained ". . . His touch is neat, but has not the brilliance displayed by our virtuosi from the very first bars. . . . He plays very quietly, with none of that dash and daring that generally distinguish the artist from the amateur."

Writing home to his parents, Chopin reported " It is said here almost unanimously that I play too softly, or rather, too tenderly, for the public. They are used to the big drum of the virtuosi. . . But I would rather they said I was too gentle than too violent."

A second concert was given a week later for which Count Maurice Lichnowsky, one of Beethoven's friends, offered him the use of his own piano —a slightly more resonant instrument. The tour concluded with visits to Prague, Teplitz, where he was entertained by Prince Clary and played an improvisation before a dazzling array of princesses, countesses, and whatnot ; and finally to Dresden.

He was at that time madly in love with a student at the Warsaw Conservatoire, Constantia Gladkowska. In a letter to his friend, Woyciechowski[1] he pours out his feelings : " I have found, perhaps to my misfortune, my ideal, whom I venerate faithfully and truly. It has already lasted for six months, and I have not yet spoken a syllable to her of whom I dream every night. It was with thoughts of this beautiful creature that I composed the Adagio of my new concerto, as well as the valse which I wrote this morning and am sending you. Note the passage marked with a cross. Nobody but you knows what it means. . . ."

It should be noted that this infatuation did not prevent him flirting with the lovely nineteen-year-old Mlle. Blaherka, when he was in Vienna, nor with the two princesses he found at Antonin when a little later he went to stay for a week with Prince Radziwill.

Chopin completed his Concerto in F-minor (now known as the Second Concerto, because it was not published until 1836) early in 1830 and played

[1] Quoted by Karasowski in *Friedrich Chopin* (Dresden, 1877).

it at his first great concert in Warsaw. It is in three movements, Maestoso, Larghetto and Allegro vivace, and the themes are given out by the orchestra so that the soloist can develop them. Here is Frederick Nieck's impression :
". . . the piano interrupts the orchestra impatiently, and then takes up the first subject ; it is as if we were transported into another world and breathed a purer atmosphere. First there are some questions and expostulations, then the composer unfolds a tale full of sweet melancholy in a strain of lovely, tenderly-entwined melody. . . . But the contemplation of his grief disturbs his equanimity more and more, and he begins to fret and fume. In the second subject he seems to protest the truthfulness and devotion of his heart, and concludes with a passage, half upbraiding, half beseeching, which is quite captivating, nay more, even bewitching in its eloquent persuasiveness. . . ."

Chopin declared that he wrote the Larghetto of this concerto while thinking of Constantia, so we must overlook its effusiveness.

The Concerto in E-minor (Opus 11) was finished during the summer of 1830 and was introduced to the musical *élite* of Warsaw on October 11th, Chopin's third and last concert in that city. Just before he left on November 1st his friends gave him a banquet at which he was presented with a silver goblet filled with Polish earth. At the sight of this he was moved to tears, for he had a curious presentiment that he would never see his native land again.

He met his friend Woyciechowski at Kalisch, and then proceeded by way of Breslau, Dresden and Prague to Vienna, where he felt sure he would be warmly received and well supported in the concert hall. But he was quickly disillusioned. Haslinger, who had already published his Variations on *La ci darem la mano*, showed no desire to publish any more of his music, and there was a new manager at the Kärnthnerthor Theatre who proved equally unhelpful when Chopin tried to negotiate terms for a concert. Then to depress him still further there came news of the revolution in Poland, which had broken out on November 30th. Woyciechowski, with whom he was sharing rooms, insisted upon returning to Poland immediately. Chopin would certainly have gone back with him had he been strong enough to enter the army, for he was already trying to stifle recurrent attacks of homesickness.

We find Chopin writing to Matuszynski on Christmas Day : " The many dinners, soirées, concerts and balls which I have to go to only bore me. I am sad, and feel so lonely and forsaken here. But I cannot live as I would ! I must dress, appear with a cheerful countenance in the *salons* ; but when I am again in my room I give vent to my feelings on the piano, to which, as my best friend in Vienna, I disclose all my sufferings. I have not a soul to whom I can fully unbosom myself, and yet I must meet everyone like a friend."

CHOPIN

After the departure of his friend Woyciechowski, Chopin moved to cheaper apartments in the house of Baroness von Lachmanowicz. His mode of life there is well described in a letter that he wrote to his parents at the time : " I live on the fourth floor, in a fine street, but I have to strain my eyes in looking out of the window when I wish to see what is going on beneath. You will find my room in my new album when I am at home again. Young Hummel[1] is so kind as to draw it for me. It is large and has five windows ; the bed is opposite to them. My wonderful piano stands on the right, the sofa on the left ; between the windows there is a mirror, in the middle of the room a fine, large, round mahogany table ; the floor is polished. . . . Early in the morning the unbearably-stupid servant wakes me ; I rise, get my coffee, and often drink it cold because I forget my breakfast over my playing. Punctually at nine o'clock appears my German master ; then I generally write ; and after that, Hummel comes to work at my portrait, while Nidecki studies my concerto. And all this time I remain in my comfortable dressing-gown, which I do not take off until twelve o'clock. At that hour a very worthy German makes his appearance, Herr Liebenfrost, who works in the law-courts here. If the weather is fine I take a walk with him on the Glacis, then we dine together at a restaurant, *Zur böhmischen Köchin*, which is frequented by all the university students ; we then go to one of the best coffee-houses, as is the custom here. After that I go visiting, return home at nightfall, get into evening dress and go to some soirée. I arrive home again at eleven or twelve—never later—then play, laugh, read, lie down and dream of you, my dear ones."

It was only the friendship of other talented artists that kept Chopin in Vienna even for this short spell. Among these we find Sigismund Thalberg, whom he admired but frequently criticized : " Thalberg plays famously, but he is not my man," Chopin declared. " He is younger than I, pleases the ladies very much, makes pot-pourris on *La Muette*, produces his *forte* and *piano* by the pedal and not with his fingers, spans tenths as easily as I do octaves, and wears diamond studs. Moscheles does not at all surprise him ; therefore it is no wonder that only the *tuttis* of my concerto have pleased him. He, too, writes concertos."

Chopin found it impossible to give a concert himself in Vienna and had to be content to take part in one given by Madame Garzia-Vestris in the Redoutensaal. It is significant that in the newspaper announcement his name was followed by " pianoforte-player " in parenthesis.

He left Vienna on July 20th, 1831, and went by way of Linz and Salzburg to Munich, where a month or so later he played his E minor Concerto at a morning concert in the hall of the Philharmonic Society. A report in *Flora* said that he showed " an excellent virtuosity in the treatment of his

---

[1] A son of the composer of that name.

instrument " and that as well as mature technique " one noticed especially a charming delicacy of execution, and a beautiful and characteristic rendering of the motives."

Shortly afterwards, he was in Stuttgart, where he heard that on September 8th the Russian army had captured Warsaw. This news flung him into the depths of despair, and it is said that he wrote his passionate Étude in C-minor in an attempt to express the grief that had overwhelmed him.

The distraction he needed came when a little later he moved to Paris and plunged into its rich, if somewhat turbulent, artistic life. Here he met, among others, Cherubini, Rossini, Baillot, Kalkbrenner, Mendelssohn, Berlioz, Bellini, Liszt, and Franchomme, the famous 'cellist, with whom he enjoyed a life-long friendship from that time.

Kalkbrenner was the greatest pianist on the continent in those days, for Liszt and Thalberg had not yet reached their zenith. On December 16th Chopin wrote to Woyciechowski : " You may easily imagine how curious I was to hear Herz and Hiller play, but they are nothing compared with Kalkbrenner. Honestly speaking, I can play as well as Herz, but I wish I could equal Kalkbrenner. If Paganini is perfect, so also is he, in quite a different manner. His repose, enchanting touch, and smoothness of playing I cannot describe : one recognizes the master in every note—he is a giant who throws all other artists into the shade. When I called upon him, he begged me to play something. What could I do ? As I had heard Herz, I took courage, sat down at his instrument and played my E minor Concerto, which charmed the people of the Bavarian capital so much. Kalkbrenner was astonished, and asked me if I were a pupil of Field. He said that I had the style of Cramer, but the touch of Field. It amused me to note that Kalkbrenner, when he played to me, made a mistake and did not know how to go on, but it was wonderful to hear how he found his way again. Since this meeting we have been seeing each other daily : either he calls on me or I on him. He wanted to teach me for three years and make a great artist of me. I told him that I was well aware what I lacked, but would not imitate him, and that three years were too much for me. He has convinced me that I play well only when I am in the right mood, and less well when this is not the case. This cannot be said of Kalkbrenner : his playing is always the same. When he had watched me for a long time he came to the conclusion that I had no method ; that I was indeed on a very good path, but that I might easily go astray ; and that when he ceased to play, there would no longer be a representative of the grand pianoforte school left. I cannot create a new school, however much I may wish to do so, because I do not even know the old one. But I know that my tone-poems have some individuality in them, and that I always strive to advance. . . . But many who dissuade me from taking lessons are of the opinion that I play as well as

Kalkbrenner, and that it is only vanity that makes him wish to have me for his pupil. That is nonsense. Whoever knows anything about music must think highly of Kalkbrenner's talent, although he is disliked as a man because he will not associate with everybody. But I can assure you that there is in him something higher than in all the virtuosi whom I have yet heard. I have said this in a letter to my parents, and they quite understand it. Elsner, however, does not comprehend, and regards it as jealousy on Kalkbrenner's part that he not only praises me, but also wishes that my playing were in some respects different from what it is. In spite of all this I can tell you confidentially that my name is already distinguished among artists here."

Chopin's great aspirations at this time are reflected in a letter to Elsner in which he says " I am known here and there in Germany as a pianist ; several musical journals have spoken highly of my concerts, and expressed the hope of seeing me soon take a prominent position among the leading pianoforte virtuosi. I had to-day an opportunity of fulfilling the promise I had made to myself. Why should I not embrace it ? I should not like to learn pianoforte-playing in Germany, for there no one could tell me precisely what I lacked. . . . Three years' study is far too much. Kalkbrenner, when he had heard me several times, came to see that himself. From this you may see that a true, meritorious virtuoso does not know the feeling of envy. I would certainly make up my mind to study for three years longer if I were certain that I should then reach the aim which I have always kept in view. So much is clear to me : I shall never become a copy of Kalkbrenner ; he will not be able to break my perhaps bold but noble resolve to create a new art-era. If I now continue my studies I do so only in order to stand at some future time on my own feet. . . ."

The result of this was that Chopin went to Kalkbrenner for a little while, but then apparently found some excuse for discontinuing the lessons. They remained friends, however, in fact it was Kalkbrenner who helped Chopin to organize his first concert, which was given in Pleyel's Rooms at 9, Rue Cadet, on January 26th, 1832. Financially, it was a failure, but Fétis in the *Revue Musicale* proclaimed : " Here is a young man who, by giving himself up to his natural impressions, and taking no model, has discovered, if not a complete revolution in pianoforte music, at least a part of what composers have been seeking in vain for a long time, namely, an abundance of original ideas of a type to be found nowhere else. This does not mean that M. Chopin has the great gifts of Beethoven . . . I speak of pianists' music and it is by comparison with the latter that I find in M. Chopin's inspirations the sign of a renewal of forms that may exert in time great influence over this branch of the art. As an executant also the young artist deserves praise. His playing is elegant, easy, graceful, and possesses brilliance and neatness."

Liszt was present at this concert and spoke very highly of the young pianist. He described Chopin thus : " His whole person was harmonious. His glance was intelligent rather than dreamy ; his soft, shrewd smile had no touch of bitterness. The fineness and transparency of his complexion charmed the eye, his fair hair was silky, his nose slightly aquiline, his movements well-bred, and his manners bore such an aristocratic stamp that one involuntarily treated him like a prince. His gestures were frequent and graceful. His voice was always toneless, and often indistinct ; but he was not very tall, and was slightly built. . . ."

Chopin's second public appearance was on May 20th at a charity concert given by the Prince de la Moskowa, but he was rather overshadowed by Brod, the brilliant oboist on this occasion. Nevertheless, he soon became recognized as one of the best pianists in France, and his services as a teacher were eagerly sought by the aristocracy of Paris. He moved with ease in the highest society, a familiar and distinguished figure at the soirées of princes, ambassadors and other noblemen. At the same time he was loved and respected in the more humble artistic circles, and was always a good friend to the little groups of his compatriots that used to meet in the French capital. A quotation from a letter written at about this time by Orlowski to a friend should be noted here : " Chopin is well and strong ; he is turning the heads of all the women : the men are jealous of him. He is now the fashion, and I have no doubt that we shall soon be wearing our gloves à la Chopin. But he is consumed with yearning for his country."

He played at several concerts with Liszt, but found little pleasure in concert-giving, and was apt to hold aloof from the public at this time. " The crowd embarrasses me " he told Liszt, " I feel stifled by their breathing, paralysed by their curious glances, mute before their strange faces. But as for you, you are intended for them by fate, for if you cannot win your public, you have the power to stun them."

In the summer of 1835 he went to Carlsbad to meet his parents, who were staying there for a while, and then went through Dresden to Leipzig, where he met Clara Wieck (afterwards Clara Schumann), and Robert Schumann. For the next couple of years he spent practically the whole of his time in composition and teaching, leaving an open field for the visit of Thalberg, who was then acclaimed as the most brilliant pianist in Paris (Liszt was then in Switzerland, and his return to the French capital in order to prove his superiority over Thalberg is told elsewhere in this book).

Constantia Gladkowska had married somebody else, and Chopin was at that time causing comment by his various short-lived love affairs in Paris, although he would have married another Polish woman, Maria Wodzińska, if her parents had not objected. It is said that his Ballade in G-minor was written as an expression of this unhappy affection. After his death a bundle of Maria's letters to him were found tied up with pink ribbon and labelled " Moja bieda " (my misery).

It was probably to help him get over this affair that Camille Pleyel and Stanislas Koźmian brought him to London in July, 1837, but he was then in poor health, and expressed no desire to move in artistic or fashionable circles here. Indeed, he preferred to stay in the capital incognito, and was introduced to James Broadwood as M. Fritz. As soon as he touched the piano, however, his identity became known, and we find that Mendelssohn wrote to Hiller on September 1st : " Chopin is said to have suddenly turned up here a fortnight ago ; but he visited nobody and made no acquaintances. He played one evening most beautifully at Broadwood's[1] and then hurried away again. I hear he is still suffering very much." Moscheles, in his diary, also referred to his visit, explaining Chopin's reluctance to meet people by saying that every conversation aggravated his chest-complaint.

Liszt had then become acquainted with George Sand, the novelist, and on one occasion happened to mention the name of Chopin to her. She immediately became interested in the Polish musician and began pestering Liszt for an introduction, despite the fact that Chopin had frequently expressed his dislike of literary women generally. Eventually, Liszt took her with the Comtesse d'Agoult to Chopin's rooms one evening when the pianist was entertaining a few friends. Subsequently, the novelist met Chopin at a soirée held by the Comtesse at the Hôtel de France, but made a bad impression upon him, for on the way home he said to Hiller, " How repellent that woman Sand is ! Is she really a woman ? I am almost inclined to doubt it. . . ."

He was perhaps trying to conceal his feelings, and said this merely to mislead Hiller, for he was soon to change his attitude. On the other hand, one could scarcely expect this delicate young man who had, according to Liszt, all manner of feminine graces, to take immediately to this Amazonian woman. Heine described her as a beautiful woman ". . . even a distinguished beauty. Like the genius which manifests itself in her works, her face is rather to be called beautiful than interesting . . . the features of George Sand bear rather the impress of a Greek regularity. Their form, however, is not hard, but softened by the sentimentality which is suffused over them like a veil of sorrow. The forehead is not high, and the delicious chestnut-brown curly hair falls parted down to the shoulders. Her eyes are somewhat dim, at least they are not bright, and their fire may have been extinguished by many tears, or may have passed into her works, which have spread their flaming brands over the whole world. . . . The author of *Lélia* has quiet, soft eyes, which remind one neither of Sodom nor of

---

[1] Broadwood's house in Bryanston Square.

Gomorrah, . . . an ordinary straight nose. A good-natured smile plays usually around her mouth, but it is not very attractive ; the somewhat hanging under-lip betrays fatigued sensuality. The chin is full and plump, but nevertheless beautifully proportioned. Also her shoulders are beautiful, nay, magnificent. Likewise her arms and hands, which, like her feet, are small. Let other contemporaries describe the charms of her bosom ; I confess my incompetence. The rest of her bodily frame seems to be somewhat too stout, at least too short. Only her head bears the impress of ideality ; it reminds one of the noblest remains of Greek art, and in this respect one of our friends could compare the beautiful woman to the marble statue of the Venus of Milo, . . . she even surpasses the latter in many respects : she is, for instance, very much younger."

Heine then goes on to describe her voice, which he says is " dull and faded, without sonority, but soft and agreeable. The naturalness of her speaking lends it some charm. . . . She has nothing whatever of the sparkling *ésprit* of her countrywomen, and nothing of their talkativeness. She is taciturn rather from haughtiness because she does not think you are worth wasting her cleverness upon. . . . George Sand never says anything witty. . . ."

Throughout 1837 George Sand was living at Nohant, and frequently pressed Chopin to go and stay with her. Balzac, who visited her there described how she would sit in her dressing gown after dinner smoking cigars, and mentioned that she had not a single grey hair in spite of her terrible troubles.[1] It is quite possible that Chopin visited her sometime during the summer of that year, but there is little reliable evidence.

In March, 1838, he appeared at a concert given in Rouen by one of his fellow-countrymen, Orlowski, and a report of his performance by Legouvé in the *Gazette musicale* describes his success as " immense." It also urges him to return to public life, to " give his beautiful talent to all," for he had rarely been heard in the concert-hall for the past two or three years.

George Sand had to return to Paris for a while that spring because of the lawsuit in which she was engaged with her husband, and she frequently saw Chopin. Then the doctor who was attending her son Maurice said that the child would have to spend the next winter in a warmer climate, and she decided to visit Majorca. Chopin was also ordered " air, exercise and rest," for some of his friends believed him to be consumptive, and he agreed to accompany her.

The novelist set out with her two children and a maid during the following November, and arranged to meet Chopin at Perpignan. If he decided not to come, she would then proceed without him. Chopin, we are

---

[1] She had contracted an extremely unfortunate marriage, and was seeking a divorce. Incidentally, she was thirty-three at that time.

told, then left Paris mysteriously, telling only a couple of intimate friends of his destination.

They arrived at Palma in due course, but had been there barely a couple of days when the weather changed for the worse and a deluge of rain made their rented villa uninhabitable. Then they found shelter in the abandoned Carthusian monastery of Valdemosa, where they were able to rent three rooms and furnish them sparsely. Chopin caught a severe cold and became a difficult invalid. Some idea of his condition may be gained from a letter he wrote to Julius Fontana : " I cannot send you the MSS. as they are not yet finished. During the last two weeks I have been as ill as a dog. . . . Three doctors, the most renowned in the island, were called in for consultation. One smelt what I spat, the second knocked whence I spat, the third sounded and listened when I spat. The first said that I would die, the second that I was dying, the third that I had died already. . . . I had a narrow escape from their bleedings, cataplasms, and suchlike operations. Thanks to Providence I am now myself again."

Chopin was at this time writing the Preludes, which he completed at the end of 1838 and sent to Fontana on the following January 12th. His health grew steadily worse, and they decided to return to France as soon as the weather improved. " Our invalid did not seem to be in a state to stand the passage, but seemed equally incapable of enduring another week at Majorca " George Sand wrote. " The situation was frightful ; there were days when I lost hope and courage. To console us, Maria Antonia and her village gossips repeated to us in chorus the most edifying discourses on the future life. ' This consumptive person ' they said, ' is going to hell, first because he is consumptive, and secondly because he does not confess. . . . We shall not bury him in consecrated ground.' "

They left Palma in a boat that carried over a hundred pigs, which were regarded as far more important than the passengers, and when they arrived at Barcelona, Chopin was " spitting basins full of blood, and crawling along like a ghost." Fortunately, the French ship *Méléagre* was stationed there, and the commandant allowed Chopin to be taken on board so that he could receive attention from the ship's doctor. The haemorrhage was then stopped, and as soon as he was well enough, the French consul's carriage took him to an hotel. A week later they sailed once more in the *Phénicien*, and on their arrival at Marseilles towards the end of February, George Sand wrote to Madame Marliani " At last I am back in France ! Another month and Chopin and I would have died in Spain ; he of melancholy and disgust, I of rage and indignation."

They stayed in Marseilles a couple of months while Chopin's condition was improving, and then returned to Nohant to settle down quietly. " In the evening " George Sand wrote, " Chopin plays to me in the twilight.

After which he falls asleep, at the same time as the children." For the next seven years they spent their winters in Paris and most of their summers at Nohant.

When Chopin got back to Paris in the autumn of 1839 he took apartments in the Rue Tronchet and resumed teaching. The house that George Sand had taken for herself was some distance away in the Rue Pigalle : a distance which both found to be inconvenient. To those who were curious about her relationship with Chopin, the novelist always posed as a sort of benevolent nurse, fairy godmother and whatnot ; and the fact that she never regarded herself as anything so sordid as his mistress may be gleaned from her own amusingly delicate statement :[1] " He began to cough again, and I saw myself forced either to give in my resignation as nurse, or to pass my life in impossible journeyings to and fro. In order to spare me these, he came every day to tell me with a troubled face and feeble voice that he was wonderfully well. He would ask if he might dine with us, and then go away in the evening shivering in his cab. Seeing how he took to heart this exclusion from our family life, I offered to let him one of the *pavillons*, a part which I could give up to him. He accepted joyfully. He had there his room, received his friends there, and gave his lessons without incommoding me. Maurice had the room above his ; I occupied the other *pavillon* with my daughter."

Moscheles arrived in Paris that autumn and met Chopin. They played the former's E-flat major Sonata for four hands so well that Comte de Perthuis happened to mention the performance at Court. King Louis Philippe forthwith commanded them to repeat the Sonata before the Royal family at St. Cloud. This event has already been described in some detail in the chapter devoted to Moscheles so I need add no more here, except to say that the King presented Chopin with a gold cup and saucer, and gave Moscheles a travelling case.

The next event of importance was on April 26th, 1841, when Chopin gave a concert at the Salle Pleyel. Here is what Liszt wrote about it in the *Gazette musicale* : " Last Monday at eight o'clock in the evening, M. Pleyel's rooms were brilliantly illuminated ; innumerable carriages brought incessantly to the foot of a staircase covered with carpet and perfumed with flowers the most elegant women, the most fashionable young men, the most celebrated artists, the richest financiers, the most illustrious noblemen : a whole *élite* of society, a whole aristocracy of birth, fortune, talent and beauty.

" A grand piano was open on the platform ; people crowded round, eager for the seats nearest to it, . . . saying to one another that they must not lose a chord, a note, an intention, a thought of him who was to sit there.

[1] *Histoire de ma Vie.*

And people were right in being thus eager . . . because he for whom they waited . . . was not only a clever virtuoso, a pianist expert in the art of making notes, not only an artist of great renown, he was all this and more . . . he was Chopin. . . .

". . . Only rarely, at distant intervals, has Chopin played in public ; but what would have been for anyone else an almost certain cause of oblivion and obscurity has been precisely what has assured to him a fame above the caprices of fashion, and kept him from rivalries, jealousies, and injustice. Chopin, who has taken no part in the extreme movement which for several years has thrust one on another and one against another the executive artists from all quarters of the world, has been constantly surrounded by faithful adepts, . . . all of whom . . . have not ceased to spread abroad his works and with them admiration for his name. Moreover, this exquisite, altogether lofty, and eminently aristocratic celebrity has remained unattacked.

" For Monday's concert Chopin chose those of his works which do not comply with the classical forms. He played neither concerto, nor sonata, nor fantasia, nor variations ; but preludes, studies, nocturnes and mazurkas. Addressing himself to a society rather than to a public, he could show himself as he is : an elegiac poet, profound, chaste and dreamy. He did not need to astonish or to overwhelm : he sought for delicate sympathy rather than for noisy enthusiasm. . . . From the first chords there was established a close communication between him and the audience. Two studies and a ballade were encored, and had it not been for the fear of adding to the already great fatigue which betrayed itself on his pale face, people would have asked for a repetition of the pieces of the programme one by one."

This warm tribute from one so great as Liszt—himself the greatest pianist of the age—placed the art of Chopin on the pinnacle from which it has never been dislodged.

Within a year, he had given another concert, notwithstanding his dislike of playing in public. It took place in the same hall on February 21st, 1842, and the programme consisted of three mazurkas, A-flat major, B major and A minor ; three studies, A-flat major, F minor, and C minor ; the Ballade in A-flat major, four nocturnes, a prelude in D-flat, and an impromptu in G.

In the following autumn Chopin and George Sand left the Rue Pigalle and took adjacent apartments in the Square d'Orléans. From then until 1845 there is little of importance to record but the fact that the severe winter of 1844-5 aggravated Chopin's consumptive tendencies. He continued his activities as a composer, of course.

What qualities contributed to his technique as a pianist ? Niecks mentions first the suppleness and equality of his fingers, and the perfect independence of his hands. " The evenness of his scales and passages in all kinds of touch was unsurpassed, nay, prodigious " declared Mikuli. His hands were small, light and delicate, yet they could expand in a most remarkable fashion to cover a third of the keyboard. He always believed that the position of the hand was the first essential to be considered when trying to acquire a good touch. Kleczynski tells us he trained the hand with infinite care before allowing it to start reproducing musical ideas. " In order to give the hand a position at once graceful and convenient . . . he would make the pupil drop it lightly on the keyboard so that the five fingers rested upon the notes E, F-sharp, G-sharp, A-sharp, and B. This was for him the normal position." These notes he would make the pupil play as a five-finger exercise, first in a light staccato, then heavier staccato, then accentuated legato, then finally in the normal legato style. He would then make the pupil repeat the process with the left hand on F, G-flat, A-flat, B-flat and C.

These exercises occur normally in the scales of B major and D-flat major respectively. Consequently they were the first scales his pupils would be asked to practise—and always staccato at first. " Then," according to Kleczynski, " by the various gradations of mezzo staccato, accentuated staccato, etc. . . . lifting the fingers high, and by the mere play of the muscles, they arrived at passing the thumb without allowing the hand to lose its horizontal position. Next, the hand was allowed to proceed to more difficult scales, to arpeggio passages, in which even the very wide intervals are stretched as they occur, without effort, and even without lifting the fingers very high. I know by experience that by this means one arrives at an even and sure touch." Suppleness was Chopin's great objective in this. He would stand by his pupil repeating over and over again " Facilement, . . . facilement. . . ." (easily, easily). Stiffness and jerkiness would exasperate him. On one occasion when a pupil played some arpeggios in a clumsy, jerky fashion, he jumped up from his chair and ejaculated " Qu'est-ce ? Est-ce un chien qui vient d'aboyer ? " (What is that ? Has a dog been barking ?) He was always very irritable, but tried hard not to show anger in front of a pupil. He would often get up, stand behind the pupil with a wretched expression upon his face, and in an effort to control himself, would break his pencil into pieces.

Chopin always warned his pupils against practising too much. One lady, thinking it would please him, said that she had been practising for six hours a day since her last lesson. He immediately displayed irritability at such foolishness, and told her never to do more than three hours a day.

He made his pupils use Clementi's *Préludes et Exercises*, particularly the second volume, which he esteemed very highly. Other such books used by his pupils included Cramer's *Études* and Clementi's *Gradus ad Parnassum*, but he was also very fond of prescribing the Suites of J. S. Bach and various fugues from *Das Wohltemperirte Clavier*.

CHOPIN

Being deficient in physical strength, Chopin made a speciality of the *cantabile* style, and he always insisted upon smooth playing by his pupils. One of his sharpest and most sarcastic criticisms was " He cannot play two notes legato." He would emphasize the value of ensemble playing if first-rate performers could be found to co-operate, and of listening to good singing if the pupil could not sing himself. His pupils were invariably urged to go as frequently as possible to the Italian opera, and to pay special attention to the singers' phrasing and expression. Bad phrasing on the piano, he told Mikuli, sounded to him exactly like someone reciting, in a language he did not understand, a speech that had been laboriously memorized. " The musician who phrases badly " he would say, " shows that music is not his mother-tongue, but something quite foreign and unintelligible to him."

Concerning Chopin's much-discussed *tempo rubato*, let us see first what Liszt said about it : " In his playing the great artist rendered enchantingly that sort of emotional trepidation, timid or breathless, that seizes the heart when one believes oneself to be in the presence of supernatural beings. . . . He always made the melody undulate like a light boat borne on the bosom of a mighty billow, or else he would give it a wavering motion, like an aerial apparition suddenly arising in this tangible and palpable world. He indicates this in his compositions . . . by the words *tempo rubato* : stolen, broken time, at once supple, abrupt and languishing . . . like a cornfield rippling under the soft pressure of a warm breeze, like tree-tops bent hither and thither at the whim of a capricious gust."

Mikuli's description was less poetical : " While the singing hand, either irresolutely lingering or, as in passionate speech, eagerly anticipating with a certain impatient vehemence, freed the truth of the musical expression from all rhythmical fetters, the other, the accompanying hand, continued to play strictly in time." Niecks also quotes the music critic of the *Athenæum* as saying : " He makes free use of *tempo rubato* : leaning about within the bars more than any player we recollect, but still subject to a presiding measure such as presently habituates the ear to the liberties taken." But let us not imagine that Chopin tolerated any rhythmical slovenliness, for Madame Streicher assures us that he detested any sign of languor, dragging of the time, misplaced *rubato* and exaggerated *ritardando*.

During his first few years in Paris, Chopin always used an Erard piano. Then he was presented with a Pleyel, and preferring its very light touch, would use no other make of instrument, if he could avoid it. When he visited England he invariably used a Broadwood ; a make of which he spoke appreciatively on several occasions.

We now come to Chopin's closing years. To what extent his premature end was hastened by the breach in his relations with George Sand can only be surmised, but the trouble started in 1846 when the *Courrier français* began publishing *Lucrezia Floriani* in which George Sand represented Chopin as Prince Karol, a delicate and charming, sexless creature " something like those ideal creatures with which the poetry of the Middle Ages used to adorn Christian churches ; an angel, fair of face as a tall, sad woman, pure and slender in form as a young god of Olympus, and, to crown this union of qualities, an expression at once tender and severe, at once chaste and passionate. Nothing could be at once purer and more elevated than his thoughts, nothing could exceed the tenacity and exclusiveness of his affections or his devotion even in the smallest trifles." George Sand represented herself as Lucrezia, wearied by fifteen years of passion, yielding to him, but only out of maternal love, and nobly enduring Karol's distressing egotism. She describes the brilliant wit " with which he would torture those whom he loved. He was mocking, stiff, affected, and bored with everything. It was as if he took pleasure in biting gently, though the wound he made reached the very vitals. Or if he had not the heart to contradict and scoff, he would retire into a disdainful silence, or heart-rending sulks." Lucrezia eventually dies broken-hearted.

The fact that George Sand had become tired of Chopin was fairly obvious, and the matter culminated in a quarrel over the composer's sympathy with the novelist's daughter and son-in-law, who had been turned out of the house. There were also the novelist's amorous escapades which Chopin regarded as infidelities, and various minor quarrels with her son Maurice. Moreover, the musician's illnesses were becoming more and more frequent, and there can be no doubt that he was a very trying patient. After his illness in the spring of 1847, George Sand wrote to Grzymala : " Well, this time he has been saved once more, but how dark the future is for me in this respect also ! . . . I am well aware that many people accuse me, some of having exhausted him by the violence of my senses, others of having driven him to despair by my vagaries. . . . As for him, he complains to me that I am killing him by refusing sexual relations, whereas I know for certain that I should kill him if I were to act otherwise. . . . I have made myself his slave in every way in which I could do so without showing him an impossible and reprehensible preference over my children. . . . I have displayed prodigious patience in this matter. . . ."

Despite his failing health, Chopin was able to give a concert in Paris—his last in the capital—on February 16th, 1848, when tickets were sold for twenty francs each : an extortionate price in those days. The *Gazette musicale* reported that " the fine flower of the aristocracy of the most distinguished women, the most elegant toilettes, filled on Wednesday Pleyel's rooms. There was also the aristocracy of artists and amateurs, happy to seize in his flight this musical sylph who had promised to let himself once more and for a few hours be approached, seen and heard." Although

70

CHOPIN

Chopin was obviously very weak, the concert was a tremendous success.

One of Chopin's pupils, Jane Stirling, a wealthy Scotswoman, then persuaded him to visit London again. He arrived on April 21st, and after a short stay at 10 Bentinck Street, took apartments in Dover Street. He seems to have been drawn well into the social life of London, for he fulfilled many engagements at private houses. He played for the Countess of Blessington at Gore House, Kensington, and for the Duchess of Sutherland at Stafford House. Two matinées were given ; one at the house of Mrs. Sartoris (*née* Adelaide Kemble), 99 Eaton Place ; and the other at the residence of the Earl of Falmouth, 2 St. James's Square. Of his playing at these, the music critic of the *Athenæum* said that delicacy, picturesqueness, elegance and humour were blended to produce that rare thing, a new delight.

We may safely assume that this activity on Chopin's part was forced upon him by the necessity of making money quickly, for he was so weak that he had to be carried up the stairs at Broadwood's. Early in August he went to Edinburgh, stayed first at Calder House, the residence of Lord Torphichen, then went to the Stirling family at Keir, and to Johnstone Castle.

On August 28th, Chopin fulfilled an engagement at Manchester. Describing what it called the most brilliant concert of the season, the *Manchester Guardian* wrote enthusiastically about both his compositions and his playing, noting that his style was refined rather than vigorous, and that he had an " elegant rapid touch " rather than a firm, nervous grasp of the instrument.

A month later he was playing in Glasgow, and on October 4th in Edinburgh, although three days before he had written to Grzymala " I am getting worse every day, I feel progressively weaker ; I am incapable of composing, not because I do not want to, but for purely physical reasons, and because I move from one place to another every week."

At the end of October he returned to London, and for the first fortnight in November was obliged to stay indoors on account of a severe cold. He recovered sufficiently to allow him to attend the Polish Ball and Concert at the Guildhall on November 16th. The few items he played at this concert— his last public appearance—were almost ignored. The audience swept into the concert room hot and excited from the dancing and seemed to pay little attention to the pallid young man who, in the last stages of exhaustion drew delicate and almost inaudible melodies from the piano. The newspapers did not even bother to mention him in their reports. Thus concluded the career of one of the greatest virtuosi the world has ever known.

He was still in London early in January, 1849, but wrote to Grzymala saying that he would go mad or die if he had to stay a day longer.

Back in Paris later that month, he burned most of the manuscripts he had started, leaving only a Nocturne and a short valse, and as he grew weaker, stopped giving lessons. The months dragged on. During the summer he moved from the Square d'Orléans to second-floor apartments in the Rue de Chaillot which gave him a splendid view over Paris. " His weakness and his sufferings had become so great that he could no longer let anybody hear him play the piano, nor could he compose ; even the slightest conversation made him alarmingly tired " we are told by Berlioz.

At the end of September he moved again to 12 Place Vendôme, where his sister and the pupil Gutmann stayed with him day and night. By the middle of October he was sinking, though when on the 15th the Countess Delphine Potocka visited him, he begged her to sing to him. On the following morning he was a little better, but he died between three and four o'clock in the morning of October 17th. The funeral took place at the Madeleine on October 30th. His own Funeral March, orchestrated by Reber, was played, and Lefébure-Wély played the B-minor and E-minor Preludes on the organ. Lablache sang the *Tuba Mirum*, as he had done at Beethoven's funeral in 1827, in Mozart's *Requiem*, which Chopin himself had requested.

Liszt

" WORDS cannot describe him as a pianist—he was incomparable and unapproachable. I have seen whole rows of his audience, men and women alike, affected to tears when he chose to be pathetic : in stormy passages he was able by his art to work them up to the highest pitch of excitement : through the medium of his instrument he played upon every human emotion. Rubinstein, Tausig and Bülow all admitted that they were mere children in comparison with Liszt."[1] Thus wrote a practical musician who frequently heard the playing of the greatest pianist the world has ever known—Franz Liszt.

Liszt was born on October 22nd, 1811, at Raiding, a tiny Hungarian town where his father, Adam Liszt, a man of noble Magyar descent, resided as a steward in the service of Prince Esterhazy. His mother, an Austrian named Anna Lager, was of partly German origin.

Franz (or Ferencz) was for several years a frail child, but his life was illuminated by a burning enthusiasm for music which he inherited from his father, who gave him his first lessons. Raiding was a poor overgrown village of little else but wooden huts and was therefore not an ideal environment for a young musician whose prodigious skill became a local sensation. When he was nine he gave his first public concert under the auspices of Baron von Braun, a blind pianist, at Oedenburg, a nearby town. The enthusiastic reception given to the boy induced his father to arrange for him to give a concert of his own, and this proved a tremendous success chiefly on account of his remarkable execution of a concerto by Ries, and some improvisations.

Liszt was then taken to play before the Prince and Princess. The latter was so charmed by the little boy's playing that she gave him an album in which the great Haydn himself had collected the signatures of the eminent musicians he had met. Alas ! within a little while Franz lost it.

Adam Liszt was a shrewd man, and realizing that the boy would need an expensive musical education, succeeded in arranging for him to play at a concert to be given at the Prince's palace at Pressburg. As he had anticipated, Franz delighted the Hungarian nobility that were present, and they immediately began a subscription which provided him with an income of six hundred gulden a year for six years. His father then gave up his post and took the little family to Vienna. That was in 1821.

[1] Oscar Beringer : *Fifty Years' Experience of Pianoforte Teaching and Playing.*

Vienna was then the greatest centre of musical culture in the world—Beethoven and Schubert were still living there. Adam Liszt first approached Hummel, but the distinguished pianist demanded a guinea a lesson, so Franz was sent to the aged Salieri and the pedantic Czerny. The former died soon after the Liszts' arrival in Vienna, so it was really Czerny who was responsible for Liszt's training : he was astonished at the boy's progress, and after the first few months refused to accept further payment.

Franz and his father were presented to Beethoven by Schindler, and although the immortal composer loathed child prodigies, he became very interested in Liszt. It is said that on one occasion he attended one of the lad's concerts and was so moved that at the conclusion he mounted the platform, took Liszt in his arms and kissed him. Through Randhartinger, Liszt also met Schubert.

After little more than two years' study in Vienna, Adam Liszt took his brilliant son on a tour through Munich, Stuttgart and Strasbourg to Paris. In the French capital he found fame immediately by convincing the critics that even at the tender age of twelve he could play as well as Moscheles and Hummel, the two great virtuosi of the day. Fashionable Paris rhapsodized over him : reproductions of his portrait were to be seen everywhere, and the newspapers called him the second Mozart, the ninth wonder of the world. While he was there he received further instruction from Reicha and Paer.

In 1824 Liszt came to London and was received by King George IV at Carlton House. He played at the Argyll Rooms on June 21st, and a week later at Drury Lane, where he performed one of Hummel's concertos under the conductorship of Sir George Smart and improvised a fugue on " Zitti, zitti " from the *Barber of Seville*. The following year, after a tour of the French provinces, he returned to London and played before the King at Windsor Castle.

The great popularity of the boy pianist induced many poets to submit libretti of operas. He set one of these to music—*Don Sanche*—and it was produced at the Académie Royale, Paris, in October, 1825, but it was a poor effort and had to be withdrawn after a few performances.

When he was sixteen Liszt made his third visit to England and played a concert given by the Royal Philharmonic Society, but his health caused some anxiety and he was sent to Boulogne to recuperate. It was there that his father died with the words " Je crains pour toi les femmes " on his lips, a significant remark for shortly afterwards Franz fell in love with the sixteen-year-old Caroline de Saint-Cricq, one of his pupils. Their friendship continued for some time, but on one occasion when a " music lesson " continued until after midnight a servant reported the matter to the girl's father, who turned Liszt out of the house and told him never to return. It was more than a boyish infatuation, for he was completely broken-hearted after this incident, and as a result his health was impaired for two years. By withdrawing entirely from public life he started a rumour that he had died, and actually read his own obituary in the *Étoile*. But for the financial necessity of giving lessons he would probably have spent years in such seclusion.

Liszt lived in Paris from 1823 to 1835, and therefore saw the Revolution of 1830. There he came into contact with Berlioz, Paganini and Chopin, three famous musicians who were to exert a great influence upon his life. Paganini, the amazing violinist, who was said to look like the devil incarnate, probably affected him most of all.

For nearly two years Liszt lived in quite humble circumstances with his mother while he was bringing his technique to perfection. This entailed a renunciation of public engagements, but not of the company of the three great musicians mentioned above, for with their stimulating comradeship he developed rapidly. A letter written by Chopin to a friend gives some idea of this association : " I write to you without knowing what my pen is scribbling, because at this moment Liszt is playing my Études and transporting me out of my respectable thoughts. I should like to steal from him the way to play my own Études. . . ."

Religion also occupied Liszt's thoughts at this time, and he spent many hours with his friend the Abbé Lamennais at La Chênaie, in Brittany, though his interest in spiritual matters did not prevent him from finding pleasure in an *affaire* with the Comtesse Adèle Laprunarède which lasted for the best part of 1832.

Paris had by then taken the lead as the greatest musical centre in the world—indeed, it was the home of practically all the culture of Europe, for most of the greatest writers, painters and musicians seemed to congregate there. In this wonderful environment Liszt first made the acquaintance of Schumann's music ; he prepared his piano arrangements of the nine Beethoven symphonies and discovered the operas of Weber.

A rather extraordinary, if not amusing, account of one of Liszt's recitals in Paris is given in the autobiography of Henry Reeves. The occasion was a concert attended by Reeves in 1835 : " Liszt had already played a great fantasia of his own, and Beethoven's Twenty-seventh Sonata. After this latter piece he gasped with emotion as I took his hand and thanked him for the divine energy he had shed forth. . . . My chair was on the same board as the piano when the final piece began. It was a duet for two instruments beginning with Mendelssohn's *Chants sans Paroles* and proceeding to a work of his own.

" . . . As the closing strains began I saw Liszt's countenance assume that agony of expression, mingled with radiant smiles of joy, which I never saw on any other human face except in the paintings of Our Saviour by some of the early masters ; his hands rushed over the keys, the floor on which I sat shook like a wire, and the whole audience were wrapped with sound when the hand and frame of the artist gave way. He fainted in the arms of the friend who was turning over the pages for him, and we bore him out in a strong fit of hysterics. The effect of this scene was really dreadful. The whole room sat breathless with fear, till Hiller came forward and announced that Liszt was already restored to consciousness and was comparatively well again. As I handed Madame de Circourt to her carriage we both trembled like poplar leaves, and I tremble scarcely less as I write this."

Liszt's style was invariably extravagant : he loved to stagger his audience with his extreme velocity, terrific attack and immense power, yet his runs and arpeggios were as near perfect as any mortal could hope to get them. His brutal fortissimos often resulted in broken wires and smashed hammers, yet his more delicate passages were executed with a superb touch that could bring tears to the eyes of all emotional people.

In his twenties he was an exceptionally handsome young man—tall and slim with a sensitive face more Polish than Hungarian : a favourite guest at the houses of the *élite*. It is not surprising, then, that he should have attracted the beautiful twenty-eight-year-old Madame d'Agoult, who had grown tired of her husband, Comte Charles d'Agoult, twenty years her senior. Liszt was then only twenty-two, and was so enthralled by this voluptuous woman that he readily eloped with her despite the fact that she had three young children, two of whom she left in the care of her husband. Leaving Paris bubbling with scandal about them, they moved to Geneva in August, 1835, and four months later a daughter was born, Blondine Rachel : the cause of intensified gossip in Paris to the detriment of Liszt's artistic career.

The rising reputation of Thalberg as a pianist was partly responsible for Liszt's decision to return to Paris a year later : continued absence would have made it easy for Thalberg to challenge the great virtuoso's acknowledged supremacy. Liszt reached the French capital with the Comtesse d'Agoult in December, 1836, to find Thalberg's name upon everybody's lips in all the musical circles. Undismayed, he arranged to appear at a concert being held by Berlioz, and to play his own transcriptions of various pieces by that composer. The audience, little suspecting that his technique had become even more remarkable during his absence, gathered in a sceptic frame of mind, but within fifteen minutes they were gasping with astonishment. Sir Charles Hallé was present, and we have his personal testimony : "At an orchestral concert conducted by Berlioz, the *Marche au Supplice*, that most gorgeously instrumented piece, was performed, at the conclusion of which Liszt sat down and played his own arrangement, for piano alone, of the same movement, with an effect even surpassing that of the full orchestra, and creating an indescribable *furore*. The feat had been duly announced in the programme beforehand, a proof of his indomitable courage.[1]"

Hallé tells us on the previous page of his first acquaintance with Liszt's playing : " Such marvels of executive skill and power I could never have imagined. . . . Chopin carried you with him into a dreamland in which you would have liked to dwell for ever ; Liszt was all sunshine and dazzling splendour, subjugating his hearers with a power that none could withstand. For him there were no difficulties of execution, the most incredible seeming child's play under his fingers. One of the transcendent merits of his playing was the crystal-like clearness which never failed for a moment even in the most complicated and, to anybody else, impossible passages ; it was as if he had photographed them in their minutest detail upon the ear of the listener. The power he drew from his instrument was such as I have never heard since, but never harsh, never suggesting ' thumping.' "

Thalberg happened to be out of Paris at this time, but he returned to the capital in the following March and arranged a concert at the Conservatoire. Liszt accepted this as a challenge and arranged one at the opera house, where to an audience many times larger than that drawn by his rival he played Weber's *Concertstück* and his own Fantasia on Pacini's *Niobe*, and convinced the musical world for all time of his supremacy.

After this, Liszt refreshed himself with a brief *affaire* with Chopin's mistress, George Sand, the famous French novelist, but it appears that Madame d'Agoult was not long in bringing him to heel, for she went to Italy with him soon afterwards and resided on the shores of Lake Maggiore. While they were there another daughter, Cosima, was born.

At Milan, Liszt one day walked casually into a music publisher's establishment and began playing the piano. The publisher rushed from his private office exclaiming " Quest' è Liszt o il Diavolo " (That is Liszt or the Devil). Whereupon Liszt acknowledged his identity and the meeting led to a series of concerts in the city.

They moved on to Venice, and there Liszt heard of the plight of the peasants who were suffering great hardships after the catastrophic flooding of the Danube. He went to Vienna forthwith and gave ten concerts within a month, thereby raising a large sum of money which he handed over for the relief of the stricken peasants. Incidentally, these concerts were also a tremendous artistic success, and he rose to even greater heights of fame. Notwithstanding malicious reports of his love affairs, he was invited to play before the Emperor Ferdinand and the Empress Anna Carolina of Savoy.

A third child, a boy named Daniel, was born, but soon afterwards Liszt and Madame d'Agoult began to drift apart, though the final separation did

---

[1] *Life and Letters of Sir Charles Hallé.*

not come until some five years later. Liszt then pursued his career as a virtuoso with rather more diligence—though he was also active as a composer—and started with a series of recitals in Vienna on behalf of the Beethoven Memorial to be erected at Bonn. He had been so disgusted at the small response to the appeal issued by the Memorial Committee that he undertook to bear the entire expense of the Memorial on condition that Bartolini, the finest sculptor of the day, be given the order.

Some idea of his fame may be gained from an incident at Pressburg, where the nobility were so unanimous in their desire to hear him play that the Prince Palatine of Hungary had to cancel a levee because he was warned that it clashed with Liszt's concert, and that if he persisted in holding it on that day, nobody would attend!

A great ovation awaited Liszt at Budapest, where the Sword of Honour was girded on him by Count Festetics. The tour finished with a series of magnificent banquets and the award to him of a patent of nobility by the Hungarian diet.

It is interesting to note that even after he had been given these honours he was coldly received when he made his next tour to England, on account of his relations with Madame d'Agoult, although he was received at Buckingham Palace by the Queen and the Prince Consort, and played before them.

A contrast is provided by his next visit to Berlin. Here, the King of Prussia, Frederick William IV, attended most of his concerts, and the public became so obsessed with Liszt's genius that wealthy and fashionable women followed him about merely to scramble after his cigar ends, which they kept as souvenirs! There is no doubt that he found a vain satisfaction in playing up to this mania. He wore his hair so long that it brushed his shoulders, and had a fascinating habit of shaking it back with a toss of his finely-shaped head while he was playing. It would invariably fall forward while he was making his bow, thus giving him an opportunity of running his fingers through it with a graceful sweep of the arm. He was the typical showman, with plenty of tricks to please his public ; a vain, egotistical creature whose affectations would have been trying to the more sober-minded man had they not been relieved by many fine qualities of character. His kindness and generosity were as well-known as his sixty waistcoats.

When he was at the height of his fame as a virtuoso he played before the Sultan Abdul Medjid at Tcheragan Palace, but he would never fawn upon persons of high rank. Indeed, he had no qualms about slighting even royalty when they displeased him. On one occasion, for instance, he refused to play before King Louis Philippe because he disliked the King's management of public affairs. " But do you not remember the time when you played at my house as a little boy, when I was still the Duke of Orleans ?

Things have greatly changed since then!" the King exclaimed. Liszt replied coldly: "Yes, your Majesty, but not for the better."

He snubbed Frederick William IV because of some trifling matter, by calmly throwing away a priceless gift of diamonds that had been presented to him. Perhaps the greatest sensation of all was when he sharply rebuked the Tsar of Russia, Nicholas I, for trying to carry on a conversation while he was playing. This audacity on the part of a mere musician caused as much scandal in the courts of Europe as his amatory adventures.

We now approach the end of his career as a virtuoso, for in 1847 he gave a series of recitals at Kiev and met there the twenty-eight-year-old Princess Carolyne of Sayn-Wittgenstein, who was living apart from her husband. Within a few weeks she instituted divorce proceedings so that she could marry Liszt.

The great pianist then decided to cease playing in public. His last recital was given in October of 1847 at Elizabetgrad, the city we now know as Stalingrad, after which he never again played for money. But before I conclude with a summary of his later life, I would like to quote a few remarks made by his contemporary von Lenz: "Liszt is a phenomenon of universal musical virtuosity . . . an apparition not to be compressed within the bounds of the house drawn by schools and professors. Liszt is the past, the present, and the future of the pianoforte. . . . When Liszt thunders, lightens, and murmurs the great B-flat Sonata for Hammerklavier by Beethoven, this Solomon's Song of the keyboard, there is an end of all things pianistic ; Liszt is making capital for humanity out of the ideas of the greatest thinker in the realm of music." Rather later, Prosniz wrote : "Liszt is the father of modern pianoforte virtuosity. He developed the capacity of the instrument to the utmost ; he commanded it to sing, to whisper, to thunder. From the human voice as well as from the orchestra he borrowed effects. Daringly, triumphantly, his technique overcame all difficulties—a technique which proclaimed the unqualified dominion of the mind over the human hand."

In 1849 he went to Weimar as musical director at the Grand-Ducal Court and stayed there for eleven years, distinguishing himself as a conductor as well as a composer. He did much to promote the performance of works by his more progressive contemporaries, and it is significant that Wagner's *Lohengrin* was given its *première* under his direction.

His marriage to Princess Carolyne was stopped by the Vatican, and in 1865 he again became absorbed in religious matters to the extent of taking minor orders in the Church. This had an effect upon his compositions, but did not prevent him from continuing his work as a teacher.

His ordination provoked a certain amount of cynicism among those who knew him well. Gregorovius wrote shortly after the ceremony

"Yesterday I saw Liszt clad as an Abbé. He was getting out of a hackney carriage, his black silk cassock fluttering ironically behind him. Mephistopheles disguised as an Abbè. Such is the end of Lovelace."

All this piety evidently made him feel the need of a little diversion, which he found in yet another *affaire*, this time with one of his pretty young pupils, Agnes Klindworth of Hanover.

The last twenty years of his life were spent chiefly in Rome, though he still found plenty of activity at Weimar and frequently visited Budapest. In 1886 he went on a " Jubilee Tour " to celebrate his forthcoming seventy-fifth birthday, visiting Paris on the way to London, where he arrived on April 3rd, for a performance of *St. Elizabeth* in the St. James's Hall. He attended the rehearsal on the following day, and in the evening delighted everybody by improvising brilliantly on themes from that oratorio. On the following Wednesday it was performed under Sir Alexander Mackenzie's direction, and on the Thursday evening Liszt was received by Queen Victoria at Windsor Castle. He played her various works of his own and Chopin's Nocturne in B-flat minor No. 1.

A great reception in his honour was given at the Grosvenor Gallery on April 8th, and once again he found it impossible to disregard requests to play : he went to the piano and gave an astonishing performance of the Second Hungarian Rhapsody and the finale of Schubert's *Divertissement à l'Hongroise*. While he was in London he also went to a concert of his own works at Crystal Palace, dined with the Prince of Wales at Marlborough House, attended the London début of Frederic Lamond at the St. James's Hall on April 15th, and went to a gala performance of *Faust* at the Lyceum, where he met Irving and Ellen Terry.

He never saw his seventy-fifth birthday, however, for later in the summer he caught a chill and died at Bayreuth on July 31st.

Clara Schumann

(CLARA WIECK)

THE life story of this superb pianist, wife of the illustrious composer Robert Schumann, opens at Leipzig, the great musical centre in which her father, Friedrich Wieck had settled as a teacher of the pianoforte and married Marianne Tromlitz, a gifted woman capable of accepting public engagements as a pianist.

Clara Josephine was born on September 13th, 1819, and showed no sign of musical precocity during her early years. She was also backward in learning to speak, a singularly quiet, pensive little child with a wistful face, dark eyes and dark glossy hair. Just before her fifth birthday her parents separated, and she was assigned with her two brothers[1], Alwin and Gustav, to the care of her father. He taught her to play the piano in the hope that some sort of musical talent would emerge, and it seems that he gave her a good general musical education at the same time. To his great surprise and gratification her musical ability developed rapidly : she acquired an excellent ear and experienced no difficulty in playing and memorizing quite difficult and elaborate passages. An hour's lesson every day was supplemented by short periods of practice alone, often as much as a further two hours a day.

By the time she reached her seventh birthday she had not only acquired a good elementary knowledge of the art but had also developed strong fingers capable of free, independent movement and at the same time great delicacy of touch. Her father then allowed her to increase the time allotted each day to practising, and to study her first concerto : Hummel's G-major, Opus 73. She mastered this with amazing ease, and within a few weeks was making a start on the Mozart Concerto in E-flat : a work that she interpreted so well that shortly before her eighth birthday she was invited to play it with a small chamber orchestra of eight players. This could scarcely be called her first public appearance as the small audience consisted chiefly of friends, but it made her a figure of special interest to the many musicians with whom her father was acquainted.

With her father she spent a fortnight in Dresden in the summer of 1828 and played to several musicians who had expressed interest in her. On

---

[1] A third brother, Viktor, died before he was four years old.

the following October 20th she made her first important public appearance in Leipzig when at the Gewandhaus she played a duet with another of her father's pupils. The *Allgemeine Musikalische Zeitung* reported, " It was with particular pleasure that we listened to the performance of the very talented nine-year-old Clara Wieck . . . her future may be anticipated with high hopes."

Friedrich Wieck was apt to allow his enthusiasm to run away with him to the extent that he became suspiciously like a slave-driver in his desire to push his daughter along the road to fame, but the pensive little girl evidently had a will of her own, for she frequently revolted. The following incident recorded in her diary took place while she was playing a set of variations for him : " My father, who has so long vainly hoped for a change of mood on my part, remarked again to-day that I am still so idle, negligent, unmethodical, self-willed, etc., especially in pianoforte playing and practising . . . that he tore the copy to pieces before my eyes and from to-day will not give me another lesson." Within a week, we are told, the incident was completely forgotten by the irascible teacher.

Meanwhile, Clara's general education was proceeding apace : she proved to be an intelligent child, and had been going regularly to school since her sixth birthday. Wieck seems to have discouraged her interest in reading on account of the strain placed upon her health by the intensive musical training. He married for the second time in 1828, and Clara gained not only a loving, cultured and sympathetic step-mother, but also two half-sisters : Marie and Cecilia. The former also became an accomplished pianist.

In the same year, Robert Schumann, a keen amateur musician, matriculated at the University of Leipzig as a law student, and on discovering that the students' club was a poor place for recreation, decided to take music lessons for a while from Wieck. He was then eighteen, son of a bookseller, and an excellent pianist—a highly-imaginative, emotional youth quite unsuited to the legal profession.

Wieck was delighted with his brilliant new pupil, although the young man's musical education lacked the old-fashioned " grounding " that he believed to be so vitally important. Schumann was always a trifle impatient when Wieck tried to instruct him in theoretical matters ; he was, he said, " as a simple pupil of nature," and preferred to extemporize and compose n blissful ignorance of the laws of harmony. The lessons were later terminated by Wieck on account of " other engagements," but we may safely assume that he lost patience with Schumann, who in any case was going to Heidelberg in the spring of 1829.

In the autumn of that year Clara was taken by her father to hear Paganini, the great violinist, when he visited Leipzig. Clara was invited to play before the eminent artist at his hotel, and he spoke highly of her possibilities. Early in 1830 she made another visit to Dresden and astonished everybody by her splendid technique, while at a concert given before Princess Louise at the Saxon Court she surprised her father even more than the audience by playing a dazzling extemporization upon a given theme. Then she was invited to play before the King and Queen ; an honour which caused Wieck some anxiety in case too much praise from persons of exalted rank would have a bad effect upon her.

To everybody's surprise, Robert Schumann returned to Leipzig in the autumn of 1830 announcing that he had abandoned his legal studies and intended to become a professional pianist. He returned to Wieck as a pupil, and accepted an invitation to live with the family, much to the delight of Clara and her two brothers. Schumann and Wieck still had differences of opinion and on one unfortunate occasion the ex-law student hinted that he hoped to go to Hummel for lessons at a later date. Wieck evidently flew into a rage, for Schumann wrote to his mother : " I was alarmed at his outbreak of anger, but we are now on good terms again, and he treats me affectionately as though I were his child. You can scarcely imagine his burning zest, his judgment and understanding of art ; yet when he speaks in his own or Clara's interest, he is as unmannerly as a peasant."

Clara was then working at harmony and counterpoint with Cantor Weinlich, and was able to write four-part songs quite well. In November, 1830, she gave a concert at the Gewandhaus which once more drew high praise from the music critic of the *Allgemeine Musikalische Zeitung*. Two months later she was in Dresden again playing with the court orchestra with such brilliance that somebody started a rumour that her cruel father made her practice for twelve hours a day, standing over her with a stick !

In the summer of 1831 Schumann took a course of harmony and counterpoint with Heinrich Dorn, the Director of Music at the Leipzig theatre. The Wieck household was then buzzing with excitement over a new composition by a young Pole almost unknown at that time : Frédéric Chopin. Schumann had reviewed the Variations on *La ci darem la mano* for the *Allgemeine Musikalische Zeitung*, and as a result, Clara was busy preparing it for her next concert : the first of a tour that was to take her outside of her native Saxony for the first time.

With her father she arrived in Weimer on September 25th and met Geheimrath Schmidt, who arranged for her to meet the famous poet Goethe, then an octogenarian. Goethe gave her a bronze bust of himself, and in a letter to a friend, described her as " a remarkable phenomenon." *Hofmarschal* von Spiegel invited her to play before the Grand Duke and the court circle, and then she gave a public recital in the town hall that was acclaimed as a triumphant success.

Their journey took them through Erfurt, Gotha, Arnstadt, Cassel, Frankfurt and Darmstadt—by road in a horse-drawn carriage, of course. At Cassel she met Ludwig Spohr, and was able to play to the composer the first piece of Chopin he had ever heard. Commenting on her performance, he said : " If it is not now very unusual to find a child of Clara Wieck's years possessed of great mechanical dexterity on the pianoforte, she is probably the first who has united with it sound interpretation, correct accentuation, complete distinctness, and the finest tone shading. Her facility is such that she masters the greatest difficulties with a certainty and ease possessed only by the greatest virtuosi of our time." Nevertheless, at Frankfurt, the musical *élite* received her coldly : she played remarkably well, but they showed little interest.

Clara and her father arrived in Paris on February 15th, 1832, very weary after a long journey and found the great city more concerned at that time with politics than music. A few recitals were given in half empty halls, and then the appearance of cholera sent most of her likely patrons out of the city in great haste. It seemed hopeless, so the little pianist and her father returned home on May 1st, after more than seven months' absence.

Schumann had by then moved to apartments of his own, but his daily visits to Wieck's house ensured that he was always on the spot when music-making or musical discussions were in progress. He was a highly tempera-mental young man, and suffered from fits of depression and lassitude that were apt to be irritating to his companions. Dorn, for instance, had lost patience with him, but in Clara, despite her youth, he found a good friend whose understanding and sympathy gave him just the encouragement he needed. They compared their compositions and were of considerable help to each other. Clara, incidentally, was then studying composition with Dorn.

Clara's first appearance at one of the great Gewandhaus subscription concerts was made on September 30th, 1832, when, at the age of thirteen, she played the Moscheles G-minor Concerto, and Herz's *Jägerchor* variations. The audience's delight was unmistakable, and this great success changed her position from that of an entertaining child prodigy to that of the youngest of the celebrated virtuosi whose names have made the history of the pianistic art.

Robert Schumann was th passing through one of the most difficult periods of his life. He had injured his right hand in a foolish attempt to increase the flexibility and strength of certain fingers by artificial means, and had been obliged to abandon his plan to become a professional pianist. He toyed with the idea of giving up music altogether and reading theology, but ultimately decided to try his fortune as a composer.

In the spring of 1833 Clara was giving concerts of her own at the Gewandhaus. An announcement in the *Leipziger Tageblatt* of April 28th tells us : " . . . Clara Wieck will by general desire perform Chopin's *Bravura Variations*. These will be followed by the first movement of a symphony by Robert Schumann, a young pianist and composer resident here who has already made a favourable impression by several interesting and original compositions."

Throughout the summer the days rang with the laughter of the high-spirited students who gathered at Wieck's house in the Reichstrasse : music and poetry was in the air from morning till night, and what could have been more natural than the ripening of the friendship between the young composer and the fourteen-year-old pianist ? We find Robert writing to his mother thus : " Clara is as faithful to me as ever ; is just what she was, high-spirited and romantic—runs and jumps and plays like a child, and, again, says the most significant things. It is delightful to see how quickly the gifts of heart and mind are developing, and yet, as it were, leaf by leaf. As we were returning lately from Connewitz (we walk for two or three hours nearly every day) I heard her saying to herself ' Oh, how happy I am, how happy ! ' Who would not like to hear this ? " That lovely summer inspired Schumann's *Impromptus on a theme by Clara Wieck* (Opus 5).

Autumn brought an entirely new venture which can best be explained in Schumann's own words written twenty years later when he was preparing his *Collected Writings:* " Towards the end of the year 1833 a number of musicians (for the most part young), used to meet every evening as if by chance for social intercourse and for the interchange of ideas on the art which was to them the meat and drink of life—music. The musical conditions of the time cannot be said to have been satisfactory. Rossini still ruled the stage, Herz and Hünten almost exclusively the pianoforte. Mendelssohn's star was, indeed, in the ascendant, and wonderful things were reported of a Pole, Chopin ; but it was not until later that the influence of these masters became effectively established. One day the idea was suggested in the circle of young hotheads : let us not look on idly ; let us bestir ourselves in the cause of the poetry of art. From this thought resulted the first pages of a new musical periodical."

The *Neue Zeitschrift für Musik* was first issued in April, 1834 (a year in which Clara spent most of her time in study) by Schumann, Wieck and two other friends, through Hartmann, a bookseller of Leipzig. This journal did a great service to music for many years.

Then there came to Wieck's house a new pupil, Ernestine von Fricken, a beautiful and voluptuous blonde of seventeen, and as Clara was still little more than fourteen, it was almost inevitable that Schumann and Ernestine should find mutual attraction. Clara did her utmost to hide her feelings, but when in the summer of 1834 she had to go to Dresden to continue her studies with Reissiger, who had succeeded Weber as Kapellmeister of the

German opera there, the little pianist went with a very heavy heart. Her letters from there to Schumann brought only belated replies full of banter.

Ernestine left Leipzig in the autumn—wearing Schumann's engagement ring. Clara's feelings can be too easily imagined to require description, yet she could see that as soon as Schumann was deprived of Ernestine's alluring presence he began to doubt the wisdom of his choice. Even after visits to his *fiancée* this doubt remained, for he found in her not a strong companion but a weak reflection of his own emotional nature, and although their engagement lasted several years, he eventually allowed Count von Zedwitz to win her affections.

After nearly a year's retirement from public life, during which time she was studying assiduously, Clara Wieck gave a concert in Leipzig on September 11th, 1834 : two days before her fifteenth birthday. It is of some importance because she brought Schumann's name as a composer for the pianoforte before the public for the first time by playing his Toccata in C-major, a work written in 1830 while he was still a student at Heidelberg. Schumann had revised it, transposing it from its original key—D-major.

Wieck then took his daughter on a tour through northern Germany, and at Magdeburg seems to have encountered some little difficulties, for he wrote to his wife[1] : " It is a wonder that I am alive to-day after the anxiety and vexation of yesterday ! Imagine : there were six hundred people again, and in the first part (Chopin's concerto) the keys of the pianoforte began to stick. It passed off, however, in spite of a thousand alarms. During the pause I was obliged to take out the keyboard in the presence of the whole public and see to the keys. This succeeded. Now comes the second part. The pedal sticks : what am I to do ? Clara plays on, but does not dare to raise the damper because it would not fall again, and so I have to press it down a hundred times before the public during the performance."

Writing from Hamburg, Wieck declares that Clara was received with loud applause, but that Zollner, reporting the concert in the *Hamburg Abendzeitung* had described Chopin's works as " unintelligible foppery and musical nonsense ! "

Clara's longing for Schumann's companionship might possibly have had something to do with a decision to shorten the tour, for they returned to Leipzig in April 1835. But the faithful little girl was again to be disappointed, for when she entered the room in which he was working he scarcely bothered to greet her. " I went to Augusta, who was with us then, and said with tears ' I prefer him to every one, and he has not even looked at me.' " It seems that Schumann had been more attentive than she had imagined, however, for in a letter to her in 1838 he refers to the occasion thus : " I still remember how I first saw you at twelve o'clock midday :

[1] Kohut : *Friedrich Wieck.*

you seemed to me taller, more distant. You were no longer a child with whom I could laugh and play. You talked so intelligently, and I saw in your eyes a secret gleam of love."

The summer days of 1835 brought back the companionship they had hitherto enjoyed, and the autumn led to a music season in Leipzig exceptionally thrilling to the young musicians, for Mendelssohn came to settle in the city as conductor of the Gewandhaus concerts. Moreover, Chopin visited Leipzig and Clara was able to play one of Schumann's sonatas to him, but her most vivid memory of that season was quite unrelated to music : Schumann kissed her for the first time—on the stairs !

The sweet consciousness of his love had a wonderful effect upon her. She radiated a new tenderness, and in her playing emerged the emotions that had been suppressed in those trying days when it seemed that the one who meant everything to her had been lost for ever.

When Wieck discovered his sixteen-year-old daughter's entanglement with this impulsive young composer, he was extremely angry. He bitterly reproached Clara for wanting to marry so early, for he was sure that such a step would mean the end of a most promising career, and wrote an insulting letter to Schumann. The young man was grievously upset by Wieck's violent opposition, and we find his feelings expressed in the Sonata in F-minor (Opus 14) which he wrote at the time.

Determined to stop the affair, Wieck forbad them to meet, or even to write to each other. Shortly afterwards, one of Schumann's earlier sonatas was published and he sent Clara a copy in the hope that she would somehow reply indicating her loyalty. To his dismay, he merely received a packet of his own letters with a request that he should return hers, and he was plunged into despair. Finding solace in his beloved pianoforte, he began composing the magnificent Fantasia in C-major (Opus 17), whose first movement is a memorial to the surging tumultuous sorrow that made him pour out his emotions upon the instrument. Some years later he told Clara that " the first movement is, I think, the most passionate thing I have composed : a deep lament for you."

Clara apparently submitted to her father's will—we must not overlook her extreme youth—but there is also a strong possibility that knowing Robert's impulsiveness, and bearing in mind the ease with which he had bestowed his affections upon Ernestine von Fricken, she wished to test his loyalty. Moreover, her father had discovered that Schumann's engagement with Ernestine had not been officially broken, so Clara wrote to her for an explanation of her present relations with the composer. She was evidently satisfied, and decided to wait and see what would happen.

By the time she was seventeen, Clara had fulfilled her father's dearest hopes : she had won the esteem of most of the greatest composers in the land and had become recognized as one of the finest exponents of Bach, Beethoven and Chopin. Early in 1837 she made her first visit to Berlin, where she appeared first at the Royal Opera House, and then at the Hotel de Russie. The *Preussische Staatzeitung* reported : "A considerable reputation had preceded the arrival of the pianoforte virtuoso Clara Wieck, and it was most brilliantly justified by the young artist's performance on the occasion of her recent concert . . . it was not mere technical facility that we were called upon to admire, but playing of irresistible charm that so captivated the attention that one almost forgot to notice the triumphant skill by which the greatest mechanical difficulties were vanquished. The artist has become so completely one with her art that it inspires her whole being . . . the tone of her instrument seems to breathe forth the spirit of the pianist."

It is significant that at each concert in Berlin she played at least one of her own works. She also seems to have caused a flutter in some of the critical coteries because she had the audacity to play from memory works of the great masters—a practice considered to be very bad form in those days— and dared to introduce the works of Beethoven into her programmes.

On her return to Leipzig her Concerto (Opus 7) was published and a copy was sent to Schumann for review in his journal. The composer felt he ought not to comment upon this work, so he passed it on to C. F. Becker, who stupidly reviewed it in a very tactless, patronizing manner and suggested that as the composer was a lady it would be ungallant to find fault with it. This distressed Clara, but she felt no bitterness, and did not hesitate to choose Schumann's recently-published *Études Symphoniques* for her next concert. This act induced Robert to write to her : " Firmly as I believe in you, yet the strongest courage may be disconcerted if one hears nothing at all of the person one holds dearest in all the world. And this you are to me. A thousand times have I considered everything, and everything tells me that it must come right if we resolve and persevere. Write the simple word ' yes ' if you will personally give your father a letter from me on your birthday. . . . He is well disposed towards me now, and will not reject me if you beg for me. . . ."

Clara replied : " You ask only for a simple ' yes ' ? Such a little word, but so weighty ! Yet shall not a heart so full as mine of unspeakable love be able to utter this little word with the whole soul ? . . . Nothing shall make me falter, and I will show father that a youthful heart can also be steadfast. . . ."

Wieck visited Schumann and told him that under no circumstances whatever would he give his consent. Clara received a letter afterwards : " Your father was terrible . . . the coldness, the bad will, the inconsistency . . . I am not to be allowed to see you once. . . . It is in vain that I seek a worthy well-grounded reason for your father's refusal. As if you would be injured as an artist by an early betrothal, that you are too young, or the like ! . . . believe me, he will try to throw you to the first man who has sufficient money and title. . . . You must counter everything by your goodness, and if that does not succeed, by your firmness. I can do nothing except keep silence. . . . Oh, how distracted I feel. . . ."

They continued to meet in secret until October 15th, 1837, when Clara started on a tour of Austria. In Prague she played Chopin's *Arpeggio Étude* in E-flat, and her own Concert Variations on a theme from *Il Pirato*. She had thirteen recalls that evening, and wrote to Robert, " I have never known such enthusiasm ! You may imagine I really did not know what to do. . . . The thought of you so inspired my playing that the public became inspired too . . . the people here seem almost crazy."

Even this great triumph, after which congratulations and invitations to banquets were showered upon her, did nothing to soften her father's heart ; indeed, Wieck actually wrote again to Schumann threatening to find a husband for Clara elsewhere if he persisted in his suit. This incredible attitude becomes even more difficult to understand when one considers that Schumann was then beginning to find fame. Liszt, for instance, had praised his work with great enthusiasm.

Clara and her father were both disappointed with Vienna, which at that time was in a very unprogressive mood musically. Before her concert there the newspapers speculated whether " the modest young artist who in Germany is placed beside Chopin and Liszt " could hold her own against the popular Thalberg. Clara's diary supplies the answer : " My triumph ! . . . the public consisted of the *élite* of the most distinguished and most musical people in Vienna. . . . I satisfied the connoisseurs and the amateurs, and was recalled twelve times in all."

It is worth noting that she was bold enough to include Bach fugues in her programmes : a great risk because such items were not favoured by the reactionary Viennese audiences in those days, yet the applause was almost hysterical, and she was invited to play before the Empress and other members of the Royal family.

Equally surprising was her decision to play the Beethoven *Appassionata* Sonata : a very daring move upon the part of one so young, yet this, too, the audience swallowed with delight and clamoured for more. After the sixth and last concert in Vienna, the local correspondent of the *Allgemeine Musikalische Zeitung* considered that her playing had created a sensation comparable only with that aroused by Paganini or Lipinski. On the following March 15th she again played before the Empress, who remarked, " She is a great virtuoso : I have never heard such playing, but I am still more pleased by her personality." Clara was then given the honorary position of chamber musician (*K. k. Kammervirtuosin*)—a title of distinction which imposed no specific duties. This honour, shared by Paganini, Thalberg and Pasta, was generally reserved for artists of mature age and Catholic faith.

Clara then wrote to Robert suggesting that her father might view their romance more favourably if Schumann would agree to live in Vienna after their marriage, for there they would both have a better chance of earning a regular income. Robert agreed, but Wieck still stubbornly refused to give his consent. " I sometimes have the terrible thought that I no longer love father," she wrote from Dresden on July 8th, " but must it not arouse bitter feelings, must it not be deeply wounding to hear one's dearest . . . spoken of slightingly ? . . . But when the time comes rely on me ! "

The great tour of the 1838-9 season took her to Paris again, where she met Berlioz " a quiet man with very thick hair and eyes continually cast down." Her success in the French capital was slightly less sensational than in Vienna because her father's insensate opposition to her engagement had kept her in a state of perpetual agitation that had proved detrimental to her health.

Meanwhile, Robert Schumann had tried his fortune in Vienna, found that conditions there were unfavourable, and returned again to Leipzig. He then prepared a petition to obtain statutory consent to their marriage, so that the ceremony could be arranged without Wieck's permission. Clara signed this on June 15th, 1839, and the lawsuit opened in the middle of the following month. The court decided that an attempt should be made to reconcile the litigants, but Wieck refused to compromise in any way and poured out a most amazing stream of slander. He also appropriated the whole of Clara's savings and even refused her access to her personal belongings. She spent her twentieth birthday in Berlin, where Robert visited her with a copy of his recently-issued Sonata in G minor (Opus 22).

The lawsuit was not resumed until the middle of the following December, and Clara had to appear in court with Robert, who was attacked by her father in such violent language that the presiding justice had to order him to be silent on several occasions. The proceedings, to use Clara's own words, " cut me to the soul . . . they have broken the tender bond between father and child. I feel as though my heart were broken also."

Wieck's vile accusations against Schumann wounded the composer very deeply. He wrote to Clara : ". . . if you imagine that it may become possible later to reconcile me with your father, renounce all hope of such things. . . . There are laws of honour as binding as those of love. . . . Bad words and bad men are an abomination to me."

Clara gave a series of concerts early in 1840 under conditions of almost intolerable mental strain relieved only by the great kindness of those who flocked to hear her play as she toured through northern Germany, and by the news that the University of Jena had conferred a doctorate upon Schumann. Wieck, meanwhile, had continued to spread insulting lies about the composer and had to be checked by a libel action.

Not until the following August 1st did the court sanction the marriage, and after a memorable appearance at a concert given by the Grand Duke and Duchess of Weimar to the Empress of Russia, Clara agreed to become Robert's bride on September 12th—the eve of her twenty-first birthday. The good-natured composer then withdrew the proceedings against her father.

The wedding took place at Schönefeld, and Schumann presented his bride with a specially bound copy of *Liederkreis* (Opus 25) which had just been published. Only her mother and one friend attended the ceremony, but other guests arrived later, and Clara's own record of the party that evening reads: " There was a little dancing, and on every countenance an expression of quiet content. It was a beautiful day, and even the sun, which had lately been obscured, shone mildly on us as we drove to the wedding as though to bless our union. Nothing occurred to disturb us during the day, and so let it be noted in this book as the happiest and most significant day of my life. . . ."

Clara and Robert settled in their new home in Leipzig " a quiet but pleasant dwelling in Inselstrasse." Clara's deep love for her husband made her realize that her first duty was now to him, and that her art must take a second place. In the first few years of their married life the conflicting claims were bound to cause some unrest in her mind, but she never wavered in her domestic duties. She continued to practise her art, adding to her repertoire as regularly as in the past, and she gave frequent concerts in Leipzig and other towns in that part of the country. It was her longer tours that became more rare.

The first eighteen months were spent chiefly in Leipzig. Clara gave several concerts at the Gewandhaus and continued in her efforts to introduce the work of her great contemporaries into her programmes. Schumann was at that time engrossed in the writing of his first symphony (B-flat). The diary that has helped so much in this narrative now became a joint affair. Clara recorded one week in January, 1841: " It is not my turn to keep the Diary this week; but when a husband is composing a symphony, he must be excused from other things. . . . The symphony is nearly finished, and although I have not heard any of it, I am extremely delighted that Robert has at last found the sphere for which his great imagination fits him."

The symphony was completed on the 26th of that month, for on the previous day Clara recorded: ". . . Robert has just about finished his symphony; it has been composed mostly at night—my poor Robert has spent some sleepless nights over it. He calls it *Spring Symphony*. A spring poem . . . gave the first impulse to this creation."

It was first performed on March 31st at a concert given by Clara in the Gewandhaus in aid of the orchestra's pension fund. Mendelssohn conducted, and although there were a few slight mishaps on account of the difficulty of certain parts, it was as great a success as the various items played by Clara. Schumann himself related : " Happy, unforgettable evening. My Clara played everything in such a masterly manner and in such an elevated mood that everyone was charmed. And in my artistic life, too, the day has been one of great importance. My wife recognized this, too, and rejoiced almost more in the success of the Symphony than in her own achievement. Forward, then, with God's guidance, on this path. . . ."

On the following September 1st, a daughter, Marie, was born, and twelve days later Schumann completed the Symphony in D-minor, which after revision ten years later became known as the No. 4. In the following year they made a tour to Hamburg, where Clara was warmly welcomed and the First Symphony performed. Clara then proceeded to Copenhagen alone while her husband returned to his work at Leipzig. That summer they both went into Bohemia and were presented to Prince Metternich at Königswart.

April 1843 brought a second daughter, Elise, and also the discovery that they had been living above their income, so they planned the Russian tour of which they had been talking for some time. At the end of that year Schumann received the following letter :

> Dear Schumann,
>
> Tempora mutantur nos et mutamur in eis.
>
> In the face of Clara and of the whole world, we can no longer keep apart from one another. . . . We were always united where art was concerned—I was even your teacher—my verdict decided your present course in life for you. There is no need for me to assure you of my sympathy with your talent and with your fine and genuine aspirations.
>
> In Dresden there joyfully awaits you
>
> > Your father,
> > Fr. Wieck.

Thus the estrangement was happily concluded.

During the first few days of 1844 Clara and her husband visited Robert Schumann's brother Carl at Schneeberg, left the two babies with him, and on January 25th set out by way of Berlin and Könisgberg for St. Petersburg and Moscow. At St. Petersburg Clara played with Henselt her husband's variations for two pianos during a soirée given by Prince Oldenburg, and the First Symphony was played at a concert arranged by Counts Joseph and Michael Wielhorsky, two eminent connoisseurs of music.

CLARA SCHUMANN

In the same year Schumann gave up the editorship of the *Neue Zeitschrift*. He was full of plans for visiting England—he even talked of settling permamently in London—but these came to nought when a serious illness overtook him in the middle of August. At about the same time Niels Gade was invited to succeed Mendelssohn as conductor of the Gewandhaus, and although Schumann would not have accepted the post, he felt very offended because he had not been invited to do so. Because of these two factors, Clara and her husband decided to move to Dresden in the autumn, and they took a house there in the Waisenhausstrasse.

The Concerto for Pianoforte and Orchestra Opus 54, which Schumann had begun in Leipzig as a " Phantasie " was completed in Dresden in the summer of 1845. Clara recorded on June 27th : " Robert has composed a beautiful last movement for his Phantasie in A-minor for pianoforte and orchestra, so that now it is a concerto, and I shall play it next winter. I am very glad about it for I always wanted a large bravura piece by him." A month or so later she made the note : " Robert has finished his concerto and passed it over to the copyist. I am as happy as a king to think of playing it with orchestra." The first performance of this glorious work was given by Clara not in Dresden but at a Gewandhaus concert in Leipzig on January 1st, 1846. Its great success was soon repeated in Dresden, however, and before long virtuosi all over the world had added it to their repertoire.

Throughout these years Clara's art was maturing unimpeded by domestic duties. Four more children were born : Julie in 1845, Emil in the following year, Ludwig in 1848 and Ferdinand a year or so later.

In 1846 she met Jenny Lind and found that she had " a genius for song such as can appear scarcely once in centuries. . . . Her singing comes from the very depths of her being, there is no straining after effect, no passion that takes by storm, it pierces one's heart, there is sadness, a melancholy in her way of singing which moves one whether one will or not. . . . There is beauty in all she does . . . her voice is not large."

Vienna was visited that year, and Clara insisted upon playing her husband's compositions, which meant nothing to the Viennese. Four concerts were given in two months : the first two just paid their expenses, but there was a deficit of a hundred florins on the third. A substantial profit was made upon the last concert only because Jenny Lind sang, and the people flocked to the hall to hear her lovely voice.

The same year brought the first serious alarm about Robert Schumann's health : an irritation of the aural nerve caused great distress and anxiety. At about that time their friendship with Liszt was becoming somewhat strained by that composer's eccentricities. Finally, in June, 1848, the Hungarian composer offended them so much by praising Meyerbeer at the expense of their friend Mendelssohn during a visit that Schumann burst into a rage and caused a breach in their relations that lasted some two or three years.

The Schumann family moved to Düsseldorf in 1850, but Robert's illness became progressively worse. Four years later his entire brain became affected and driven to distraction by the pain, he attempted to drown himself in the Rhine. He was rescued, however, and had to be put into a mental hospital. Clara's grief at the thought of her great creative genius being put away in this manner was reflected some years later when she wrote : " . . . my glorious Robert in an asylum ! How was it possible for me to bear it ? . . . I was forbidden even to clasp him once more to my heart. . . ."

Brahms came over from Hanover to console her, and it was chiefly his great kindness that sustained her through the terrible years that followed. By September, 1854, financial difficulties had added to her worries and she was obliged to resume her work, though she wrote after a concert at Utrecht : " It is incredibly difficult to appear in public when one's heart is torn with grief."

Her first visit to England was made in April, 1856, when she played at some of the Philharmonic Concerts under Sterndale Bennett. She was very surprised to find that " no more time is allowed for the rehearsal than for the performance, so that of course things cannot go very well." Bennett, she discovered, was " a nice man but no conductor."

Among the many provincial towns she visited were Manchester, Liverpool and Dublin, but inadequate rehearsals were to be found everywhere. " They call it a rehearsal here if a piece is played once through, but no one thinks of looking at it carefully." These remarks might well apply in certain quarters to-day ! " . . . the public puts up with it. It is the artists' own fault : they allow themselves to be treated as inferiors in English society." Writing of the taste of the average English audience in those days she recorded : " They will not hear of any newer composers than Mendelssohn, who is their god."

Clara Schumann played before Queen Victoria on June 18th and gave several recitals to high social circles. She was playing at a soirée given by Lady Overstone when she discovered to her horror that the guests were talking. Stopping in the middle of a piece she informed them that she would not continue until there was perfect silence in the room.

Returning home she heard that Robert's condition had suddenly become worse. At the mental hospital she discovered that he had lost control of his limbs and was sinking rapidly. He embraced her with great difficulty and died in her arms on July 29th, 1856.

Clara Schumann then went to live with her mother for a while in Berlin. Plans had to be made for the future of her career, and it is significant that notwithstanding the Philistinism she found here, she made long tours in

CLARA SCHUMANN

England year after year playing for the Philharmonic Society and the Musical Union in London and with most of the similar organisations in the provinces. For twenty years she continued her career as a touring virtuoso until, in 1876, she accepted an appointment as principal teacher of the pianoforte at Hoch's Conservatoire, Frankfurt. Even then occasional tours kept her in the public eye. Her last visit to England was in March, 1888, when she played in London. Noteworthy also was her tour in Russia during 1864.

In March, 1896, she sustained a slight stroke, and in less than two months she had another of greater severity. She died on May 20th, 1896, and was buried in her husband's grave at Bonn.

Clara Schumann was loved by all her fellow-musicians, and substantial sums were raised for her assistance when illnesses interfered with her teaching and recital work. There are still people in this country who can remember her as a rather " dumpy " old lady in a bonnet. She used to seat herself at the piano with great ceremony and would spend at least five or ten minutes in arranging her gown. More often than not she would get up just as the conductor was about to start a concerto, go and speak to him, and then return to her seat to take another ten minutes arranging herself.

For all that she was always greeted with tremendous applause, and her playing revealed no traces of personal display : it was marked by her clear perception of the composer's will and the emotions she brought into her interpretation. Fiery or tender passages were particularly impressive. The unusually beautiful tone she produced seemed to please everybody : her fortissimos were produced by heavy rather than percussive playing—they had the grandeur of the heavy reeds of a fine organ, being singularly free from harshness.

Clara Schumann's repertoire included almost everything of a high standard from Scarlatti to Brahms, but she was undoubtedly greatest in the execution of her husband's works. Towards the end of her life her declining strength robbed the more powerful passages of their full force, but that was about the only criticism one could make.

Anton Rubinstein

Bülow used to call Anton Rubinstein the "Michelangelo of Music." Other people, irritated by his vanity, described him differently, but the fact remains that he was an extraordinarily clever pianist. We are told that he could make the piano sing like the human voice, or thunder like a mighty organ, but that, like most other highly-coloured reports of the playing of the virtuosi, we swallow with the customary condiment. He was also a prolific composer—some of his minor works still survive—and had a very high opinion of his own musicianship. " I play as a musician, not as a virtuoso," he used to say.

He was born on November 16th, 1829, at Vichvatìjnetz, a village on the Dniester, near the frontiers of Podòlsk and Bessarabia, and received his first music lessons at the age of five from his mother, Kaleria Christofòrovna, a well-educated woman from Prussian Silesia. His father, Gregòri, was a Russian, born in Berdìchev, and derived a modest income from tracts of land leased in the Vichvatìjnetz region. Anton was one of a large family, and his earliest recollections were of their removal to Moscow in a large covered wagon which carried the servants as well. In that city they rented a house by the river Iòwza.

His remarkable talent for music soon became apparent, and his mother devoted more and more time to his training. Unfortunately, his studies were based only upon the compositions of such virtuosi as Moscheles, Kalkbrenner, Czerny and Clementi : he learnt nothing of the works of the great masters ! After a while, however, his mother approached Alexander Villoing, one of the finest piano teachers of the day, and persuaded him to hear the boy play. He was amazed at Rubinstein's precocity, and said he would gladly take over his musical education free of charge. To a family of limited means this was too good an opportunity to lose, so Anton went to Villoing for five years.

His first public concert was given in Moscow when he was only ten, and the enthusiastic reception made Villoing decide to take him on tour as a boy prodigy. Thus he was barely in his " teens " when he was touring all over Europe. At Paris in 1840 he played before Liszt and Chopin and gave his first performance at court to the Grand Duke Constantine. Liszt, who was then at the zenith of his popularity, was greatly impressed and advised Villoing to take him to Germany so that he could complete his musical education at one of the best centres.

ANTON RUBINSTEIN

The whole of Europe was obsessed with "virtuoso-mania" at that time, and the craze provided wonderful opportunities for the promoters of infant prodigies. Rubinstein, with an inadequate musical education, was taken around Holland, Norway, Sweden and other countries and exploited to the full. He came to London and played before Queen Victoria, astonishing the court by his nonchalant attitude and complete lack of shyness in even the most exalted circles.

On the whole, Villoing was a good teacher, but like so many of his type, concentrated upon technical skill rather than good musicianship. He was most particular about the correct position of the hands and the production of good tone, and being the possessor of a vile temper, would attack his pupils with his fists if they displeased him.

Returning to Russia in 1843, Rubinstein was summoned to the Imperial Palace at St. Petersburg, received like royalty, and asked to perform before Emperor Nicholas. At that time he was a slavish imitator of Liszt : he even practised his manners and affectations, his trick of tossing back his long hair, the way he held his hands, and so forth. All this evidently helped to win the affection of his admirers, for he received many elegant and costly gifts.

But child prodigies grow up and thereby lose most of the fascination that to some degree compensates for their imperfect musicianship. The public that worship the prodigies are notoriously fickle, and give little thought to the young artists as soon as they cease to be popular. This was what the young Rubinstein had to learn in the later stages of adolescence. The family moved to Berlin in 1844, and it was there that he succeeded in getting one of his early compositions published : a short study for the piano. Two years later he went to Vienna, chiefly because Liszt was there, for he hoped that the great composer would be willing to help him. But Liszt received him coldly, and told him that " a talented man must win the goal of his ambition by his own unassisted efforts."

In Vienna, Rubinstein encountered his greatest difficulties. He had a number of letters of introduction from the Russian ambassador and his wife, but they seemed to make no impression. He therefore decided to open one of them and discover the cause. To his dismay he read : " To the position which we, the ambassador and his wife, occupy, is attached the tedious duty of patronizing and recommending our various compatriots in order to satisfy their often-times clamorous requests. Therefore, we recommend to you the bearer of this, one Rubinstein." He flung the rest of the letters in the fire and watched them burn.

So the youth who had once been a court favourite and darling of hundreds of sentimental, wealthy old ladies, had to take an attic and start earning his own living by giving cut-price piano lessons. In these Spartan conditions his creative urge flourished, and he wrote some hundreds of piano pieces, many of which became very popular in later years. He also augmented his slender income by writing magazine articles, yet he often had insufficient money to buy proper meals.

He was obliged to live in poverty for about eighteen months then quite suddenly Liszt remembered him and decided to call. He climbed up to the attic followed by the retinue of companions and servants known as his " courtiers "—they included a doctor, an artist and at least one prince in somewhat reduced circumstances—and was horrified at the conditions in which the youth was trying to work. Rubinstein accepted an invitation to dine with him chiefly because he hadn't eaten for three days.

Liszt probably helped him in a number of ways, and in 1848 he was in Berlin again, mixing with the " Bohemian " community of artists and writers. He became involved in the revolution of that year, and as there seemed to be little chance of making much progress in the German capital, he decided to return to Russia. At the frontier the Russian customs officers seized his case of manuscripts because at least one anarchist had invented a code that looked very much like music when written upon ruled music paper. He heard nothing more from them, and six months later happened to look in a secondhand music shop and saw his manuscripts for sale! The shopkeeper calmly explained that he had bought the lot at an auction sale of waste paper.

Settling for a while at St. Petersburg, he was able to support himself by giving piano lessons until he was engaged by the Grand Duchess in 1852 as accompanist to the palace singers. Two years later he had re-established himself sufficiently to embark upon a tour of Germany, France and England. Just as he was getting really popular in those countries he made a dreadful *faux pas* by publishing a magazine article in which he spoke of Glinka as being comparable to Beethoven. In those days even the poorer specimens of Beethoven's work were sanctified by the concert audiences, and a veritable tornado of abuse and vitriolic criticism swept down upon him.

Nevertheless, Rubinstein climbed steadily upward and in 1861 founded the Russian Musical Society at St. Petersburg, a body which became the nucleus of the St. Petersburg Conservatoire in the following year. He did excellent work as the first Director of this academy : daily concerts were given to raise funds, and everything possible was done to establish the rights of the professional musician. Outside the courts, the musical life of the nation was at such a low ebb that there were extremely few truly professional musicians in the country. An instance of the attitude of society towards music may be found in the following incident. During an ecclesiastical registration in the Kazan Cathedral, Rubinstein was asked to record his name, rank and vocation. He said he was a musician, but was informed by a superior deacon that there was no such profession. He protested, but the deacon merely asked the profession of his father. Rubenstein supplied the information and saw himself registered as " son of a merchant of the second guild."

He maintained his connection with the Conservatoire until 1867, when his hasty temper provoked a serious dispute among the staff, and he resigned. Resuming the life of a travelling virtuoso he had no difficulty in drawing large audiences in Europe, and was therefore able to look even further afield. In 1872 he started a lengthy concert tour of America with Henri Wieniàwski, the violinist. They made well over two hundred appearances, and went as far as New Orleans. The American idea of an artist's life—non-stop money-making—did not appeal to Rubinstein at all. He wrote afterwards : " May Heaven preserve us from such slavery ! Under these conditions there is no chance for art—one grows into an automaton simply performing mechanical work ; no dignity remains to the artist, he is lost. . . ." Two or three concerts were given every day, and there was barely time for meals and the changing of clothes. An offer of over half a million francs for a second tour was rejected outright.

A little anecdote obtains about this particular tour. Arriving in a certain town, Rubinstein happened to see that Wieniàwski was billed in slightly larger type than that used for his own name. He flew into a rage, accused the violinist of having issued instructions to that effect, and swore he would never speak to him again. So they played together day after day without a single word passing between them.

Rubinstein had no illusions about the mentality of the bulk of the audiences that paid him homage, and he was often bitterly critical of their taste. Brachvogel said of him : " No artist has ever shown to his audience so merciless a front. Both his programmes and his attitude are absolutely uncompromising. At first sight one is conscious of something stern, even inimical in his bearing towards his audience, as though a chasm were fixed between them . . . but gradually the sense of hostility vanishes and the great artist conquers once and for ever. Rubinstein has no idea of descending to the level of popular taste ; he can only raise his audience to his own plane. . . . He has the head of an inspired sphinx, upon whose face not even the paroxysms of enthusiasm call forth a smile. If the colour of life did not illuminate it, his face might be of stone. Those who have heard his playing will never forget it."

Rubinstein often declared that as a result of his travels he had come to the conclusion that of the German people at least fifty per cent. understood music ; of the French, sixteen per cent. ; but of the English—" the least musical of all people "—two per cent. ! One cannot help wondering what those figures would be if he were here to-day. He was always ready to acknowledge the magnificent hospitality he received in this country but insisted that " the ignorance of music in England is exceeded only by the lack of appreciation."

The proceeds of the great American tour enabled him to acquire an estate in Russia—at Peterhof—and to marry the beautiful Vièra Tchékuànov in 1865. They had three children.

During the season of 1885-6 he carried out a long-cherished plan to give a series of concerts illustrating the gradual development of piano music. The complete series of seven concerts was played in each of the following cities : St. Petersburg, Moscow, London, Vienna, Berlin, Paris and Leipzig. Special morning performances were also given for the benefit of music students.

Early in 1887 he returned to his former post as Director of the St. Petersburg Conservatoire, and drew up a new constitution for it. Noteworthy, I think, is the scheme he prepared to make each of the fifty-two governments of Russia assume responsibility for musical education and to establish opera in every important city. Little did he think that a Communist regime would eventually accomplish this ambitious dream.

He was a good teacher, though rather fond of telling young ladies what experience they required to be able to put real emotion into their playing. One of his pupils recorded that he would love to take a piece and play it for her, increasing the emotional intensity more and more towards the culmination, and muttering all the time : " More emotion, you see . . . more emotion . . . more emotion." On one occasion the little demonstration was just reaching its climax when he struck a wrong note. "Ah ! " he sighed, gazing up into her eyes, "*Too* much emotion ! " A psychologist might have had a lot of fun probing into Rubinstein's emotional life.

His repertoire embraced almost everything of importance from Handel to his own works. Levensohn, who was also one of his contemporaries, declared : " His passionate temperament often carries him beyond the lawful boundaries ; for instance, he takes too rapid a *tempo* in the *prestissimo* of Beethoven's Sonata Opus 109, hindering the listener from following in detail this desperate shriek from the soul ; he always plays Chopin's F major Ballade too rapidly . . ." On the other hand, we are told that ". . . in Chopin's Nocturne Opus 37 the heart-rending cry is interrupted by a succession of Palestrina-like chords. In Rubinstein's rendering it is as if these chords were played on the organ . . . these religious strains fail to soothe the suffering soul, and the desperate cry is renewed, and grief resumes its sway."

Speaking of Rubinstein's technique, Levensohn explains that he set at defiance the formerly accepted methods : " How is one to play the rapid octave accompaniment of the Schubert-Liszt *Erl König* ? Any professor will tell you to do it with a light wrist and with the middle fingers extended. What does Rubinstein do ? He curves the middle fingers and raises the wrist, so that the fingers that play the octaves, instead of falling sideways on the keys, strike with their tips as with a hammer. By this method the octaves are played with ease and freedom, whereas in the rendering of other pianists one is always sensible of the effort. There is no living pianist who could imitate this."

He was very distressed at the popular conception of *tempo rubato* in the works of Chopin and was frequently engaged in disputes with other prominent musicians upon the subject of the interpretation of the classics. Another contemporary, Hanslick, wrote of his skill thus : " His youthful and untiring vigour, his incomparable power of bringing out the melody, his perfection of touch in the stormy torrents of passion, as well as in the tender long-drawn notes of pathos, his wonderful memory . . . these are the qualities that amaze us in Rubinstein's playing. His rendering of the Chopin B-flat minor Sonata is indeed wonderful ; he plays the first movement tempestuously, giving to it the atmosphere of passionate gloom ; the funeral march is stern and sustained ; the mighty *crescendo* at the beginning of the trio and the gradual *decrescendo* after it, is a brilliant innovation of his own. But in the *finale* he takes such an astounding *prestissimo* that all accents are lost, and only a grey cloud of dust seems to hover before the dazed listener, who simply waits for the last note that he may open his eyes and draw a breath of relief. Therefore young virtuosi must beware of imitating the excesses of Rubinstein's playing, rather learning how to play with expression, keeping all the while a strict watch over *tempo*."

Rubinstein invariably played from memory at recitals, chiefly because he was short-sighted and had difficulty in reading music unless he bent very close to the copy. He said in later life that the fear of being " let down " by his memory used to haunt him whenever he was playing a concerto : " the strain of memorizing everything is like the torture of the Inquisition." Incidentally, the London critics censured him for playing a concerto without a score : such a practice was then considered to be bad form.

He excelled in producing a beautiful tone from his instrument and obtained remarkably smooth effects by his clever use of the pedal. He would tell his pupils to forget about *striking* the notes, and to imagine, instead, that they were singing them. Few pianists of his period could manipulate the sustaining pedal with skill comparable to Rubinstein's. " The more I play the more convinced I become that the pedal is the soul of the pianoforte " was one of his more significant remarks.

He played for the last time one day in January 1889 at Moscow. As he made his final bow to the audience he closed the piano, locked it, and making a pathetic gesture of farewell, disappeared for ever from the concert hall. He died at Peterhof in 1894.

Leschetizky

Most musicians would probably agree that in the history of music—and of the pianistic art in particular—Leschetizky's great reputation as a virtuoso has become overshadowed by his fame as one of the world's greatest teachers of the pianoforte. Through his many pupils, and, in turn, through their pupils, this fame is still spreading, whereas personal recollections of his playing will in a few decades cease to exist.

He was born near Lemberg, Poland, on June 22nd, 1830, in the shadow of the great castle of Lancut, a treasure-house of antique porcelains, bronzes and other works of art, where his father was music teacher to the famous Potocka family. As soon as he was able to walk he was allowed to play upon the terraces and grassy slopes that surrounded the castle, but invariably frequented one particular spot : the bank beneath the windows of the music room. Here he would spend hours listening to the pieces played by the young countesses under his father's direction. He longed to be able to make music like this, but alas ! his father's piano was always kept locked. One day he discovered that by pulling back the green curtains beneath the keyboard he could work the notes from below, and in this novel fashion learned to play some of his favourite melodies by ear. It was not long before his mother found him amusing himself in this manner, and delighted with his zeal, persuaded his father to give him lessons.

By the time he was ten Theodore Leschetizky was a favourite in the drawing rooms of all the nobility in the neighbourhood : he could play so well that three or four times a week he was invited to tea ; a fascinating little prodigy always ready to entertain the other guests. In later years, he used to tell the most extraordinary stories of the life of the great aristocratic Polish families. There was for instance a certain noblewoman who had at least half-a-dozen maids of honour. In her anxiety to preserve the virginity of these young ladies she kept two curious dwarfs, grotesque little men dressed up in musical-comedy uniforms, who were compelled to spend their lives spying upon the girls. The slightest flirtation was duly reported, and as a result the maid concerned was brought to her mistress and caned like a troublesome schoolgirl !

What intrigued Leschetizky most of all in the great Polish and Russian households, however, was the trained and domesticated Lithuanian bear that most families kept in the kitchen. He was generally a very docile animal and would perform simple domestic tasks as efficiently as any human. He was often given the job of pounding sugar or nuts in a mortar, and would sit for half-an-hour laboriously manipulating the pestle with an intense, pensive expression upon his face. Turning the spit before the roaring fire was another job for Bruin, and the sight of him helping one of the male servants cut wood with a two-handed saw was too good an entertainment to be missed. One bear of Leschetizky's acquaintance was a very unprincipled fellow : he would watch the cook pour out a glassful of cognac to flavour a pudding and immediately her back was turned, would walk casually up to the table and swig it off as coolly as Tommy Handley's Colonel Chinstrap !

Leschetizky was brought up under the strictest of parental discipline : he was allowed no toys, and the slightest misdemeanour brought a thrashing from his father. As a child he found pleasure in reading Goethe and Schiller.

His first public appearance was made at Lemberg when he was about nine. He played a Czerny concertino in a hall infested with rats : they could be seen running about during the performance. After the concert a friend presented him with an air-gun, and he insisted upon going back to the hall to hunt the rats with it.

He could not have been much older when he was invited to play before Prince Metternich. This notorious aristocrat was so charmed by the boy's playing that he told him to choose anything in the room as a memento of the occasion. Leschetizky's father, standing by, cast an envious eye around the sumptuous chamber with its priceless vases, jewelled ornaments, costly antiques and pictures, and began to speak on the boy's behalf. " Not a word, please," the Prince interrupted, " let the little fellow choose for himself." The young pianist had already decided. He went over to the window and picked up a gaily-painted toy left by one of the Prince's children : an artcile worth a few francs ! His father never got over it.

At eleven he went to play before Karl Czerny, one of the greatest teachers of the day, and then became one of his pupils. Czerny was of course an eminent virtuoso, and as there is no biography of him elsewhere in this book It would, I think, be worth while to quote Leschetizky's impression of him :[1] " He was rather short in stature, with woolly hair and bright, expressive brown eyes which fairly shone behind his spectacles. He was of a high order of intelligence ; he was deeply interested in politics, and spoke seven languages . . . a pupil of Beethoven and Clementi and besides being himself an eminent pianist was, with Hummel, at the head of the ' school ' of piano-playing founded by Mozart. His manner of teaching was something like that of an orchestral director. He gave lessons standing, indicating the different shapes of tempo and colouring by gestures. The chief aim of my father's instruction had been the development of musical feeling and

[1] Quoted by Comtesse Angèle Potocka in *Theodore Leschetizky* : New York 1903

taste ; Czerny insisted principally upon accuracy, brilliancy and pianistic effects. I played a great deal of Bach under him . . . some pieces by Thalberg, and above all, those of Beethoven. Czerny taught that Beethoven should be rendered with freedom of delivery and depth of feeling. A pedantic, inelastic interpretation of that master made him wild. He allowed me to play Chopin just as I pleased, and though he appreciated the great Polish composer, he sometimes said his works were sweetish. Again, he would become enthusiastic and say that they were ' famose Musik.' Czerny did not fully recognize the value of the later Beethoven sonatas ; Mendelssohn he understood."

Czerny, in due course, presented Leschetizky to Liszt. " Liszt had a charm of manner, a certain gracious cordiality without a tinge of condescension ; he seemed to see into everyone's mind and feel with him. . . . I was about to sit down when he stopped me saying, ' Wait a minute, my boy, notice this name attentively.' I read the name : Richard Wagner. The book was the score of *Rienzi*. ' That man will some day make the world hear from him,' said Liszt."

In the same year he played to Thalberg. " He was handsome, refined in his manners and very aristocratic in his ways." Then he was presented to Prince Esterhazy who invited him to perform at his court at ten ducats a time, and met Anton Rubinstein, but his mother disapproved of this great virtuoso's " not particularly refined language, his precociousness and frankly-expressed cynicism, especially regarding women."

Leschetizky had an exceptionally beautiful singing voice as a boy : its lovely quality and fine power attracted the attention of Salvi, the celebrated tenor, for whom he sang airs from the works of Donizetti and Bellini like an accomplished opera singer. Through Salvi he met Donizetti in person, and showed him some of his efforts at composition. The composer criticized these but showed far more interest in the lad's skill at the keyboard : he took him to Schönbrunn and got him an audience with Emperor Ferdinand and the Archduke Charles, who invited him to play and afterwards to take part in several of the imperial concerts.

At fourteen, Leschetizky was a self-supporting musician, well-known in a dozen large towns and with many influential friends. He began taking pupils and rented two rooms—one for use as a studio—next door to the house his father had taken in Vienna. He still seemed quite a child to all who knew him, chiefly on account of his luxuriant curls, a considerable asset to any child prodigy.

Within a year he had fallen in love with Mlle. Angri, a famous singer, and in the hope that she would regard him as a young man, and possibly as a suitor, he had his hair cut short and acquired a manly (but very ill-fitting) jacket. A few days later he had to appear with her at a joint-recital, and on the appointed evening presented himself at the door of her dressing room conscious of a man-about-town feeling. When he entered she took one look at him and burst into an uncontrollable fit of laughter. He was so furious that at the concert he played like a demon, and won a great ovation from an astonished audience.

With such early success, Leschetizky might easily have grown into a capable but very dull and conventional virtuoso, for there were plenty of them about at that time, and as they enjoyed no small measure of public adulation, they were quite content to rake in the money and give little thought to their art. But then he met Julius Schulhoff, who altered the entire course of his artistic career.

They became acquainted at a soirée in Vienna. Here is Leschetizky's own account of the event : " I well remember that drawing room filled with musicians and critics, all in expectation with regard to the artist of the day. He was of course asked to play and acceded with charming simplicity. After trying the piano and preluding a little he began a composition of his own— *Le Chant du Berger*. Under his hands the piano seemed like another instrument. Seated in a corner, my heart overflowing with indescribable emotions, I listened. I began to foresee a new style of playing. That melody standing out in bold relief, that wonderful sonority—all this must be done to a new and entirely different touch. And that cantabile, a legato such as I had not dreamed possible on the piano : a human voice rising above the sustaining harmonies ! I could hear the shepherd sing, and see him. Then a strange thing happened. He had finished, and had awakened no response ! There was no enthusiasm ! They were all so accustomed to brilliant technical display that the pure beauty of the composition and interpretation was not appreciated. . . . Schulhoff's playing was a revelation to me. From that day I tried to find that touch. . . . I practised incessantly, sometimes even on the table-top, striving to attain firm finger-tips and a light wrist, which I felt to be the means to my end. I kept that beautiful sound well in my mind, and it made the driest work interesting. I played only exercises, abandoning all kinds of pieces. . . . In the meantime, Schulhoff had conquered Vienna. Heard in a large hall, his playing produced the proper effect. . . . At the end of three months I went back to my work feeling less dry. I had attained my result."

Leschetizky used to acknowledge that at seventeen his technique was more brilliant than at any time afterwards. " While I worked on my exercises I never allowed my thoughts to wander from my task." He practised diligently for three hours a day and then, as a recreation and to broaden his mind, would study subjects unrelated to music.

During the revolution of 1848 he was wounded in the right arm, and the treatment he received in Vienna brought on congestion of the muscles.

After two weeks of acute pain he went to Greifenberg to consult the eminent physician Prisnitz, who prescribed a curious form of treatment that consisted chiefly of wrapping the patient's body in wet sheets. However, within five weeks he was cured.

Then he went to Italy. At Venice he happened to see the most ravishingly beautiful woman he had ever set eyes upon. She was lying in a gondola, and without a thought for the consequences he jumped into the boat and sat down beside her. She was of noble birth and lived in fear of a tyrannical guardian, but permitted Leschetizky to visit her in secret that evening so that he could play to her. He did—until dawn, and eventually to continue the story in Leschetizky's own words, " One day she told the old Count that she was going to spend two weeks with her mother. Her guardian consented, little dreaming where she was actually going. We lived our idyll on the Isola Madre, in a deserted fisherman's hut. We were happy with a poetic happiness. Alas ! it was to last but two weeks. . . . I was determined to cast all aside and entreated Giulia to become my wife. But she answered gently and sorrowfully that our lives could not be united. She even extracted from me a promise never to write to her or make any effort to seek her out again. Our love was to be like a beautiful dream . . . and standing on the beach, watching the boat that carried her off, I wept with the passionate bitterness of a man's first woe."

His next journey took him through Finland into Russia to play before the Emperor and Empress on several occasions. At one of these court performances, Rachel, the world-famous tragedienne, read La Fontaine's *Les Deux Pigeons*. Later in the evening the Empress was standing near her and happened to drop her handkerchief, but to her intense annoyance, Rachel pretended not to notice it, and a courtier had the " honour " of restoring it to its owner. Leschetizky asked Rachel why she did not take the opportunity of serving the Empress. She replied scornfully, " Why should *I* stoop for her ? "

Leschetizky then settled for a while in St. Petersburg and accepted an appointment as inspector of music at the Smolna Institute, an exclusive establishment for the education of the daughters of the highest nobility, under the patronage of the Empress. He also held a private music class of his own which was later embodied into the St. Petersburg Conservatoire founded by Rubinstein in 1862. At about the same time he received yet another appointment : concert-master at the court of the Grand Duchess Helen.

In 1856 he married Anna Carlowna de Friedebourg, a very charming contralto, but within a year or two it became perfectly obvious that they were an ill-matched pair, and they sought a divorce. Some years later Annette Essipoff, then only a schoolgirl, entered his class at the Conservatoire :

a remarkably intelligent and attractive child who eventually graduated with Tschaikovsky in 1869. They both received the coveted gold medals : the first to be awarded by the Conservatoire. Annette soon became a most beautiful young woman and was made all the more attractive to Leschetizky by her phenomenal success as a pianist. All Europe and the more civilized parts of America paid her tribute. So of course he fell in love with her, and they were married in 1880, after having lived together for some time and surviving an attack of typhoid that compelled them to move to Vienna.

Leschetizky had by then reached his maturity as a virtuoso, having made highly successful tours in Germany and Russia, and one or two appearances in London. Many of his recitals were given jointly with either Auer or Sarasate, the eminent violinists. His fame as a teacher was also spreading far and wide ; one of his greatest triumphs being accomplished when he brought out his famous pupil Paderewski.

His Wednesday afternoon " class concerts " had become quite an institution, for at these he assembled over a hundred pupils among whom one could meet such promising people as Schnabel and Paula Szalit. The true genius of Leschetizky emerged, however, at the private lessons, when the pupil, after careful preparation by one of his assistants, would play two or three pieces for the great man to criticize. The strain of this ordeal can be well imagined, for at such an opportunity he would weed out the less satisfactory pupil. On one occasion a rather supercilious young man rattled off a Beethoven sonata with all the self-confidence in the world. Leschetizky sat in silence, and then as the young pianist played the final chords he got up and went forward proffering his right hand. " Good-bye ! " he said with a chilly smile. The young man stared in blank astonishment. " Good-bye ! " Leschetizky repeated. " We shall never meet again at the piano. A man who could play that with such bad feeling would murder his own mother." One had to approach the work of the great composers with a feeling of profound reverence to please him.

The pupil would generally come to the piano and find a dish of dried beans on one side and an empty plate on the other. While the student played, the master would transfer one bean from the dish to the plate for every good point that emerged, but would reverse the process for every fault. Happy the pupil who discovered a large plateful waiting for him at the end !

So much has been said about the " Leschetizky method " that one feels almost disappointed to find that he had no strikingly original system, and certainly no short cut to success. The position of the hand, upon which he insisted, might be described thus : rather low, pliable wrist ; high knuckles, curved fingers with firm tips, and a light thumb. " There is no method for the wrist except to get the easiest way to the next note," he would say.

" You cannot teach the method of technique, because every hand is different. There are no mysteries in technique : the mysteries and secrets come when you begin to play systematically and rhythmically."

He detested unrhythmical playing, and disapproved of " standard " fingerings—" artificial," he called them. Every pianist should decide his own fingering for himself, for one man's fingering would be another man's frustration. Incidentally, although he found difficulty in remembering the faces of all his pupils, he never forgot their hands.

One of his favourite precepts was " Train your eye and your ear, and the rest will take care of itself," and to this he would often add, " When once you listen to your own playing as if you were listening critically to somebody else, and find yourself unhappy or dissatisfied, then it is that your real study begins." He always believed that the true artist could rarely, if ever, feel satisfied with his work. This did not mean that one could not find happiness in one's work—far from it—but that the happiness should be found in the striving after perfection rather than in the accomplishment. A good point, I think, which many of us would do well to bear in mind.

When his pupils were preparing concertos, Leschetizky would invariably play the orchestral part on a second piano, not only as it should be played, but also as a bad orchestra would perform it. He was careful to warn his students against inferior orchestras and incompetent conductors, and would generally tell them of an experience he had when a conductor complained that they had played the concerto in question a dozen times during the past couple of months but never at Leschetizky's speed. The great pianist stood up and said, "Am I the soloist or not ? When I play the melody, you are merely the accompanist, and you will work at my speed or not at all."

He had a marvellous memory, yet he frequently admitted that he dreaded the lesser-known concertos lest it should fail him. When a pupil once asked him what he would do if such a catastrophe occurred, he said, " I think I should do the same as a certain other pianist of international reputation once did : he suddenly stopped playing in the middle of the first movement, stood up, glared at the conductor and shouted, ' I refuse to continue until this piano is properly tuned.' While the tuner was trying to discover some minute imperfection, the pianist calmly returned to his dressing room, had a glass of vodka, and spent twenty minutes studying the score ! "

Leschetizky always prided himself that his pupils were musicians first and pianists after. He rarely paid compliments, and during the lessons smoked strong cigars. When questioned about the " Leschetizky method " he once said, " I have no method : if I had it would be based upon the mental delineation of a chord."

It must be admitted that he showed more tolerance to inefficient young lady pupils than to men, chiefly because he found difficulty in resisting a beautiful face or a voluptuous figure. One of his pupils, who was a most luscious creature in her " teens," said that he once stopped her in the middle of a Chopin study, took her hands, sighed, and said " Why not get married instead ? " " But Professor," she blushed, " I've been married a month ! " Undeterred, he went on, " Well, then, go and have a baby, you'll enjoy it much more than trying to play the piano."

His marriage with Annette Essipoff lasted twelve years, and was then dissolved. Two years later—in 1894—he married another of his pupils, Donimirska Benislavska, and while I am on the subject of his matrimonial affairs I might as well record that in 1908 he took a fourth wife, a Polish pupil named Maria Rozborska. One would have thought that with this pleasant variety of women he would have been quite satisfied, but no, his private life was not all that could be desired by the parents of his pupils.

He insisted upon strict discipline among his pupils—musical discipline, I mean—and they were not allowed to accept engagements without consulting him, so that he could consider the music they proposed to play. He would never allow them to perform, in public, music that was too difficult or in any way unsuitable for them.

Brahms and Leschetizky had a mutual contempt for each other's piano compositions. Brahms once told him that his works were suitable only for " sweet sixteen." Leschetizky retorted, "And your piano stuff shouldn't be played by anybody under ninety." Nevertheless, they were great friends, and the pianist had the utmost respect for the Brahms symphonies. His relations with Rubinstein were equally cordial and frank : he often said that he felt like spitting in Rubinstein's face because of his interpretation of certain classics, yet they always enjoyed each other's company.

Leschetizky was probably one of the first musicians to propound the theory that all the arts are related—a theory beloved by some of our more progressive artists at the present time. Knowledge of one art, he declared, could inspire understanding of the others, and he would urge his students to study the various modes of expression employed by each sphere of art in the manifestation of each emotion, and above all, to compare them intelligently. Happiness, for example, could be expressed in a variety of ways by the musician, the poet, painter or sculptor, and the musician could benefit by trying to understand the medium of expression used by each. Then he should go deeper and understand the basic instincts that produce the emotion, and its derivatives. A fascinating study for those who care to devote a little thought to it.

The declamatory nature of the pianist's art, Leschetizky would insist, made it comparable with that of the actor, and he would ask his students to compare their shading of tone with the expressions of an actor's voice. Then he would suddenly produce a fine picture and make them compare its lines to the phrasing of a piece of music being played on the piano. This method of teaching was probably responsible for the wonderful perception and deep feeling portrayed in the work of many of his students when they went forth to win their laurels in the concert halls of Europe and America.

To-day, they still talk of their wonderful master, that intensely dynamic character whose personality was made up of the oddest mixture of qualities. One attribute he lacked was patience when it came to the toleration of dull people : he could endure fools and failures, freaks and fanatics, but never the type of person devoid of ideas and individuality. He detested regularity of hours and any trace of routine in life. " Study should not be regulated by the clock if you find pleasure in your work " he was heard to say on one occasion.

His favourite form of recreation was to wander aimlessly in the streets and parks of Vienna at night : he was often out until three or four in the morning. Strolling home at dawn one morning he met a pupil going to mass. He smiled dreamily, observed " You can learn so much from the peace of night " and passed on.

Early in the year 1915 he had one or two operations upon his eyes, and died that autumn. He was in his eighty-sixth year.

Busoni

THERE may be some diversity of opinion concerning the value of Busoni's compositions, but on his skill as an executant all responsible critics are unanimous : he was one of the few world-famous pianists whose musicianship allowed them to be classed with Rubinstein, Liszt and Paderewski.

His father, Ferdinando, was a clarinettist, a self-educated virtuoso of Corsican origin, who spent most of his life travelling chiefly because his quick temper made it almost impossible for him to hold any orchestral appointment for long. This odd, interesting character married a pianist named Anna Weiss, and together they toured Italy until their son Ferruccio was born on April 1st, 1866. Typical of the father was his insistence upon the array of Christian names given to the boy at his baptism : Ferruccio Dante Michelangiolo Benvenuto—after the illustrious Tuscans who had borne these names !

At the earliest possible moment the two musicians sent Ferruccio with a nurse to his grandfather at Trieste, and resumed their tours. Eventually two or three considerable successes in Paris made Ferdinando decide to set up his home in the French capital, and as soon as this was done the boy Ferruccio was fetched so that he could grow up under the influence of his mother. With incessant practice, concerts, household duties and a son to rear, Anna's time was fully occupied, but she apparently coped with it all in high spirits, for a letter to her niece is full of enthusiasm for her little boy :[1] ". . . He gives me plenty to do ; he is as lively as can be, and has to be watched continually. . . . He jumps and dances and gets up on to the chairs ; he is a regular *moto perpetuo* and often makes my hair stand on end for fright. You can imagine how between the music of my own pianoforte and the ' music ' of that little imp I often do not know where I am ! He is very big and strong for his age and uncommonly clever. You should see him at the pianoforte and how prettily he puts those dear little hands on the keyboard. He tries to imitate me, lifts his head and says, ' What a lovely thing Daddy's playing ! ' Ferruccio plays scales *glissés*."

When he was only four he was working studiously at the piano, learning to play the violin, and accompanying his mother's practice on a toy flute ! " He is all music and when he hears a beautiful melody he dances and jumps for joy and is quite beside himself."

[1] Quoted in full in *Ferruccio Busoni* by E. J. Dent.

111

Ill-health and rumours of war made their sojourn in Paris a short one, and various difficulties then made it necessary for Anna and her son to reside for a while in her father's house at Trieste while Ferdinando toured alone. This was not a propitious arrangement, and neither mother nor son was happy there, so when Ferdinando returned he took rooms in the Via Geppa opposite the Turkish Consulate.

Unfortunately for Ferruccio, his father's return brought another sort of trouble : the shrewd musician could see in his son's remarkable musical precocity a potential source of income, and resolved to exploit it as soon as possible by intensifying the child's training.   This process has been described by Busoni himself : " My father knew little about the pianoforte and was erratic in rhythm, so he made up for these shortcomings with an indescribable combination of energy, severity and pedantry.   For four hours a day he would sit by me at the pianoforte with an eye on every note and every finger.   There was no escape and no interruption except for his explosions of temper, which were violent in the extreme.   A box on the ears would be followed by copious tears, accompanied by reproaches, threats and terrifying prophecies, after which the scene would end in a great display of paternal emotion, assurances that it was all for my good, and so on to a final reconciliation—the whole story beginning again the next day."

At the age of seven, little Ferruccio appeared with his parents at a concert and played the first movement of Mozart's Sonata in C-major, Schumann's *Povero Orfanello* and *Marcia del Soldato*, and Clementi's Fourth Sonatina (F major).   His success may be judged from the fact that four months later he gave a concert of his own when he played two fugues by Handel, Schumann's *Knecht Ruprecht* and a Theme and Variations by Hummel.

His father must, however, be given the credit for having introduced him to the wonders of Bach, upon whose works much of his training was carried out.   In an epilogue to his complete edition of Bach's Clavier Works, Busoni acknowledges this : " I have to thank my father for the good fortune that he kept me strictly to the study of Bach in my childhood, and that in a time and in a country in which the master was rated little higher than a Carl Czerny.   My father was a simple virtuoso on the clarinet, who liked to play fantasias on *Il Trovatore* and the *Carnival of Venice* ; he was a man of incomplete musical education, an Italian and a cultivator of the *bel canto*. How did such a man in his ambition for his son's career come to hit upon the one very thing that was right ?   I can only compare it to a mysterious revelation.   He educated me in this way to be a ' German ' musician and showed me the path which I never entirely deserted, though at the same time I never cast off the Latin qualities given to me by nature."

BUSONI

Soon after his ninth birthday Busoni gave several local concerts—at one of these he played the Mozart Concerto in C minor with his father conducting—and was then taken by his father to Vienna. " We went to the Hotel Erzherzog Carl—the hotel for princes and celebrities—and were lucky enough to meet Rubinstein. My father managed to have me introduced to him. . . . He never met anybody at a cafe or in the street without telling him all about ' my son.' And he would end by bringing the stranger back to the hotel, bursting in and dragging the new acquaintance along with him. . . . The stranger was always described as a most distinguished gentleman —until my father came to know him better. The acquaintance generally resulted in his becoming ' the fool ' or ' that disreputable fellow ' or something else of the sort. If he accommodated my father with a small loan of money he might revert to being ' a thoroughly good man,' for the state of the exchequer was then, and always was, the weak point of my father's administration."

Busoni went to the Conservatoire as a student while he was in Vienna, but derived little benefit from the casual and disinterested teaching of his professor : he learnt far more about music from the many operas and concerts to which he was taken. Incidentally he heard Brahms play the piano, but thought little of him as a pianist, although he had every admiration for his compositions. " Music is performed here by the yard, just like shopkeepers measuring out cloth " he wrote to his mother. He had already started composing, and at that time was working upon an Overture for orchestra.

At a concert given on February 8th, 1876, he played the Haydn D major Trio, a Mozart Rondo, Hummel's Theme and Variations and several little pieces of his own. A critic who called him the " Tom Thumb of pianists " described him as a " most delightful duodecimo edition of Liszt, Rubinstein, Brahms or any other long-haired composing virtuoso." Soon after this concert the lad became ill and had to be taken back to Trieste.

Convalescence at Gmunden, the popular health-resort in Upper Austria, during the summer, provided an opportunity for Busoni to play before the Emperor and Empress, the Queen of Hanover and the Archduchess Elizabeth. Back in Vienna for the following winter, Busoni met Liszt and heard him play.

Another illness contracted by the twelve-year-old pianist compelled the little family to move again, this time to Graz, where Busoni seems to have enhanced his reputation as a second Mozart with the assistance of a young man named Wilhelm Kienzl ; an admirer who did much to stir up local interest in the boy. In that town he also commenced his life-long friendship with Otto von Kapff, a journalist-poet.

Towards the end of 1878 a tour of Klagenfurt, Bozen, Trent, Arco and Rovereto was made with considerable success notwithstanding Ferdinando's absurd extremes in his anxiety to boost his son as the second Mozart. The poor lad was bullied into such stunts as playing improvisations on tunes supplied by members of the audience, and suchlike : grossly unfair demands upon a lad whose musical education had been decidedly patchy. Busoni soon began to realize that as well as being the principal earner of the family he was the only member of the trio with a sense of responsibility and discretion.

Equally unfortunate was a concert given at Graz in November, 1879, when he conducted a performance of his own *Stabat Mater* for solo voices, chorus and string orchestra. This work was a crude, childish attempt at a form of composition far beyond his powers. The only good that came out of it was the formation of a committee of sympathetic people who, recognizing the talent that Busoni undoubtedly possessed, desired to take upon themselves the responsibility of his education—it was obvious that he was urgently in need of proper training.

The boy was therefore sent to Dr. Wilhelm Mayer, who was then living in Graz and who, despite his dislike of infant prodigies, had become interested in Busoni. From this accomplished teacher he received a thorough grounding in harmony, counterpoint, orchestration and composition, and caught his great enthusiasm for Mozart and Bach. " When he mentioned Mozart's name, his thoughtful face assumed an expression of almost fatherly confidence and happiness, while his eyes betrayed a deep inward amazement. It was perhaps Rémy's[1] greatest achievement, at any rate the most fruitful achievement for his pupils, that he stamped the picture of Mozart so profoundly upon our minds."[2]

Busoni completed Mayer's two-year course in fifteen months, and in April, 1881, his committee arranged a farewell concert for him. At this he played Schumann's Concerto, the Beethoven Sonata Opus 111, and several of his own compositions, including a Prelude and Fugue for the piano.

The next event of importance in his life occurred about a year later when after he had given a series of five concerts at Bologna, the Accademia Filarmonica conferred a diploma for composition and pianoforte-playing upon him : a rare distinction for a youth of sixteen.

It was perhaps this honour that made him decide to try his fortune once again in Vienna in the following year. His first concert there brought him a profit of four hundred florins : the programme included Bach's *Italian Concerto*, the Beethoven Sonata Opus 111, Schumann's *Études symphoniques*, Chopin's *Andante Spianato* and the *Polonaise Brilliante*. But there were many disappointments. His other concerts were not particularly successful and the Philharmonic Committee postponed their trial of his Suite for

---

[1] Mayer used the pseudonym " W. A. Rémy " on his compositions.
[2] Ferruccio Busoni : *Von der Einheit der Musik.*

Orchestra again and again. When finally it was tried on October 4th, 1884, it was rejected by a majority of one vote : most of the orchestra had voted against it despite the enthusiasm that Richter, the conductor, had shown for it. This was a great blow to Busoni, for he had been relying with confidence on the acceptance of this to make a favourable impression upon Baroness Todesco who was at that time acting as his patron and paying him a hundred florins a month. It is true that she was reassured when she heard him play in public, but it was some months before he got over this bitter disappointment. Writing to his father he said : "Although I was and am still very annoyed, yet I have tried to take the matter calmly and not feel discouraged, but maintain confidence in my talent, and persevere. All that was humanly possible for the success of my plans was done—I have no cause to blame myself, I neglected nothing, left nothing undone. I worked hard, I went everywhere and waited in antechambers, I was my own copyist and porter."

His next move was to Leipzig, which for a few years had snatched from Paris the honour of being the greatest musical centre of Europe. Here, they had heard of no Italian pianist since Domenico Scarlatti, but on the whole received him sympathetically, though several of the critics disliked his treatment of the classics.

It was also in Leipzig that in 1886 he met Grieg who introduced him to Delius as " a most remarkable pianist—and perhaps something more." Gustav Mahler was there, too, but Busoni's close friendship with him did not start until several years later.

For many years Busoni's financial position was precarious, chiefly on account of his lazy father who preferred to live a life of idleness on his son's earnings than to work for his own living. His compositions helped him over the periods when concert engagements were few, but some idea of his need for a steady income may be gained from his acceptance, at the age of twenty-two, of a teaching appointment at the Helsingfors Conservatoire without knowing even where Helsingfors was situated ! His first lonely weeks there were not improved by the discovery that most of his pupils at the Conservatoire had scarcely heard of Bach, Mozart, or Beethoven ! He wrote to a friend saying that he felt like a clown with a troop of performing geese in a circus. The other teacher of the pianoforte was a gentleman of such high intellect that he spent most of his time reading and positively enjoying the sort of short stories that are written for young servant girls. However, Busoni gave several recitals in the town and made a very good impression with Beethoven sonatas, works of Bach, Mozart, Handel and later, Liszt, Grieg and various compositions of his own.

As one would imagine, he lost no time in getting back to a more congenial environment during the holidays. This generally meant Leipzig, where he continued to make useful contacts. There, in 1888, he met Christian Sinding, who had just completed a piano quintet. On learning of Busoni's ability as a pianist, he asked him to play this work at its first performance in Leipzig. It was received with great enthusiasm by everybody except the critics, one of whom, occupying the most conspicuous seat in the house, ostentatiously ate sandwiches while the quintet was being played.

The critics at Hamburg, who had hitherto been caustic, were much more encouraging when he gave his next concert in that city in January, 1889. The programme included the first of his own transcriptions of the organ works of J. S. Bach, and one critic complimented him highly on his " wonderful reproduction of the full soft organ tone on the pianoforte."

It is curious how a chance encounter in the most unlikely place can suddenly affect the entire course of one's life. When Busoni returned to Helsingfors for the ensuing term he felt thoroughly dissatisfied with his academic post, indeed with Finland and everything connected with it. He felt sure that no good could come out of his stay there. One Monday in March he was feeling particularly depressed when one of his pupils, a young man named Edi Fazer, persuaded him to go to the *tableaux vivants* with him. The performance, in aid of a charity, was followed by a supper and dance, during which the student introduced him to Gerda Sjöstrand, the daughter of a Swedish sculptor who had come to live in Helsingfors. They fell in love almost at once, and within a week announced their engagement.

In the summer of 1890 Busoni accepted an appointment at the Moscow Conservatoire. He arrived there early in September, and a few weeks later Sjöstrand followed with his two daughters for the wedding. Gerda was a Protestant, and the only person who would marry them was a German Protestant pastor who had planned to leave Moscow for his holidays on the very morning the bride was due to arrive. Busoni met Gerda at the station, drove her straight to the pastor's house, and married her on the spot.

Moscow in those days was notorious for its fabulously rich nobility and its masses of poverty-stricken workers and filthy beggars. To make matters worse, most of his colleagues at the Conservatoire were jealous of him—he had won the Rubinstein prize for composition that summer—and disliked working with a foreigner. Busoni and his wife had found a couple of unfurnished rooms less dirty than the average and made a home, but the young professor still had to keep his parents, who saw no reason for economy when their son was in a good position. His first public concert in Moscow was a great artistic success but barely paid its expenses, and throughout the term he became more and more dissatisfied with the conditions in which he lived and worked. It is not surprising, therefore, that early in 1891 he decided to accept a similar appointment at the New England Conservatory at Boston ;

several of his friends, including Hermann Wolff, the eminent concert agent, having advised him to go to America.

At Boston, however, other troubles were in store for him. The Conservatory's finances were not very sound, and almost anybody who could pay the fees was accepted regardless of talent. There was an unmistakable air of commercial efficiency about the place, but little else, and Busoni found himself giving four lessons every hour, stopping each pupil immediately his prescribed fifteen minutes had expired. He tolerated it for a year and then resigned, preferring to make a living as a travelling virtuoso. A son, Benvenuto, was born at Boston on May 24th, 1892, but a month or so later they moved to New York, a better centre from which to work.

In the 'nineties, America was not the cultured nation it is to-day, and it was not long before Busoni found himself longing for the stimulating artistic circles of Leipzig, Paris and Vienna. " In America, the *average* is better than elsewhere, but along with that there is much *more* average than elsewhere, and as far as I can see, it will soon be *all* average ! " This statement in a letter to a friend reflects his anxiety that American life would reduce his genius to mediocrity.

The summer of 1894 found him on his way back to Europe, with his wife and son, determined to settle in Berlin and to make a living as a pianist. " I have great successes as a pianist : the composer I conceal for the present." His first important concert on his return was at Hamburg in October of that year, when he played Weber's *Concertstück* and his own arrangement of Liszt's *Rhapsodie Espagnole* for pianoforte and orchestra with Mahler conducting. This was the start of a tour that took him to Leipzig, Liége and St. Petersburg. Back in Berlin in January, 1895, he enraged the critics by his interpretation of the Chopin Sonata in B-flat minor, but before he could read their remarks he was off on another tour to Helsingfors, Brussels and Christiania. This strenuous life is amusingly described in a poem he wrote at that time :[1]

" CAREER OF A VIRTUOSO."

Where is my Bradshaw ? How do I get there ?
Ah ! Page a hundred : here's the only train.
Change—can I risk it ? Three minutes to spare.
No sleeping car ? Well, useless to complain.

Next morning at eleven, half awake
And shivering, I arrive. A man comes up.
" Make haste ! Rehearsal's waiting ! You must take
A cab at once ! " No time for bite or sup.

[1] Translated and quoted by E. J. Dent in his masterly biography, *Ferruccio Busoni* (Oxford University Press.)

No time to change or wash. " You're rather late,"
Says the presiding magnate. " You must know
The rehearsal's public. We have had to wait ;
The songs were all sung half an hour ago."

Straight to the platform—play as best I can—
Hungry and dirty, fingers frozen quite—
That's done ! Why, there's the critic ! " Poor old man,
You can't expect him to go out at night."

The concert's a success—but what of that ?
The critic writes on how *he* heard me play.
Encore ? No time. I seize my coat and hat,
For to the station it's a goodish way.

Into the train just as the whistle blows—
On to the next place, supperless again,
Clammy with sweating, still in evening clothes—
To-morrow the rehearsal is at ten.

Busoni's interpretation of the classics still brought sharp criticisms, and we find him writing to one of his critics, defending himself thus : " You start from false premises in thinking that it is my intention to ' modernize ' the works. On the contrary, by cleaning them of the dust of tradition I try to restore their youth, to present them as they sounded to people at the moment when they first sprang from the head and pen of the composer.

" The *Pathétique* was an almost revolutionary sonata in its own day, and ought to sound revolutionary. One could never put enough passion into the *Appassionata*, which was the culmination of the passionate expression of its epoch. When I play Beethoven, I try to approach the *liberté, nervosité* and *humanité* which are the signature of his compositions, in contrast to those of his predecessors. Recalling the character of the man Beethoven and what is related of his own playing, I have built up for myself an ideal which has been wrongly called ' modern ' and which is really no more than ' live.' I do the same with Liszt, and oddly enough people approve in this case, though they condemn me in the other."

Busoni's somewhat ruthless interpretation of Chopin, which horrified all who had become accustomed to the tender, delicate and almost dreamy style that most pianists used in all but the most vigorous of his works, is less easily explained. Many of Chopin's compositions he never touched—the Mazurkas, for instance, but he was particularly fond of the Preludes. His intellectual approach to his art, which rigorously excluded popular sentimentality, accounted for his failure to please many of his listeners. It is significant that during a visit to Moscow, Safonoff acclaimed him as a great artist : " Tone, virtuosity, poetry—you have everything ! "

BUSONI

Mention should be made of his visit to Italy in December, 1895. He gave concerts at Milan, Verona and Parma, but his native country disappointed him as far as its musical life was concerned. One of his secret ambitions was to lead the renascence of Italian culture, but we find him writing : " It would be a giant's work to bring Italy up to the musical level at which Germany stood years ago." The landscape, food and wine were the chief consolations of this tour, which gave him an opportunity to visit his continually-complaining father at Trieste. On the way back he met Bösendorfer at Vienna, and was invited to play at a Philharmonic Concert : a pleasing compliment after his experience in that city ten years previously.

His first visit to London was made in 1897. The metropolis fascinated and impressed him, and although he found difficulty in making a start, his success was sufficient to lead to engagements in Paris and Budapest. He returned again in the following year, visited Nottingham, Manchester and Glasgow and found a large circle of friends, including Delius and Richter.

Compelled to spend most of his time in Germany, Busoni could not help observing the appalling narrow-mindedness of the German people in their appreciation of music : they were content to go on hearing the same old German masters over and over again. At the beginning of the present century he therefore decided to give one or two concerts a year of entirely new orchestral music, conducting them himself. The first took place on November 8th, 1902, and the programme included the Prelude and the "Angel's Farewell" from Elgar's *Dream of Gerontius*, the Saint-Saëns Overture *Les Barbares* and Sinding's *Rondo infinito* Opus 42. The Berlin papers were unanimous in their hostility ; some were even abusive, and one described the Elgar as " the most barren piece of senseless music-fabrication that has been heard for a long time." At the second concert the nocturne *Paris* by Delius was played, and Sibelius conducted his own *En Saga*, yet the *Berliner Neueste Nachrichten* solemnly declared that " after the complete fiasco of the second concert, the announcement that these orchestral concerts would be continued in the autumn of 1903 sounded little short of blasphemy."

Busoni was right in his anticipation that the more enlightened section of the German musical public would support him regardless of the derision of the ignorant critics, and he gave a third concert in the following January. His good work was then continued for several years, and it is noteworthy that all the new composers introduced by Busoni have since become world-famous. The last concert of this series was in January, 1909, and although the programme included César Franck's Symphony in D-minor and the Scherzo from Bartók's Suite for Orchestra (conducted by the composer) the concert was ridiculed and Bartók's Scherzo described as " another of those outrages on good taste."

MASTERS OF THE KEYBOARD

In the summer of 1904 Busoni completed his Concerto for pianoforte and orchestra with a chorus of male voices, a work in five movements with a solo part so difficult that few pianists have been able to master it. He played this himself under the direction of the eminent conductor Dr. Mück at its first performance, and it caused a riot among the audience. The majority disliked the work and showed their feelings in no uncertain manner, while a small minority tried to applaud. The *Tägliche Rundschau* described it thus : " During the five movements we were bathed in a flood of cacophony ; a *pezzo giocoso* depicted the joys of barbarians lusting in war, and a *tarantella* the orgies of absinthe-drinkers and harlots ; finally the *cantico* showed us to our horror that a composer can take seriously the facetious humour of a male-voice choral society. It was frightful."

Although he had decided not to accept further academic appointments, he allowed himself to be persuaded to accept a post at the Vienna Conservatoire in 1907 as conductor of the *Meisterklasse* for pianoforte. He began to regret his decision as soon as he got there : the class consisted almost entirely of uninteresting girl pupils who had to be taught the ordinary routine of piano playing. Even the general musical life of Vienna was not to his taste, for he wrote : " I begin to realize that the ruin of the Viennese, as regards their attitude towards art, comes from newspaper criticism. This systematic daily reading (for half a century) of *causeries* on art, witty and superficial, *short*, and all turning on an obvious catchword, has destroyed for the Viennese their own power of seeing and hearing, comparing and thinking with any seriousness. These little Viennese have something Parisian in their thirst for enjoyment and their ' superiority,' and in their chase after sensations they are often badly taken in, like the Parisians." This criticism is of special interest, I think, in view of Vienna's world-wide reputation as a centre of musical life : even this " wonderland of music " evidently had its faults.

The class had just begun to show signs of taking a really intelligent interest in its work—one or two of the young men were specially promising—when a short illness and several important concert engagements caused a temporary breach in his work at the Conservatoire. To his amazement he received a letter from the Director terminating his engagement owing to non-fulfilment of the contract. Worse still, that official allowed the newspapers to announce that Busoni had been dismissed for neglect of duty ! For the benefit of the pupils, he continued the class independently of the Conservatoire for some months afterwards.

Busoni's activities as a composer undoubtedly exercised a beneficent influence upon his career as a virtuoso : they were largely responsible for his high standard of musicianship and his deep perception into the works of other men, but at the same time, they also filled him with distaste for the inevitable artificialities of the life of a virtuoso. An interesting letter written in August, 1907, runs : " This summer I have noted one of the greatest steps in the progress of my development. With regard to my musical tastes, I began . . . by getting beyond Schumann and Mendelssohn ; I used to misunderstand Liszt, then I worshipped him. Later I was amazed at him, and then, as a Latin, turned away from him. I allowed Berlioz to take me by surprise. One of the most difficult things was learning to distinguish between good Beethoven and bad. Latterly I discovered the most recent French composers by myself, and when they became too quickly popular, dropped them again. Finally, I have come to a closer inward understanding of the old Italian opera-composers. These are metamorphoses which cover twenty years, and all through those twenty years there stood unchanged, like a lighthouse in a stormy sea, the score of *Figaro*. But as I looked at it again a week ago, I found signs of human weakness in it for the first time, and I rejoiced at the discovery that I do not stand so far beneath it as I did —although on the other hand this discovery means not only a positive loss, but it also points to the transitoriness of all human achievement. And how much more transitory must my own be ! "

The streak of cynicism and the predominating petulance in Busoni's personality made him see most of the innumerable towns he visited on his extensive tours with a jaundiced eye. As he grew older he rarely spoke appreciatively about the cities that did him homage—not that he ever had much chance of considering them because his agent or manager planned the tours so that what little leisure he had was spent in travelling. His provincial tours in England, for instance, provoked nothing but complaints of discomfort and dismal observations of the grey, depressing lives of the people in the industrial cities. Manchester he described as " an ingeniously contrived department of Dante's Hell, where travelling virtuosi, who threw away the best part of their lives for the sake of fame and money, gnash their teeth in blindness." Curiously enough, he generally seemed happy in London, but then, he never saw its grimier boroughs and never contemplated, at close quarters, dwellings in certain suburbs that stand as monuments to charlatan builders, who were allowed to rob London's workers of their life's savings. Newcastle he described as " horrible, grey and joyless." His impression of Venice on a wet day was of " an unspeakably depressing town which might have been imagined by Edgar Allan Poe." Tours through western America were generally nothing but long tales of woe. At San Francisco he found himself among a little community of German musicians : " They hold the traditions high on the Pacific Ocean, these conscientious folk ! To think what mischief that rat-hole of a Leipzig can spread ! Oh these Germans ! Oh these Bismarck-columns and fairy woods, with beer and male-voice part songs thrown in ! I think that expresses the whole of it." Even in Paris he once exclaimed, " How old-fashioned and over-ripe this Paris is ! It unites all interests and is openly indifferent to everything. I expect it is really the right place for d'Annunzio, as it was for Oscar Wilde and Meyerbeer."

In October, 1913, Busoni became the Director of the Liceo Rossini at Bologna, one of Italy's provincial schools of music. This move was undoubtedly prompted by a feeling that somebody would have to take Italy's musical culture in hand, for he had written to a friend a year previously : " Has this Italy at last come to its end, or is there to be a new beginning ? The intelligence and culture of the *élite* is very high, but the proportion of *imbecilli*, of indifference and ignorance is terrifying. Then there is the Americanism of the business and sporting world . . . and what has become of painting and sculpture, the most legitimate offspring of the country ? And a new disease has appeared : the regular visits of second-rate German conductors with ' classical' orchestral concerts. The Italians are becoming ' educated ' and consequently boring, like women who attempt intellectual conversation. The great man, Toscanini, spends his winters in the north and his summers in the south—of America. If he did his damned duty and stayed at home, people would put every difficulty in his way ; that is, unfortunately, in the blood of all Italians, owing to their little narrow towns—it is the inheritance of a past that is all too rich in tales of treachery."

Did he like Bologna ? Of course not. Everything at the Liceo was wrong, from its musical standards down to its sanitary arrangements. Within a little while he was applying for a year's leave of absence to tour America. Even the declaration of the Great War in August, 1914, was made just to annoy him. He never returned to the Liceo.

Returning to Italy because he found America *dégoût*, he discovered that it was impossible to live in his native land because that country had entered the war. Describing all Europe and America as a " monster madhouse " he sought refuge in neutral Switzerland, and for a while conducted the Zurich municipal orchestra, but he was not happy there : he found the Swiss people " dull " and he cared nothing for that country's natural beauty.

In London after the armistice he began a series of recitals at the Wigmore Hall and found favour with the musical *élite*. After one of these recitals Pachmann ran up behind him, kissed his coat tails and cried " Busoni grösster Bachspieler—ich grösster Chopinspieler." Busoni actually found something to please him : he liked the aristocratic air that London seemed to have just after the war ; its sense of dignity. He liked the Embankment, Westminster, St. Paul's, the Tower and the façade of Buckingham Palace, *but* " I look at the people less than I used to do ; their expression is very unpleasant to me." He decided that the English can be men of taste, but not artists ! A tour of the provinces filled him with " nothing but disgust," and when a friend asked if he were happy, he replied " I confess I am not." Which, of course, was just too bad.

He then settled in Berlin—in a state of melancholia, of course—and even when the young enthusiastic audiences there gave him the greatest ovations he had ever known, he was sceptical. At Hamburg for a concert, he reported ". . . the orchestra is morally and artistically in a very bad way. . . . Brecher said that Kapellmeister Pollack would ' engage ' me for next year. I said to Brecher it was a question whether I should accept an engagement. . . . Not a soul *loves* and *feels* music. Some take it as a trade, some as time-beaters, some out of vanity. I was very bad-tempered at the rehearsal. Naturally, people thought I was playing the ' star,' although they did not listen. Anyway, the ' time-beaters ' are the ones that deserve most respect, however far away from music they are."

By this time he had developed a hearty dislike of playing the piano for a living, but was obliged to do so for financial reasons. That was undoubtedly the root of his trouble, because concert-giving interfered seriously with his work as a composer, the work on which his heart was set. It continually irritated him to find that people readily acknowledged his fame as a pianist, but were less eager to consider him as a composer.

Certain eccentricities in his interpretation of the works of the old masters were apt to offend, and even horrify, a great number of those who attended his concerts, yet few could fail to be impressed by his truly marvellous technique, amazing agility and infinite variety of tone-colour. As Professor Dent says in his biography of Busoni : " He played the first prelude of the *Forty-eight*, and it became a wash of shifting colours, a rainbow over the fountains of the Villa d'Este ; he played the fugue, and each voice sang out above the rest like the entries of an Italian chorus, until at the last *stretto* the subject entered like the trumpets of the *Dona nobis* in the Mass in B-minor, though in the middle of the keyboard, across a haze of pedal-held sound that was not confusion but blinding clearness."

His Liszt was a great joy to hear, but the majority of Chopin's compositions he murdered—very impressively, I admit—with a blunt instrument. Somebody once said that he played the Trio of the Funeral March like a cornet solo ; a statement to which another horrified listener added " outside a pub." Busoni used to say " If you honestly believe that the melody is beautiful, you must sing it with all the fullness of your voice." Professor Dent calls this " severe logic."

In May, 1922, Busoni sent the Berlin critics into paroxysms of rage by his treatment of the Beethoven Concerto in E-flat. That was too much for him and he accepted no more engagements. Although he planned recitals in London some time afterwards, he never gave them. So his last appearance was at that unfortunate concert in Berlin on May 29th, 1922. " I have devoted myself too much, I think, to Bach, Mozart and Liszt. I wish now that I could emancipate myself from them. Schumann is no use to me any more, Beethoven only with an effort and strict selection. Chopin has attracted and repelled me all my life ; and I have *heard* his music too often —prostituted, profaned, vulgarized. . . ."

After that, Busoni devoted himself to composition and to his pupils. Ill-health cast its shadow upon his last few years, and he died on July 27th, 1924, at his home in Berlin, leaving his opera *Doctor Faust*, in which he had put great hopes, to be completed by Philipp Jarnach.

Paderewski

THE greatest exponent of Chopin's immortal compositions for the piano was also one of the most remarkable characters the world of music has ever known. Pianist, composer and statesman, Paderewski had a romantic personality which together with his aristocratic appearance and dazzling technique at the piano made it possible for him to earn at one time as much as a hundred thousand pounds a year. But money meant little to him : practically the whole of his vast earnings when he was at his zenith he gave away to those in need or spent in his efforts to establish the freedom of his native country.

Ignace Jan Paderewski was born on November 6th, 1860, in an old manor house in the village of Kurylówka, situated in Podolia, a former province of Poland where vast orchards were the outstanding feature of the lovely undulating country. He began to show deep interest in music when he was three : the piano had an irresistible attraction for him, and with one finger he began playing little melodies. Experiments with simple chords soon brought all the rest of his fingers into use, and he was still quite a little boy when his father discovered that he possessed unusual talent for music. His father was the administrator of various large estates in that part of the country ; a man of cultured tastes which included a great love of music. He could play the violin after a fashion, but possessed no skill as an executant. Paderewski's mother died soon after his birth.

The revolution of 1863 brought great trouble to the household. Paderewski's father, being a member of the minor nobility, was sent to prison, and the little boy, together with his sister, was placed in the care of an aunt. When his father was released a year or so later, the estates had been seized, so the family moved to Sudylkow, a wretched little place populated chiefly by unsociable Jews.

Paderewski's first piano lessons were received from one or two down-at-heel musicians of no importance, and he felt little inclination to practice : improvisation was much more exciting ! He also began composing in earnest, but his dominating desire was to write music that looked beautiful on paper —it didn't matter so much what it sounded like !

When he was twelve he performed at a charity concert with his sister, and this was followed by two or three other local events at which he played solos. The great attraction at these was when he played with a towel stretched above his hands so that he could not see the keyboard. The audience thought it was a remarkable feat.

Up to that time he had never heard an orchestra or a professional pianist, and had no idea what an opera was. So Count Chodkiewicz, one of his father's friends, took him to Kiev for a few weeks to hear some music. It was an enthralling adventure : he heard his first symphony concert, his first opera, and also went to a play for the first time in his life. Although this will read very much like a child's story, I must record that on their return journey by sleigh they were attacked by a great pack of wolves, and they saved their lives only by setting fire to the second sleigh, thus frightening the wolves away.

It was not long before a railway was laid to connect their village with Warsaw, and Paderewski travelled in the first train that ran into the city, to become a student at the Warsaw Conservatoire. Kontski, the Director, took to the boy immediately, and received him as a student without the usual examination. Then Paderewski called on Edward Kerntopf, a pianoforte maker, with the intention of buying an instrument, but the genial tradesman offered to lend him one gratuitously and invited him to board with his family while he was at the Conservatoire. The young student was of course overjoyed at the prospect of living with the large Kerntopf family : there were ten children altogether.

Paderewski's first teacher at the Conservatoire told him bluntly that he hadn't the hands to become a pianist, and was so unpleasant generally that the crestfallen lad asked to be relieved of his piano studies forthwith. Studzinski and Roguski, with whom he studied harmony, counterpoint and composition, were both congenial men who insisted that he should strive to become a composer. A second piano teacher was provided for him in due course, and told him that he had a real and natural gift as a pianist !

It was not long before the absence of a regular orchestra in Warsaw (apart from the ensemble connected with the Opera) made the Director decide to form a Polish orchestra composed entirely of the students. Paderewski thereupon started to learn to play the flute as well—but was soon told that his lips were too thick. Then he tried the oboe and clarinet, but was assured that he had no future with either instrument. So next he tried the bassoon—then the horn, and strangely enough he seems to have mastered this very difficult instrument in a matter of months. Then temptation came from the trumpet and trombone, and he was so successful with the latter that his teacher said he would make a better living with that instrument than as a pianist. Paderewski was flattered, and continued to disturb the peace of his neighbours, but he never lost interest in his first-love—the piano.

PADEREWSKI

The Director was so delighted with the orchestra that he expected all its members to neglect their normal studies in order to attend endless rehearsals. Paderewski, as first trombonist, protested that he had come to study music—to pass his examinations—but this extraordinary Director insisted that the orchestra should take priority over everything. The matter came to a head when the young trombonist arrived late at a rehearsal and was told that as a punishment he would be detained afterwards. Paderewski protested that they had no right to do this, and within a few minutes was engaged in a fracas. The result was that in his second year as a student he found himself expelled " for effrontery."

Meanwhile, Edward, the eldest son of the Kerntopf family, had taken great interest in him, and had accompanied him to all the concerts and recitals worth hearing. He was the only member of the family who did not criticize Paderewski when he announced his expulsion. Fortunately, various teachers at the Conservatoire had been in sympathy with the young rebel, and decided to protest to the authorities about the Director's sharp treatment of him. Eventually, Paderewski was recalled. Incidentally, yet another teacher of the piano on the staff told him even during his later years as a student that he should not try to play the piano, for he would *never* make a pianist!

When he was barely sixteen he went with two companions, a violinist and a 'cellist on a tour of the provincial towns. His repertoire then consisted chiefly of pieces by Chopin and Liszt. The students were fairly successful, and made a little money here and there, but experienced endless difficulties in getting a tolerable piano. Most of the small towns could offer nothing but insufferable little square pianos that emitted a truly dreadful sound even under a skilled hand. It generally meant approaching some well-to-do local resident and begging the use of his grand, and as one would imagine, the request more often than not produced only an expression of blank amazement—or worse. Even when the instrument was forthcoming there was the difficulty of getting it to the hall, and the three students were generally obliged to wheel it through the streets themselves—with the help of any kind soul who cared to offer assistance. There was no time for rehearsal : all their spare moments were occupied in the borrowing and transport of the piano ! At one town some thirty or forty soldiers lent a hand : they marched through the town with the piano on their shoulders and kept up a running commentary of ribaldry *en route*.

At one time during this tour their money ran out and they lived for ten days on one enormous loaf of bread. Later, they encountered such appalling weather that they were obliged to stuff newspapers around their vests to keep out the cold. On one road they came upon six soldiers frozen to death in the standing position : an eerie sight that Paderewski remembered for the rest of his life.

MASTERS OF THE KEYBOARD

Back once more in Warsaw, Paderewski put on a tremendous spurt with his studies and covered the last two years' work in six months. When he received his diploma in the Municipal Hall in 1878 he played the Grieg Concerto with full orchestra for the first time.

The authorities of the Warsaw Conservatoire evidently bore no malice against this rather turbulent student, for he was invited to accept an appointment on the staff as a teacher of the piano. In the following year his first composition was published : the Impromptu in F, and in 1880, despite the uncertainty of his future, he married Antonina Korsak, a young student at the Conservatoire. They found a little house, and were blissfully happy ; but a year later Antonina died in childbirth, leaving her husband with a tiny son and a small sum of money. The latter he deposited with some trustees for the child's future, but within a few years it had mysteriously disappeared—like its trustees.

Leaving the child with his mother-in-law, he went to Berlin to study composition with Friedrich Kiel, for people still told him that he would never make much progress as a pianist. Kiel insisted that he should at the same time become better acquainted with the stringed instruments, and suggested that he should take violin lessons with another teacher. This gentleman positively assured him that he had neither talent nor aptitude for music at all ! This was too much for Paderewski. He led the teacher to the piano and played him a Chopin Mazurka. An embarrassed apology followed.

Paderewski worked so hard with Kiel that his health broke down. Incidentally, Kiel told him that he should concentrate on the piano because he had remarkable talent as a pianist and would do well in that capacity !

In Berlin he met Richard Strauss and became great friends with him : he found a strange fascination in watching the incredible grimaces that the eminent German composer made while playing the piano. Berlin was over-run with music students in those days, but they were not particularly friendly because even then the Germans indulged in persecution of the Poles. Militarism was rife : civilians had to step off the pavement when German officers passed. Wagner was already a passion with thousands of music-lovers.

At the house of Hugo Bock, his German publisher, Paderewski met Anton Rubinstein, who told him that he had a brilliant future as a pianist. He also became acquainted with Joseph Joachim, the great violinist. One evening at the same house a famous Italian contralto asked him to play an extremely difficult accompaniment for her at sight, adding that she wanted it transposed a major third higher. Paderewski accomplished this almost impossible task with no more than one or two wrong notes. The thanks he received was a loud comment " What an inferior pianist you are ! "

PADEREWSKI

In 1883 Paderewski gave up his post at the Conservatoire and went again to Berlin to study orchestration with Urban. In the following year, after a short vacation in Poland when he gave a concert in the famous old university town of Cracow, he went to Vienna to study the piano with Leschetizky, the greatest teacher of the age, who told him that he *could* have become a great pianist if only he had started his studies earlier ! It should be added, however, that as the course proceeded, the eminent teacher was amazed at Paderewski's progress.

The first part of this course was a great trial to his patience : he had to start almost at the beginning again with the Czerny studies he had been *teaching* at Warsaw. Leschetizky would keep on saying " It's too late ! It's too late ! Your fingers lack discipline : you do not know how to work." Those were hard gruelling days : intensive study the whole time, day after day. What little leisure he had was spent in reading politics, a subject that had always been of the utmost interest to him.

He found Vienna a paradise for all who loved music and drama. The Philharmonic Orchestra was probably the finest in the world at that time, and the Opera scarcely less famous. He often met Brahms, who, though reticent, impressed him with his fine head, great beard, tiny feet and " a tremendous belly."

Paderewski accepted the offer of a teaching appointment at the Strasbourg Conservatoire in July, 1885, and by doing a great deal of recital work in the city had the satisfaction of finding his fame spreading rapidly to the various towns in the neighbourhood. He was very poor in those days, and had to save for weeks to visit Paris at Rubinstein's invitation to hear the latter's recital there. To his profound disappointment and great annoyance he was unable to obtain a seat and neither Rubinstein nor his agent would trouble to help him gain admittance to the hall.

When the vacation came round, the directors of the Conservatoire calmly told him that they would not pay him for the two months' holiday. He protested that a year's contract always included payment for the usual vacation, but they were adamant, and he left in disgust.

His old friend Edward Kerntopf then lent him the money to return to Leschetizky for further lessons, and soon after his return to Vienna the great teacher arranged for him to appear at an important public concert with Pauline Lucca, the famous soprano. This was Paderewski's first great opportunity, and he was a tremendous success although he had a horrible attack of stage-fright. He admitted afterwards that his whole inside seemed to be quivering with nerves ; he suddenly felt scared of everything, the public, the piano and the music ; an agonizing frame of mind that he attributed to lack of self-confidence. For subsequent concerts he worked like a slave to make doubly certain of every single phrase in the pieces he had to play, for he found it was the only way to allay nervousness. If even the briefest passage remained uncertain it would cause him such mental distress that he would spend hours in mastering it so that it could be played almost subconsciously.

The success of this concert with Madame Lucca encouraged him to go once again to Paris, and he made his début there in the Salle Erard in March 1888 before a distinguished audience that included Tschaikovsky, Colonne and Lamoureux (both famous conductors), Madame Essipoff, Princess Brancovan, Madame Trélat, Madame Dubois (Chopin's last pupil) and suchlike. Enthusiasm ran so high that the audience made him play for a whole hour after the end of the announced programme. Lamoureux went round to his dressing room immediately afterwards and engaged him on the spot for a concert. He had not entirely mastered his nerves at that concert, and the knowledge that so much would depend upon the impression he made upon the more influential members of the audience did nothing to calm him.

A second recital was demanded, but he had nothing prepared! Even so, within a fortnight he was playing the Saint-Saëns Concerto in C minor. Then he prepared Liszt's Hungarian Fantasia, which brought him an invitation to play in Brussels.

Returning to Vienna, he enjoyed another tremendous success there in 1889 : his first solo recital in that city. It was given in the Bösendorfer Hall, part of that eminent piano maker's premises. In the same year he completed the scoring of his Pianoforte Concerto, which was introduced to the Viennese by Madame Essipoff.

Engagements in Paris were now becoming so frequent that he was able to take a small apartment there in the Avenue Victor Hugo. As he became drawn further into the musical life of the capital he met such people as Charles Gounod—a wonderfully impressive personality whose white beard made him look like a high priest, and Camille Saint-Saëns, who astonished Paderewski with his profound knowledge of astronomy, philosophy and at least a dozen other subjects not usually associated with musicians. There was also the talented and wealthy Massenet, composer of such operas as *Manon* and *Thaïs*, Vincent d'Indy and the brilliant organist Widor. Paderewski frequently met Edouard Lalo in the house of Sarasate, the famous violinist, and had happy memories of evenings spent with Gabriel Fauré.

Paderewski's first tour of Holland left bitter memories. The impresario absconded without paying him his fee, and the only bright spot seemed, at the time, to be the generosity of a certain hotel proprietor who invited him and a host of other artists to a banquet. When he left the hotel on the following morning he found that the entire cost of the manager's lavish hospitality had been charged on his bill !

His next tour brought him to England. He had enjoyed three successful seasons in Paris and had arranged to come to London to give a series of recitals at the old St. James's Hall in May, 1890. When he arrived he discovered to his horror that his manager, in an attempt to force a big attendance, had been advertising him in the most extravagant terms— " Paderewski : the Lion of Paris " and so forth.

This put the music critics in a bad mood, and after his first concert, which was sparsely attended, they opened their attack with heavy sarcasm. Paderewski was very hurt ; but persevered, and his second concert was rewarded with a much better attendance, and notices less spiteful.

After a Philharmonic Concert he started on a tour of the provinces, and to the astonishment of his manager, insisted that all the handbills should bear not only the good reports, but the more acrimonious criticisms as well ! He played in all the principal towns, generally to packed houses, and then returned to a London season of no less than forty concerts.

One of his sharpest critics was Bernard Shaw, who was then writing his famous music articles in *The World*. His criticisms were as violent as he declared Paderewski's attacks to be upon the piano. He called him a harmonious blacksmith who laid a concerto upon the piano as upon an anvil, and then hammered it out with exuberant enjoyment. It should be noted, however, that Shaw was one of the very few critics who rightly praised Paderewski's vigorous playing of Schumann. The others had all become so accustomed to the aged Clara Schumann's délicate and genteel interpretation of her husband's works that they failed to realize that when Schumann indicated ff he wanted a real fortissimo. In later years, Shaw became one of Paderewski's most ardent admirers, though they never met.

While he was in London, the famous pianist met Burne-Jones. This great portrait painter was out one morning when he happened to pass Paderewski and was so impressed by his wonderful head of golden hair that he returned to his studio saying that he had seen an archangel in the streets of London. To his amazement a friend happened to bring Paderewski to his studio a few days later. He greeted him with a shout of " My Archangel," and set to work forthwith on the portrait that has now become renowned.

In the same year—1890—Paderewski made a tour through Germany into Roumania, and had the honour of playing before the Queen in her castle at Budapest. Then came a less pleasant experience that again shook his faith in concert agents. Returning to Berlin, he scored a tremendous success at a " public rehearsal " of a Philharmonic Concert under the baton of Hans von Bülow. Immediately afterwards, Wolff, the eminent concert agent who a year or two before had disdainfully refused to act as Paderewski's manager, approached him and suggested that he should manage his affairs in the future. Paderewski did not remind the agent of his previous attitude, but said that as his present manager had worked very hard for him, he felt he couldn't desert him. Wolff was dumbfounded, for he enjoyed such a high reputation that he had never been refused before in his life. At the concert, a day or two later, Paderewski was horrified to discover that the concerto which had been such a triumph at the " public rehearsal " seemed to go wrong almost at every other bar : the orchestra seemed out of time with him, and some players were actually producing wrong notes ! Then, as a last straw, while he was playing a solo in the latter part of the programme, von Bülow, who had been sitting in a conspicuous place on the platform, got up and walked out in the middle of it ! For months afterwards Paderewski pondered upon von Bülow's relations with Wolff.

Just after this incident the newspapers all began to ask indignantly what right he—a Pole—had to be playing in Berlin at all ! Paderewski told his publisher that he would never play in Berlin again, and he never did. In later years when he received enormous offers to play in the German capital, and even pressing invitations from the Emperor, he politely refused.

During his second visit to London in 1891 he received a request, signed by Sir Walter Parratt, Master of the Queen's Music, to play before Victoria at Windsor Castle. The Queen was in ill-health at the time and had to be wheeled into the hall in an invalid chair. Paderewski was amazed at her knowledge of music, and remembering that she was supposed to have taken lessons from Mendelssohn, he revised his programme at the last moment to please her classical taste. The Queen addressed him in perfect French and displayed great interest in his work. Later when she withdrew he played to the Princesses Christian, Beatrice and Louise.

Rather less pleasant was his memory of the various " at homes " he attended in England at that time. On many occasions when he obliged his hostess by playing to the other guests he was horrified to discover that people were talking while he was playing. This hurt him grievously, and he would generally stop playing, turn to the offending guests and apologize for interrupting their conversation. In many cases his sarcasm was too subtle, and after a while he refused to play at such functions : he generally demanded a fee of five hundred guineas, to discourage people from making requests.

Towards the end of 1891 he made his first tour of America under the auspices of the famous pianoforte firm of Steinway, who regarded the tour as a means of publicity for their instruments and made a generous contract which guaranteed him thirty thousand dollars and allowed him to keep everything he made above that figure.

For this tour a very large repertoire had to be prepared. He made the crossing on a dreadful little boat called *The Spray*, and felt ill most of the time. When he arrived, Steinway's representative greeted him with the tactless remark that the American audiences, having heard so many virtuosi, had become extremely exacting. He felt so discouraged that he made immediate enquiries about boats returning to England, but on second thoughts decided to stay and face these hypercritical beings.

The next shock was the discovery that he was expected to play six different concertos in one week besides a group of solos. In those early days of his career it seemed an impossibility, but suppressing his diffidence, he started practising forthwith. After his début at the Carnegie Hall, New York, on November 17th, 1891, a moderate success, he was obliged to stay up all night practising for the rehearsal of the second concert on the following morning. At the concert he had to fight back an overwhelming sense of fatigue the whole time, but he struggled through the second and third concertos and received a tremendous burst of applause. This was his first great American triumph, yet he had felt half dead all the time he was playing ! By the end of the week New York had no hall large enough to hold all the people who were clamouring to hear him.

This outstanding success was then repeated at Boston, where he was amazed at the perfection of that city's famous Symphony Orchestra. Then he proceeded by way of Philadelphia to Chicago, and was greeted by the largest audience he had ever seen in his life : well over four thousand. Little did he think that in later life he would play to colossal American audiences of as many as sixteen thousand at one time. At Portland, Maine, as soon as he entered the hall about a thousand people left their seats, stormed the platform and insisted on shaking hands with him. When he had finished this little ceremony his hands were almost numb, and he found the greatest difficulty in playing his first item.

A disaster occurred at Rochester (New York). He struck the opening chords of his first piece and almost fainted as an agonizing pain shot up his right arm. " My arm suddenly became very stiff, and the pain grew worse and worse, but somehow I got through Beethoven's *Appassionata*. I thought it was the end of everything, that my career was over, because I knew that something very serious had happened to my arm."

A surgeon was waiting for him as soon as he came off the platform, and within a few moments explained the cause of the pain : he had torn some of the tendons in his arm and injured one of his fingers. He would have to stop playing for some months at least. Paderewski protested that he had to fulfil his contract, for his career depended upon the success of this great American tour. After an argument that lasted the best part of an hour the surgeon applied dressings and a device that would enable the pianist to go on playing, but refused to accept any responsibility for the consequences. Paderewski completed his tour receiving medical attention before each concert and playing with only three fingers of his right hand.

On his return to England he still had to play at two concerts before he could receive the medical attention he needed. The specialists he consulted here told him that there was no hope of a complete recovery : his injured finger had become quite useless, and with another American tour planned, the poor pianist was desperate. He postponed the tour and decided to try an eminent masseur in Paris. In time, the strength of the right arm was restored, but the finger remained useless until Paderewski himself devised a method of exercising it. After many weeks he found he could move it, and then there was steady improvement, though for the rest of his life the finger remained much weaker than the others. This serious setback so early in his career might have made any other artist give up in despair, but Paderewski had very little money and was determined to overcome the infirmity somehow. After endless practice he was able to set out on his second American tour.

During this, another disaster occurred. He had scratched one of his fingers but thought little of it ; then he was dining out one evening when his hostess asked him to play a few pieces. After dinner he went to the piano, but as soon as he touched the keyboard he discovered that the finger had turned septic. Within a few hours it had swollen to the most alarming dimensions, and he was unable to get in touch with his doctor until the following morning. As the specialist examined the finger Paderewski informed him that he had to give a recital that afternoon.

" You're crazy ! " the doctor gasped.

" I'm sorry, but I must play this afternoon."

" Quite impossible ! " the doctor retorted.

Paderewski then explained that he had to play with a chamber music ensemble who could not possibly find another pianist and rehearse everything with him in time for the concert. The other players were young artists whose whole careers might be affected by the success or failure of this particular concert, and he was determined not to let them down. Eventually, the specialist gave in, performed a slight operation on the finger, using an anæsthetic that would minimize the discomfort during the afternoon. Before the concert took place Paderewski had printed slips placed in the seats informing the audience that the pianist had undergone a slight operation that morning. The afternoon went better than he had expected, but on the following morning several newspapers severely criticized his playing without mentioning a word about his disability.

Against his doctor's orders, he resumed his concerts about three weeks later, but on several occasions the incision opened while he was playing, and by the end of the concert the keyboard was almost covered with blood.

Returning to Europe in 1893 he decided to spend some time in composing. His *Polish Fantasia* was the result of this diversion from concert-giving, and it was first performed at the Norwich Festival before it was heard in London under Georg Henschel.

PADEREWSKI

Paderewski then made the longest tour he had ever attempted in the British Isles, visiting, among other places, Dublin, Belfast and Cork. At the end of this season he again stopped playing for a while so that he could compose the opera *Manru*.

After various European engagements, the third American tour started in 1895 : the greatest artistic and financial success of them all ; a tour that embraced California, which made a very favourable impression upon him. Los Angeles was also visited, a very small town in those days : now it is half the size of Birmingham. Incidentally, it was during this tour that he noticed many people in the audience were applauding in a novel but exceedingly disconcerting manner : by producing an unpleasant whistling noise. If Paderewski were alive to-day and could hear how this ear-splitting form of vulgarity had infected the greater part of the audiences that so often seem to be present when the BBC broadcast the more " popular " programmes . . . !

In 1897 he made his début in Rome at a concert patronized by the Queen of Italy. The first Russian tour took place nearly two years later, after a short series of concerts in Warsaw, where his return was enthusiastically fêted. His first concerts in St. Petersburg were so successful that all the newspapers acclaimed him as the successor of Rubinstein, who had died a few years previously. This had the unfortunate effect of hurting the feelings of all the great Russian pianist's former devotees, and all the members of the Conservatoire were openly hostile towards him, despite the fact that his first concert had been given in aid of the poorer students of that institution.

In Moscow he played his *Polish Fantasia*, but the performance was entirely spoilt by a drunken horn-player in the orchestra, whose antics were not unlike the extraordinary behaviour of the brass-players in some of the modern dance bands. At the Moscow Conservatoire he had arranged to play in aid of the widows and orphans of professors of that academy, but he was very annoyed to find that as soon as he walked on the platform, anti-Polish demonstrators in the audience began hissing. When Safonoff, the conductor, came in, Paderewski told him that he could not play while such a disturbance was going on. The conductor asked in mild surprise " What disturbance ? " and when the outraged pianist drew his attention to the hissing, Safonoff replied " Oh, that's nothing. Let's start ! " Paderewski, however, refused, and the police had to be called, whereupon the demonstrators mysteriously disappeared.

The concert was an outstanding success, and Safonoff invited him out to supper afterwards. After the meal they went to Safonoff's house where to Paderewski's disgust the conductor drank steadily until six o'clock the next morning.

MASTERS OF THE KEYBOARD

At one of the Moscow hotels, the great pianist was very puzzled when he found a room containing a piano with no " action " inside. The proprietor proudly explained that it was his " gold mine," because the room was used regularly by some of his wealthiest patrons who always got helplessly drunk, and then proceeded to display their high spirits by pouring champagne into the piano. The joke had become a solemn ritual. This particular instrument made it possible to retrieve the champagne and to charge heavily for damage to the piano without having to pay anybody to repair it.

After this tour, he rested for a while at the beautiful Chalet Riond-Bosson near Morges, a property he had recently acquired giving a superb view of Mont Blanc across Lake Geneva. He then married for the second time, the lady being Helena Górska, Baroness de Rosen. Another American tour followed almost immediately, and this time the hundred or so concerts took him as far as Mexico.

Paderewski's engagements and tours during the twentieth century have been too numerous to mention in detail, and we must therefore be content with a note about one or two of those of special interest, as for instance, his visits to the Spanish Court, where he was always made welcome by King Alfonso, one of his greatest admirers.

Neither Paderewski nor his wife was in good health when they visited Australia and New Zealand, so they took their family doctor with them. The physician was ill practically the whole time, and they had to nurse him ! At Melbourne the meals served in their hotel were so unpalatable that they had to go to the market every day to buy food which they cooked themselves in their rooms. One day, Paderewski, in a fit of annoyance, asked the waiter what the chef was by trade : was he a tailor or a carpenter ? The man replied solemnly " No sir, an engineer."

The trades-union mentality was so strong at Sydney that immediately they came to the end of the time allotted for rehearsal, the triangle-player, who hadn't done a thing all the morning, got up (watch in hand) and insisted that they should stop. Less than thirty more bars had to be played, but with one accord they disregarded Paderewski's polite request that they should finish the concerto.

During a tour in South Africa a lady called at his hotel just as he was dressing for a concert and pleading extreme urgency begged to see him. At last he consented, and when she was shown in she asked for his autograph ! He obliged her, but enquired why she could not have approached him at the hall after the concert in the customary manner. " Oh, I can't be bothered to come to the concert " she replied, " Besides, I'm going to a party ! "

Shortly before the Great War, Paderewski bought extensive property in California—the Rancho San Ignacio at Paso Robles—chiefly to be able to live near the Paso Robles Hot Springs. Remembering the vast orchards he loved as a child in Podolia, he began planting out innumerable fruit trees. His greatest joy was the multitude of almond trees—twelve thousand of them—that in blossom-time were an almost unbelievable sight.

But the declaration of war gave him something far more serious to think about : he started his gigantic task of raising money for relief work in Poland. Over fifty thousand pounds was raised in four months. Then his determination to deliver Poland from its miseries made him prepare himself for a career as a statesman. Some idea of the reputation he had already acquired in diplomatic circles may be gained from the statement made by Franklin K. Lane, Secretary of the Interior in President Wilson's cabinet : " I don't know Paderewski well, but I believe he is capable of rebuilding Poland. . . . He is the outstanding phenomenon of the war . . . an artist always thinks in big terms. But there is a great practical side to the job of nation-building. Paderewski has that also. That's why he is succeeding. He will become the liberator of modern Poland. . . ."

Paderewski eventually became Prime Minister of Poland in 1919, and Clemenceau, when someone commented on his change from being a world-famous pianist to the first leader of the Polish Republic, exclaimed " My God ! What a come-down ! " Although Paderewski did much to restore order in Poland, he experienced great difficulty in working with the politicians, and a year later resigned his offices. He then returned to California, after a short spell in Switzerland, to devote himself once again to music.

His first concert on the resumption of his musical career was given in the Carnegie Hall on November 22nd, 1922, and as Gutzon Borglum said : "A cry of joy arose throughout the country." Alexander Fried wrote : " Five years in the purgatory of earthly experience have given Paderewski's art fresh power, new significance. His art is purer than when he left it ; his understanding seems broader and more mellow. He resumes his music refreshed and inspirited." The vast crowd that was packed into the hall demanded encore after encore, and refused to leave at the end of the concert even after the management, in despair, had extinguished all the lights for about five minutes to show that they meant to close the building. It was hours afterwards when the last few people left the hall.

Paderewski came to England on a concert tour in 1923 and then made a tour of France, Belgium and Italy, playing in aid of war charities. A total of over a million francs was raised in this manner. Two years later he gave a series of concerts in England to swell the funds of the British Legion, and was afterwards created a Knight Commander of the Order of the British Empire. His other philanthropical gestures are far too numerous to mention in detail : he founded innumerable scholarships ; in fact he gave away practically the whole of the vast fortune that before the Great War had earned him the reputation of being the richest musician in the world. Of his untiring efforts to assist distressed musicians during the years of the great economic depression in the early nineteen-thirties I can mention only the magnificent recital he gave in the Albert Hall in January, 1933.

In 1936 he appeared in the English film *The Moonlight Sonata*. Although his wonderful personality dominated the film throughout and made it one of great interest to all music-lovers, the general effect was rather spoilt by the sentimental and " popular-press " attitude of the producers. Unfortunate in a different way are some of the gramophone records he made in his closing years, for they do not give a true indication of this great man's genius : his fingers became weak after he had passed his seventieth birthday.

What this splendid, amiable character thought when his beloved Poland was again ravaged by war in 1939 we must leave to our imaginations. It probably hastened his death, which occurred in New York on June 29th, 1941.

Ernest Newman once wrote that no other pianist could reveal so acute a sensibility to the poetic content of music as this incomparable virtuoso. During his later years, Paderewski was often criticised for the tone he drew from his instrument, but even if these criticisms were justified, they did nothing to affect his great reputation. As an exponent of Chopin, he was supreme, for in that composer's works he could see the Poland he loved with a passionate sincerity. When he opened the Chopin Centenary Festival in Lemberg on October 23rd, 1910, he said : " No man, however great, can be above his nation or beyond his nation. He is seed of her seed, a portion of her, blossom of her bearing, fruit of her ripening. . . ."

He once told an interviewer that his success was due " one per cent to talent, nine per cent to luck, and ninety per cent to hard work. Work is the main secret of success." He always subjected himself to rigid discipline.

Paderewski believed that to produce the finest effects, a pianist must identify himself absolutely with his work, yet at the same time must put his own personality resolutely into his interpretation of the composer's idea. His *tempo rubato* was sharply criticized by Bernard Shaw, but he insisted that it would be absurd to play Chopin, Schubert, Schumann, Brahms, Liszt and Grieg without *tempo rubato*. With Bach and Handel, of course, the case was entirely different. Incidentally, he always maintained that it was impossible to become a good pianist without studying Bach : " the universal genius."

His work as a composer brought him more joy that any amount of praise for his talent as a pianist. He believed that creative work—in any sphere— could alone bring supreme satisfaction. It could defeat death. The ideas of the creative man, he would say, are eternal, and in presenting them to others, man could reach the apex of his purpose.

PADEREWSKI

Another little sidelight on his character is provided by an event which took place during one of his American tours. He had just completed a recital when he learnt that a small party of nuns who had been longing to hear him had arrived too late owing to some duties they had been obliged to perform. He promptly invited them to accompany him to the private railroad car that he always used when travelling in America, and there he played the whole programme through again for them, although he was feeling quite exhausted.

He was always very tolerant with the many American business men who tried to " cash-in " on his name. Some of his friends were most annoyed when a large confectionery firm began selling " Paderewski Candy " in all the towns he visited, but when he was told that all the street urchins were walking about eating it he merely remarked that he hoped they wouldn't make themselves ill.

Journalists have already said enough about his exquisite silk shirts, and so forth, but it would perhaps be worth adding that he was very fond of visiting the cinema and could play a good game of billiards and bridge. Finally, he was always ready to tell jokes against himself. One of his favourites was about the two policemen who were on duty at the doors of one of the New York concert halls when he was giving a recital. One pushed his head through the door of the foyer and addressed his colleague standing just inside the hall. Here is their conversation :

" What's that guy Paderooski doin' now ? "

" Nothin'."

" Nothin ? "

" No, 'ee ain't doin' nothin', 'ee's just playin' the pianner."

Rachmaninoff

NOBODY who heard Rachmaninoff's bold, masterly playing of such favourites as the *Waldstein* and *Appassionata* Sonatas of Beethoven, the Chopin B-flat minor Sonata, or of the Liszt transcriptions of Bach, will easily forget this brilliant twentieth-century pianist. Opinions may differ on the value of his contribution to the pianistic art, by which I mean, of course, the influence that as an artist he exerted upon those who have followed after him ; but who will deny that on the concert platform he was one of the finest executants one could wish to hear ?

Sergei Vassilyevitch Rachmaninoff was his full name, and, like so many Russian names, you can spell it in half-a-dozen different ways without being incorrect. He was born on April 2nd, 1873, son of an aristocratic landowner who had resigned his commission in the Cavalry Guards of the old Imperial Russian Army to retire to his estate in the Novgorod district, and to indulge, as an amateur, in the various musical activities that appealed to him. Rachmaninoff's mother, Lyoubov Boutakova, came of a wealthy family, and was also very interested in music, in fact she gave him his first lessons when, at the age of four, he expressed a desire to learn to play the piano. What the average child takes two years to accomplish at the piano, Rachmaninoff did in a couple of months, and he was soon playing quite difficult works to visitors. Anna Ornazkaya, an ex-student of the St. Petersburg Conservatoire was then engaged as his teacher.

His father wanted him to enter the exclusive military academy at St. Petersburg : he loathed the idea of his son's adopting the " proletarian " profession of music, but his mother was equally insistent that he should go to the Conservatoire that had been founded by Anton Rubinstein in the same city. While they were debating the matter, Rachmaninoff succeeded in getting a scholarship to the latter institution, and as his father had by that time squandered most of the family fortune, the question was decided by the boy himself.

When the official abolition of the serfdom deprived his father of the unpaid labour he had been using on the estate, the family moved to a modest flat in St. Petersburg. It was at about this time that his parents separated.

Rachmaninoff was not the ideal student. He frequently permitted himself to enjoy prolonged periods of idleness, and due partly to his grandmother, who always spoilt him, became thoroughly lazy. He often cut his lectures to visit the ice-rink. Nevertheless, he was invariably chosen to play at the students' concerts, and his general interest in music never became dull. It must be remembered, too, that the teachers at the Conservatoire at that time were not a very encouraging or inspiring group. Rachmaninoff was so bored by the interminable, monotonous exercises he had to play that he began improvising extensively. One of his favourite recreations in music was to spend an hour or two at the Cathedral of St. Isaac listening to the fine liturgical music. He would then go home and turn it into cash by playing it from memory, with suitable improvisations, to his grandmother, who had a pleasant habit of tipping him liberally whenever he played to her.

His mother was sufficiently shrewd to see that he was wasting much of his time, so she took him to see his cousin Siloti, who had already distinguished himself in the world of music. He advised her to send Rachmaninoff to study with Sverev at Moscow.

This recommendation was carried out forthwith, and at the age of twelve Rachmaninoff found himself in that city, with a very heavy heart. Sverev was an extremely severe teacher, and when he lost his temper with a pupil he would not hesitate to attack him with his fists or fling at his head anything within reach. Moreover, he worked twelve hours a day and expected his pupils to do likewise. He also disliked sentimentality in his pupils' parents, and for that reason insisted that their visits should be only very occasional, while the boys themselves were rarely allowed to go home, even during the holidays. On the other hand, his enthusiasm for music and drama and his boundless generosity richly rewarded the keen students who resided at his house : they were taken to every first-class symphony concert, the opera, and to the first nights of all plays of any cultural value.

Rachmaninoff was only thirteen when Anton Rubinstein visited Moscow to conduct his opera *Demon*. During his stay he visited the Conservatoire, and Sverev arranged for Rachmaninoff to play Bach's English Suite in A-minor to him. For years afterwards, Rachmaninoff had vivid memories of this great ordeal, and never forgot Rubinstein's playing of the Beethoven Sonata in F-sharp (Opus 78) afterwards. This, and the series of great recitals given by the famous pianist in Moscow in the following year, enabled Rachmaninoff to become acquainted with Rubinstein's wonderful use of the pedal ; a use which, it will be recalled, he always justified with the maxim, " The pedal is the soul of the piano."

The tendency to idle away his time disappeared when Rachmaninoff began studying harmony with Arensky, an accomplished teacher who took great interest in him because he could see that he possessed outstanding ability. With Arensky's encouragement he began composing, and it was not long before his Study in F-sharp, though somewhat mediocre, impressed

Sverev enough to make him mention Rachmaninoff to Tschaikovsky, who being a fairly frequent guest at Sverev's house already knew the boy by sight. This was the start of a most valuable friendship and induced the great composer to give Rachmaninoff permission to arrange his *Manfred* Symphony for two pianos.

At the last examination in the harmony course Rachmaninoff won the highest marks ever obtained in the history of the Conservatoire. Consequently, it was presumed that he would devote himself to composition in the future, and arrangements were made for him to enter Taneiev's counterpoint class.

Troubles came in his sixteenth year. He was still residing with Sverev and sharing a room with another pupil ; an arrangement which he disliked more and more as he grew older, so he asked his teacher if he might be given a room of his own. He evidently caught Sverev in an ill-tempered mood, for the request led to a quarrel which resulted in Rachmaninoff's departure to live with an aunt who also happened to live in Moscow. Then he was foolish enough to bathe in the river on a chilly September morning, and for months afterwards was troubled with malaria. His condition grew worse and worse during the ensuing term, and eventually his aunt was obliged to call in one of the most famous doctors in Moscow, Professor Mitropolsky, whose diagnosis revealed brain fever. He was compelled to stay in bed until well after Christmas, and when ultimately he was allowed to get up, he discovered to his dismay that he had lost his facility for composing. Fortunately, his skill was not long in returning, for in his final examination at the Conservatoire his setting of the one-act opera *Aleko* made such a favourable impression upon Sverev that although he had not spoken to his pupil since their quarrel, he went up to him, kissed him and gave him his gold watch and chain. Rachmaninoff was very touched by this gesture, and wore the gift until the end of his days.

He was then awarded the " Great Gold Medal," the highest honour the Conservatoire could offer, and his name was inscribed upon its Roll of Honour. Only two other pupils had been distinguished in this manner since the foundation of the college.

Gutheil, an enterprising publisher, then offered to print several of his works, and acting upon the advice of Tschaikovsky, Rachmaninoff opened negotiations with him for the outright purchase of the compositions concerned. When Gutheil offered five hundred roubles, Rachmaninoff nearly had a fit : his income had been fifteen roubles a month, and Gutheil's offer seemed a colossal sum to receive all at once.

Aleko was produced in the spring of 1893 at the Grand Theatre, Moscow. Tschaikovsky was present and led the applause from his box. At about the same time Rachmaninoff gave his first public recital as a pianist : he played

Rubinstein's Concerto in D-minor for a fee of fifty roubles at a concert given at the Electric Exhibition. The most important event of that year, however, was the publication by Gutheil of the pianoforte pieces Opus 3, which included the famous Prelude in C-sharp minor. Little did Rachmaninoff realize that this would in time conquer the whole world ; that millions of amateur pianists would make it their *pièce de résistance* !

In those days he had no definite plans for the future : he certainly did not anticipate a career as a virtuoso, although one of his earliest tours was as accompanist to the violinist, Mlle. Teresina Tua. It was a profitable engagement, but he cut it short because he could not endure the monotony of playing her trivial repertoire over and over again.

He was then occupying himself chiefly with composition, but his First Symphony was a catastrophe : as soon as he heard it being rehearsed he knew it would be a failure. Cesar Cui, writing in one of the St. Petersburg newspapers said, " If there were a Conservatoire in hell, Rachmaninoff would gain the first prize for his symphony, so devilish are the discords he has dished up before us." Many years later—in May, 1909—Nikisch conducted it in London at one of the Royal Philharmonic Society's concerts.

The Prelude in C-sharp minor became a great favourite in England, and chiefly on account of this the Royal Philharmonic Society sent him an invitation in the autumn of 1898 to perform at one of their concerts. He was given a great welcome in London : he conducted his Fantasy for orchestra, *The Rock*, and played various piano pieces, including, of course, the Prelude that had won him favour. He had been so depressed by the critics' attitude towards his works in Russia that his triumphant success in London astonished him, and he was more than gratified when Francesco Berger, the Society's secretary, invited him to return the following year to play his Concerto No. 1. Rachmaninoff said he would rather write a Second Concerto expressly for the occasion and settled the engagement forthwith.

Although this encouragement exhilarated him at the time, his old apathy set in again when he got back to Moscow, and the engagement was never fulfilled. His despair became so serious that eventually a psychologist had to be called in to restore him to a normal frame of mind.

On April 29th, 1902, he married Natalie Satin, his cousin, in Moscow, and together they visited Bayreuth, Vienna and Italy ; a honeymoon paid for by the sale of a dozen songs. Then they settled in a flat in Moscow close to the Strastnov Convent.

In the autumn of 1905 he became a conductor of opera on the staff of the Imperial Theatres in the same city, and caused a sensation by demanding that the conductor's rostrum be moved from its old place behind the prompter's box to the centre of the orchestra. He also stopped members of the orchestra sneaking out of the orchestra pit during the performance merely to smoke. A year later he moved to Dresden to live for a while in a different environment.

His Second Concerto was at length completed, but it was 1908 before it was heard outside Russia. In that year he received an invitation to play it at a concert given by the Vienna Philharmonic Society. For the next few years his career was threefold : composer, pianist and conductor, and in that capacity he visited Paris and Berlin.

His first journey to America was made late in 1909, and his Third Concerto was written specially for this tour in which he had to appear as pianist or conductor at twenty concerts given by the Boston Symphony Orchestra. The Concerto was first performed in New York with himself as soloist under the conductorship of Damrosch, and a little while afterwards he repeated it under Gustav Mahler's baton. Rachmaninoff never forgot the amazing care and devotion with which Mahler rehearsed this Concerto: every detail received his expert attention, and he detained the players for far longer than the allotted time for rehearsal. Other cities visited during this tour included Baltimore, Philadelphia and Cambridge (Massachusetts).

He was in England again in 1910 to conduct his Second Symphony at the Leeds Festival, and four years later made a third visit here to give a series of recitals. When the Great War broke out he was back in Russia, and during its early years intensified his activities as a pianist in order to raise money for war charities.

Realising the great blow that Russian music sustained by the premature death of Scriabin in April 1915, Rachmaninoff made a concert tour of all the principal Russian towns playing the works of this great composer.

Shortly afterwards he was asked to organize a concert in aid of the wounded soldiers. He took the Grand Theatre, Moscow, for this purpose and played three concertos in one evening : Liszt's E-flat major, Tschaikovsky's B-flat minor, and his own Second Concerto.

We now come to the Revolution of March 17th. In his *Recollections*[1] he said : "Almost from the very beginning of the Revolution I realized that it was mishandled. Already by March of 1917 I had decided to leave Russia, but was unable to carry out my plan, for Europe was still fighting and no one could cross the frontier. . . . This was to be my last summer in Russia. The impressions I received from my contact with the peasants, who felt themselves masters of the situation, were unpleasant. I should have preferred to leave Russia with friendlier memories.

" The outbreak of the Bolshevist upheaval still found me in my old flat in Moscow. I had started to re-write my First Concerto for pianoforte, which I intended to play again, and was so engrossed with my work that I

---

[1] Published by George Allen and Unwin, Ltd.

did not notice what went on around me. Consequently, life during the anarchist upheaval, which turned the existence of a non-proletarian into hell on earth, was comparatively easy for me. I sat at the writing table or piano all day without troubling about the rattle of machine guns and rifle-shots. . . . The anarchy around me, the brutal uprooting of all the foundations of art, the senseless destruction of all means for its encouragement, left no hope of a normal life in Russia. . . .

". . . Three or four days after the shooting in Moscow had begun I received a telegram suggesting that I should make a tour of ten concerts in Scandinavia. . . . I had difficulty in obtaining a visa from the Bolshevists. . . . Later I heard that I was the last to receive permission to leave Russia in a ' legal ' manner. . . . I travelled to St. Petersburg by myself. . . . My wife, with the two girls, followed later, and together we took the train which carried us via Finland to the Swedish frontier : I was allowed to take with me only the most necessary articles and not more than five hundred roubles for each member of the family. . . ."

They crossed the frontier on a peasant's sledge during a dense blizzard and arrived in Stockholm on Christmas Eve to find it gay with festivities. Rachmaninoff played in all the principal towns of Sweden, realizing that his hands now afforded him the best means of earning a livelihood.

Here we come to the turning point of his career, for it was during this tour that he decided to become first and foremost a professional pianist. Most of his playing in the past had been of his own works. Now, this decision entailed the preparation of an extensive repertoire made up chiefly of the works of other composers, so he took a house in Copenhagen and made a start on the great task before him.

While he was preparing this repertoire he received a telegram from America inviting him to accept the conductorship of the Boston Symphony Orchestra, but he refused the offer. At the same time, however, he realized what boundless possibilities the United States offered him, and he made up his mind to go there in any case.

With his family he crossed the Atlantic in a small Norwegian steamer and arrived at New York on November 10th, 1918. On the following day the entire population seemed to go raving mad in their celebrations of the Armistice.

Charles Ellis, one of America's greatest concert agents, had recently lost a highly remunerative contract with Paderewski, who was then too engrossed in politics to give piano recitals, and consequently Ellis was on the lookout for another great pianist. But even this enterprising manager did not foresee the great welcome that the American people would give to Rachmaninoff on his return to their concert halls. For his first concerts he chose only the works of the great masters : Schumann's *Carnival*, the Chopin Sonata in

B-flat minor, and the Beethoven *Appassionata*, for instance, and nothing could have given greater pleasure to the Americans. Then he began his long association with several of the great American orchestras as a concerto pianist, finding in Stokowski the conductor he had dreamed of, and in the Philadelphia Symphony Orchestra an almost unbelievable perfection of musicianship.

In 1928 he toured Europe once again, visiting London, Paris, Vienna, Prague, Budapest, Berlin and Munich, and reaching the apex of his fame. Extensive tours on both sides of the Atlantic in the years that followed, and frequent recording sessions, made him neglect his composing to a great extent, and therefore he became known primarily as a pianist, although he had three symphonies and the same number of concertos to his credit. During his few years in America he wrote nothing whatever. In 1931 he bought a small estate on the shores of Lake Lucerne and went there frequently for periods of rest and recreation.

My last personal recollection of him in England was when he played at the Queen's Hall on March 10th, 1934, a magnificent programme that included works of Mozart, Beethoven, Chopin, Debussy, Liszt and one or two of his own compositions. Perhaps the most memorable were the Chopin Ballade in G-minor and the Beethoven Sonata in C-sharp minor.

It is perhaps worth recording that on one occasion when he played one of his own concertos in London a critic declared in all sincerity that his tempi had been all wrong ! I might also add that the Royal Philharmonic Society awarded him its coveted Gold Medal in March, 1932.

One of Rachmaninoff's happiest memories was of the day when, as a young man of twenty-four, he was introduced to Tolstoy. The great writer lectured him in a fatherly way upon mastering all the little troubles of life, and spoke of the value of having confidence in oneself and determination to follow one's chosen path. Rachmaninoff himself once told a pupil that the most difficult obstacle in an artist's life was the one that perplexed him when trying to get his feet upon the first rung of the ladder. It often seemed so formidable that in many cases the artist would lose hope at the very outset.

Shortly before the Second World War the *Revue Musicale Belge* quoted a statement made by Rachmaninoff in an interview concerning his *Recollections*, from which I have quoted. These memoirs are really " as told to O. van Riesemann," but Rachmaninoff said, " Riesemann states that I dictated it all. If so, something must have gone wrong with my mind at the time."

Not until his closing years did this great pianist turn again to composition. His Third Symphony was written in 1936, he revised his Fourth Concerto two years later, and published his *Symphonic Dances* in 1940.

RACHMANINOFF

He never returned to his native land, though had he lived long enough to see the whole of Soviet Russia's glorious struggle in the Second World War he would no doubt have wished to renew acquaintance with the country whose soil was always dear to him. For years he was sharply critical of the Communist regime, and in 1931 his music was banned in the Soviet Union as being representative of " the decadent attitude of the lower middle class " and " especially dangerous on the musical front in the . . . class war." But as the Soviet Government became more tolerant, Rachmaninoff modified his criticisms and quite frankly acknowledged all that was praiseworthy in the Soviet's efforts to promote the welfare and culture of the Russian people. In 1939 he learnt with considerable delight that his works were being studied, performed and received in the Soviet Union with great appreciation and understanding.

He died at Beverley Hills, California, on March 28th, 1943.

PART II

SOME PROMINENT PIANISTS IN BRITAIN TO-DAY

Harriet Cohen

TAKING my selection of living pianists in alphabetical order, we come first to Harriet Cohen, who in 1938 was awarded the C.B.E. for her services to music. She was born in London of musical parents : her father composed and her mother was one of Tobias Matthay's students. Her earliest recollection of music was of playing on Paderewski's knee in the artist's room at the Queen's Hall.

When she was twelve, she won the Ada Lewis Scholarship to the Royal Academy of Music, and in the following year made her début at one of Chappell's Sunday Concerts at the Queen's Hall. Her first important appearance, however, was in 1920, when she gave a joint recital with John Coates at the Wigmore Hall. This inaugurated a career that was to take her all over the world.

She has given the first performance of several of the major piano works produced by our contemporary composers : Vaughan Williams and Sir Arnold Bax both wrote concertos for her, Béla Bartók, Ernest Bloch and E. J. Moeran have dedicated new works to her, and she had the honour of introducing William Walton's *Sinfonia Concertante* to France, Spain, Germany and America. John Ireland wrote for her his *Legend* for piano and orchestra.

Harriet Cohen is one of the few pianists who have gone to the trouble of discovering the great merit of the Tudor composers, and she has given many fine recitals of the works of William Byrd, Orlando Gibbons and others of their period. She has also included a number of Purcell's works in her repertoire. Incidentally, she broadcast works of Purcell and Bax when she played at the Washington Festival during one of her visits to America.

Spanish music has also found a prominent place in her programmes. She gave the second performance of Falla's *Nights in the Gardens of Spain*, and has now played it more than any other pianist in the world. Miss Cohen can also claim to be one of the first to have played the music of Soviet Russia in this country, a distinction that brought her an invitation to visit Russia in 1935 to broadcast from Leningrad and Moscow. Works by Shostakovich, Kabalevsky and Polovinkin were included, and these composers have since sent her several of their later compositions.

As an exponent of Bach, she has won high praise from some of the finest critics in the world. The late Adolph Weissmann, for instance, said " so

151

deeply has the spirit of the master entered into her that she has few, if any, equals as a Bach player," and Alfred Einstein declared " she is one of those chosen few who stand among the elect." When Casals, the eminent Spanish 'cellist, heard her play Bach he immediately invited her to perform a Bach Concerto with his orchestra in Barcelona. A similar invitation to play in Berlin was given to her by Dr. Furtwangler when he heard her in Switzerland. It might be added here that Miss Cohen gave the first " all-Bach " programme at the Queen's Hall in 1925.

Just before the Second World War, Dr. R. Vaughan Williams and Sir Arnold Bax presented her with a gold chain bearing leaf-shaped pendants, one for each of her more important achievements in the musical world. Another gift which she values very highly is the exquisite diamond brooch given to her by the Queen of Spain about ten years ago.

One of her most vivid memories is of the occasion when she had the pleasure of playing arrangements for four hands of various symphonies with Bernard Shaw. Another is of when she had the very unusual experience of broadcasting with a well-known dance band. She interposed items of Bach between their " numbers " ! She is very fond of dancing, by the way, and while we are on the subject of recreations, I might add that she is an ardent collector of snuff boxes.

Harriet Cohen is the Vice-President of the Women's Freedom League, and for some years has been associated with the Jewish National Fund and the Palestine Conservatoire of Music at Jerusalem. She has been a very willing helper at the various concerts organized from time to time with the object of promoting Jewish culture.

Clifford Curzon

PADEREWSKI gave his " farewell " recital in a concert hall in New York one afternoon in the early spring of 1939. Immediately afterwards, in the same hall, a young English pianist, Clifford Curzon, made his American début and impressed the critics so favourably that one of them wrote " . . . one recital marked the twilight of a great career ; the other, the dawn of what promises to be another perhaps as great in the world of pianists." Few musical careers are more interesting to watch than Curzon's, for he is a magnificent pianist endowed with a poetic temperament, and is at the same time a thoroughly sound musician.

He is a Londoner, born in 1907. At the age of twelve he entered the Royal Academy of Music and within a few years distinguished himself by winning what must be almost a record number of scholarships and prizes, including the McFarren Gold Medal. His first professional appearance in London was made at a Queen's Hall Promenade Concert at the age of sixteen, and the fact that Sir Henry Wood invited him to play during every subsequent Promenade season is sufficient proof of the good impression he made.

Two or three years of general concert work in this country made him realize the need of wider experience, so at the age of nineteen he withdrew from public life and went to Germany to study for two years with Schnabel. While I was having tea with Curzon one afternoon recently he drew a vivid picture of his student days in Germany, and in particular the sort of classes Schnabel used to hold. He was always in favour of the " class " method of teaching, for he believed that there was plenty a student could learn from the mistakes of his fellows. For four afternoons a week Schnabel would assemble all his pupils in his large music room : an impressive chamber completely lined with books he had never read and, it was said, he never intended even to look at. Apart from chairs, there was little else in it but two fine Bechstein pianos. At one of these Schnabel would sit himself while the student chosen for the afternoon's ordeal would sit at the other. The pupils came from all over the world—England, America, Russia, France, Greece and Spain were represented in Curzon's day, and there were of course people from all parts of Germany and Austria. Whatever his nationality, no student sat at the piano without the sympathy of the onlookers, for Schnabel was not an easy man to please !

153

MASTERS OF THE KEYBOARD

The lesson would start soon after two o'clock, and would rarely last for less than three-and-a-half hours—some of our twenty-minute piano teachers should make a special note of this. Schnabel had a habit of getting so engrossed in the music that he would completely ignore the clock, and as no student would dare to risk his displeasure by reminding him of the time, the lessons would often go on until seven or eight in the evening. Curzon remembers that on one occasion he was there from two o'clock until ten, but Schnabel could be so interesting that one rarely felt a sense of fatigue. Nobody seemed to mind going without tea.

Schnabel was very watchful of his pupil's *tempo*, and any controversial matters on this subject were invariably settled with the reminder: " I swallowed a metronome as a little boy." He never favoured the extensive use of that device, however.

Fashions and traditional interpretations of the classics made no impression upon him : he would dismiss them with the adage " Tradition is only a collection of bad habits." And all the pupils, sitting below a portrait of Leschetizky inscribed " with memories of beautiful and difficult hours " would nod appreciatively whether they believed it or not.

After completing his course with Schnabel and shorter periods of study with other distinguished musicians in France and Germany, Clifford Curzon made his début in Berlin and then toured in Austria, playing in Vienna before his return to this country. Although in recent years he has spent most of his time in England, the years preceding the Second World War were to a great extent given up to establishing himself in various foreign capitals and in America. This perhaps accounts for his rapid rise to eminence, for he was barely out of his twenties when the foreign critics were acclaiming him as " a master of the pianoforte."

One of his Berlin recitals produced this notice from the critic of the *Allgemeine Musikzeitung:* " His technical mastery resulting in extraordinary purity of phrasing, harmonically and architecturally, his ' purling ' scales and beautiful eloquence in declaiming ornamentation, together with an ascetically charming concentration on the spiritual content, occupied the foreground in the Beethoven Sonata, while poetry, the most essential quality of all, was shown in the positively enchanting treatment of the Schubert *Moments Musicaux,* and in the transporting rendering of Liszt's B-minor Sonata, which has seldom so enslaved me. The young pianist was forced to give repeated encores to a clamouring audience."

The years Curzon spent in building up a large concerto repertoire have been well rewarded. He is as ready to play Dohnanyi, Bloch, Prokofiev or D'Indy concertos as the better-known works of Beethoven, Brahms, Liszt, Tschaikovsky or Schumann.

CLIFFORD CURZON

For a year or so, Clifford Curzon returned to the Royal Academy of Music as a professor, but he found that it was almost impossible to fulfil his engagements as a concert pianist and to teach at the same time, and therefore felt obliged to relinquish his appointment. Only very occasionally does he give a private lesson now, yet he is interested in teaching, for he realizes the very important part the teacher plays in our cultural life. A fundamental mistake that many pianists and teachers make, in Curzon's opinion, is that they become so interested in technique (in its widest sense) that they develop a standardized technique of their own and then proceed to impose it upon everything they play. Every individual type of music demands a different technique : one might almost say that every single phrase has to be considered apart from its neighbour.

To the student pianist, Curzon says, " Work hard at the classics while you're young, but see that you are not satisfied with a ' dull ' performance of such works. This applies particularly to the Beethoven sonatas." The method Curzon recommends for learning a piece is on much the same lines as Sir Adrian Boult's system for the preparation of orchestral works[1]. This can be summarized thus : play the piece through several times regardless of mistakes to gain a thorough general impression of the work : you *must* be conscious of the work as a whole, its outline, emotion and so forth, before you attend to details. The music should then be taken to pieces, as it were, and every integral part studied and mastered separately. Finally the piece should be re-constructed and polished as a whole. At the final performance you must still be " in love " with the music : signs of tiredness or staleness can be quickly discerned by the more discriminating listener.

Difficulties of fingering are often under-rated. When he is preparing a work, Clifford Curzon experiments over and over again to find the ideal fingering : the simplest and easiest to play is *not* always the best arrangement, nor is it always the most effective. His own music bears an enormous number of markings patiently pencilled-in during practice ; he never trusts such matters to his memory. In the preparation of concertos, he frequently plays with his radio-gramophone, but thinks that this method can sometimes be overdone, and in any case should never be attempted without the most careful study of the full score.

Contrary to popular supposition, the piano virtuoso of to-day leads a very hard life if he is a conscientious musician. Curzon practises every day, for he finds that as little as three days' holiday is enough to tell unfavourably upon his work. The skill of the concert pianist is like highly polished metal : a day or two without attention and it begins to get slightly dull ; almost imperceptibly, perhaps, but lacking the brilliant freshness of its former state. Virtuosity, Curzon insists, is not as empty as some people

[1] See my biography of Sir Adrian Boult in *Conductor's Gallery*.

imagine : we are afraid of the virtuoso in this country because of our national distaste of " showing off."

He believes that the music of Chopin is apt to be over-played these days, and in any case, it is too often badly played. Schubert on the other hand is becoming neglected, and so is Liszt, whose music is pathetically misunderstood by millions of musicians to-day. We should always bear in mind the vast numbers of people who have never heard much of the work of these composers.

For the benefit of those who imagine that professional pianists bask in the " lime-light " and enjoy the stare of thousands of eyes, I might add that Clifford Curzon feels no pleasure when he is actually playing : he identifies himself so completely with the composer he is interpreting that the only sense of which he is conscious is one of profound responsibility for the control of a work of art. The pleasure and satisfaction come afterwards, when one is conscious of a job well done ; conversely, a performance marred by a blemish of some sort, however tiny, can result in a sleepless night ! Accidents *do* happen sometimes : when he was making his début in New York, for instance, his glasses fell off just as he reached the climax of the Liszt *Funérailles* ! Curzon is very short-sighted, and he had to complete the work playing upon what seemed to be almost a phantom piano. Fortunately, all went well, but this was a very unpleasant experience on an occasion of such vital importance to a young artist. Commenting on this recital the critic of the *New York Times* wrote : " Curzon, English pianist, at once established himself as an artist of prime importance. A supreme colorist, with an impeccable virtuoso technique, Mr. Curzon possessed that irresistible combination of power and tenderness, of vitality and subtle delicacy, that belongs only to the exceptionally gifted performer. . . Few pianists of the day have the perfect control of nuance in prismatic softer tints, the invariably singing tone, the velvety fortissimo with strength behind it that gave the delivery of these familiar pieces unusual appeal, aside from the wealth of poetry and imagination that informed the sensitive readings accorded them."

Clifford Curzon was married in 1931 to Lucille Wallace, the American harpsichordist, whom he had met in Schnabel's class. Their extensive work on the continent made it necessary for them to have a house abroad as well as in London, and they acquired an excellent property in beautiful surroundings near Salzburg. Although Curzon was in England when the Second World War broke out, most of his possessions, including the bulk of his music and the best of his pianos, were in Austria. Eventually a friend succeeded in posting his music to England in 2-lb. packages !

It would be impossible to relate all Curzon's experiences in wartime, but it is perhaps worth mentioning that he was once asked to play in a certain provincial town hall in England where the local authorities had concealed the name of the German piano in the interests of public morale ! He refused to play until the cloth covering the name was removed.

Curzon believes that all the arts are related, and that the musician should be able to appreciate other forms of art if he is to bring his own to perfection. He is keenly interested in painting, and among his proudest possessions are works of some of the greatest modern artists. Poetry also makes a strong appeal to him, and he reads extensively ; Henry James and George Eliot for preference. Swimming and driving are his favourite recreations, and he is interested in Yoga.

Mark Hambourg

I SHOULD think that Mark Hambourg has met more of the greater musicians than any other living artist : he seems to have gone everywhere and met everybody, and for those who wish to know the full story of his most eventful life, I can recommend his autobiography *From Piano to Forte*, which was published some years ago by Cassell's.

Son of a musician, he was born on June 1st, 1879, in the South Russian village of Bogutchar, although his father's house was at Voronesch. One of his earliest and most thrilling memories of childhood is of the way he used to stand at his father's side as the latter conducted the orchestral class at the Voronesch Conservatoire, of which he was the principal. Mark's first piano lessons were given by an aunt, but his progress soon justified personal attention from his father. He loathed practising, and did everything possible to evade the drudgery of exercises and scales, yet at the age of seven he gave his first public concert. This acted as a stimulus, for he became so keen that the piano had to be locked to prevent him from playing all day long. His father considered one hour's practice a day to be sufficient for a boy of his age.

He was then sent to the Moscow Conservatoire, where he soon outshone most of his fellow-students, though he attributes his progress not to the lessons he received at that institution, but to the private instruction he continued to receive from his father, who, incidentally, accepted a professorship there some years later.

In his autobiography he tells how, as a boy, he was engaged to play a concerto before the Grand Duke Constantine. The concert was preceded by a banquet at which Hambourg was given champagne to drink. Alas ! when he mounted the platform to play his head was " swimming." He got through the concerto without a mishap until the last movement, which he forgot entirely ! The conductor and his players stared aghast, but the young pianist calmly improvised for about ten minutes, then remembered the last few pages and concluded the concerto. He was obviously intoxicated, so the Grand Duke treated him very kindly, in fact he complimented him on his clever extemporization and presented him with a wonderful toy engine.

In the spring of 1889 his father brought him to London, acting upon the advice of a friend who assured him that there would be far greater opportunities here than in Russia. They arrived at Victoria in pouring rain, knowing not a word of English, and might have found conditions intolerable during their first few months here but for the help of a few refugees from the Tsarist regime. One of these, an eccentric engineer, incurred the wrath of some of his associates by insisting on pickling cucumbers in a humble bedroom utensil.

Paderewski happened to be in London at that time, and his agent, Daniel Mayer, asked him to hear Mark Hambourg play. He did, and spoke so enthusiastically of the boy's skill that Mayer immediately offered to present Mark as a child prodigy. His début was at the old Prince's Hall on July 12th, 1890, its success leading to another concert in the same hall a week or so later, and to a tour of the provinces. Josef Hofmann and Otto Hegner, two other child prodigies, were public favourites at that time, though the newspapers frequently printed letters complaining of the exploitation of children in this manner. Hambourg's father would have been only too glad to withdraw his son from public life so that he could receive a proper musical education, but with four other children and a wife to support in Russia, the money earned at these recitals was urgently required.

In due course the rest of the family arrived from Russia, and they took a house at Teddington for a while. Hambourg was then much in demand— " Max Hambourg, the child prodigy " he was called—but disliked all the dear old ladies who tried to kiss him and pat his head. Eventually he made Narcissus Vert, who had become his manager, inform these admirers that he could be embraced only upon the production of a large box of chocolates !

He then had the good fortune to meet Felix Moscheles the painter, son of the famous pianist, and became one of the *habitués* of that studio in Chelsea where on Sunday afternoons such distinguished characters as Oscar Wilde, G. Bernard Shaw, W. T. Stead, and Ellen Terry were wont to meet. What vivid memories he has of those days ! All very pleasant except one : Mrs. Moscheles had a habit of examining his neck to see if he had washed it, and the inspection invariably led to her performance of the ablution on his behalf—with the utmost vigour.

When he was twelve, his parents and friends all agreed that his career would suffer if he were not withdrawn from public life and given a sound musical education. Paderewski was consulted and recommended three years in Vienna with Leschetizky ; but how was the money to be found ? Discreet appeals to some of the wealthy people who had invited Mark to play in their houses, and to some of the benevolent old ladies who had insisted on kissing him, brought nothing, and the project might have been abandoned but for the generosity of Paderewski, who paid the major part of the cost out of his own pocket. So in the autumn of 1891 Mark Hambourg found himself in Vienna, a pupil of the greatest pianoforte teacher in the world.

One of the major accomplishments of his student days was the winning of the Liszt Scholarship of five hundred marks, and to this evidence of hard work I might add an equally useful achievement: the acquisition of the goodwill of almost every person of importance in the artistic circles of Vienna. Early in 1895 he made his first appearance as an adult pianist when he played the Chopin E minor Concerto at a Vienna Philharmonic Symphony Concert under Richter with great success.

He was still a student with Leschetizky when the sudden indisposition of Madame Sophie Menter, a very popular pianist at that time, brought another splendid opportunity. She was to have played Liszt's *Hungarian Fantasia* at a concert to be given in Vienna by the Berlin Philharmonic Orchestra under Weingartner, and her inability to do so at the last moment caused a frantic appeal to be made to Leschetizky. The famous teacher declared that only one of his pupils could play the piece sufficiently well to accept the engagement, a youth named Mark Hambourg, and as a result the young pianist was called from his bed before seven o'clock on the morning of the concert and told to prepare for a rehearsal. That evening the people were obviously disappointed when a mere student walked on the platform instead of the favourite Sophie Menter, but their mood changed to one of exuberant admiration as he swept through the work. A great banquet was held after the concert, and Johannes Brahms himself, the guest of honour, proposed a toast to " The youth who played this evening ! " Not at all a bad start to a professional career.

At sixteen, Hambourg commenced his first world tour. It started with a visit to Australia, where he was so successful that he was asked to prolong his stay by six weeks. At Sydney he was challenged to a duel by a hefty German ten years his senior, who accused him of flirting with his fiancée. Fortunately, he evaded this by revealing his age.

On his return to London he had a splendid opportunity to deputize for Paderewski at a Philharmonic Concert when the great pianist was suddenly taken ill. He played the Rubinstein D minor Concerto ; a work rarely heard to-day. His first appearance in Paris was in 1896, and then he proceeded to Brussels and Berlin.

In the autumn of 1898 he went to America, made his début in New York with the Boston Symphony Orchestra under the direction of William Gericke, and then commenced an extensive tour of the States. One of his less happy memories of this musical expedition was a concert in a western city where an utterly incapable trombone player was allowed to wreck a concerto merely because he was the local secretary of a musician's union. At another town, Los Angeles, he found the whole place flooded, and his first concert there was attended by an audience of three. These young men were piano students however, and were so delighted when Hambourg announced his intention

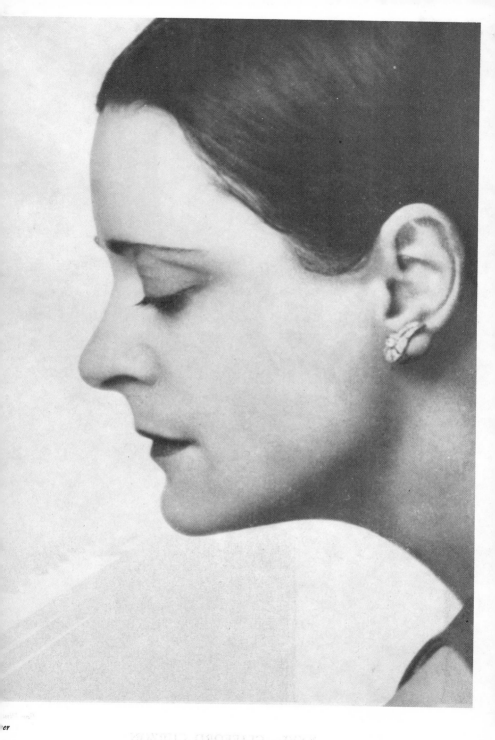

XXV.   HARRIET COHEN

Ben Pinc

XXVI. CLIFFORD CURZON

XXVII.   DAME MYRA HESS

Hay Wrights

XXVIII.   MARK HAMBOURG

XXIX.   LOUIS KENTNER

Anthony Buckl

XXX. EILEEN JOYCE

XXXI. MOISEIWITSCH

XXXII. POUISHNOFF

XXXIII. SOLOMON

Hay Wrights[o...]

XXXIV.   SOLOMON'S HANDS

XXXV. (Below) SOLOMON AT THE PIANO, from a photo by a friend

of playing the whole programme through as advertised that on the following day they proclaimed his sporting gesture to the whole town and ensured a full house for the subsequent recital.

Back in London in 1900 he continued to add to his repertoire and to his circle of distinguished friends and acquaintances. At the house of Felix Moscheles he met Lenin, Ramsay Macdonald and a dozen other people with advanced political views, while on a holiday in Scotland he made the acquaintance of Andrew Carnegie, of blessed memory, who did for this country what the politicians had failed to do, as far as education was concerned.

The following year brought Mark Hambourg's first engagements for the Promenade concerts at the Queen's Hall, which were just beginning to establish the reputation of a young conductor named Henry Wood!

Then came another American tour, visits to Poland and Russia, and pleasant spells of work and social activity in Germany. But demands on his time became so heavy that when in 1906 he was offered a tour in South Africa, he accepted chiefly because the voyage would give him a few weeks of complete rest on the way. Something like twenty recitals were given in one month at centres ranging from Capetown to Natal. Although South Africa possessed no orchestra at that time, he found a genuine love for music among the people, and had no difficulty in filling the concert halls. Johannesburg was then but an overgrown village! There were few roads, and to one concert in a small town off the railway line he was taken in a mail cart drawn by mules. This meant nine hours of perpetual jolting accompanied by drizzling rain. However the tour was so successful that he was asked to repeat it shortly afterwards.

Many of the Canadian towns were also in a very primitive state when he visited that Dominion for the first time in 1909. Touring artists to-day have no idea of the conditions that Mark Hambourg endured in his efforts to take music to such places as Winnipeg, Regina, Calgary, and Vancouver. At Moose Jaw, for instance, the town had sprung up so quickly that its water supply was hopelessly inadequate, and residents were rationed to half-a-pint of water a day. To use water for washing was unthinkable.

When the Great War broke out, Mark Hambourg organised what was probably the first concert of the war in aid of the Soldiers' and Sailors' Families Association, yet malicious people began to circulate rumours that although he pretended to be of Russian birth he was really a German, and as a result his posters were torn down in many of the towns he was visiting. The old *London Mail*—a paper long since disappeared—actually printed a rumour of this type, and Hambourg was compelled to institute libel proceedings. Proof of his Russian origin and the fact that he had been a naturalized British subject for over twenty years gave him an easy victory, and although the proceedings were extremely distasteful to him, the publicity given to the case dispelled all doubt in the minds of the public. On the morning after his victory a Scotland Yard man called at his house to detain him as an " unregistered alien ! " He showed him the morning papers announcing the damages he had been awarded, and the officer withdrew hastily.

A visit to America shortly afterwards gave Hambourg a foretaste of the great jazz craze that was to sweep the world. He also had the novel experience of hearing a negro band of forty pianos. The effect was quite pleasant until they started playing the classics in jazz rhythm. As in the Second World War, musicians from all over the world were seeking refuge in America at that time, and the large number that settled there permanently did much to build up the great musical reputation that America enjoys at the present time.

Several of Mark Hambourg's friends asked him to postpone his return to England for a week so that he could accompany them home on the ill-fated *Lusitania*. Although he was anxious to get back to London, he hesitated, but would no doubt have acceded to their request if he had not met another friend who was returning a few days earlier upon an American liner, and who persuaded him to go on it. Not one of the party on the *Lusitania* survived when the great liner went down.

One of his first tasks on returning was to give a series of afternoon recitals of old English music at the Aeolian Hall. He wished to use the famous Fitzwilliam Book, which contains the finest collection of seventeenth-century instrumental music in existence, but the only modern edition of it was published by the eminent German firm of Breitkopf and Hartel, with whom he could not of course correspond. So he was obliged to study the book at the British Museum and to memorize the pieces he wished to play. Although the modern revival of interest in our Tudor composers had not then begun, the audiences were delighted with the fine specimens of Byrd, Gibbons, Bull and Blow that he played at these recitals. Of all Hambourg's recitals during the Great War, his frequent appearances at the London Coliseum were undoubtedly the most popular, yet on these occasions he played nothing but the classics.

As soon as the war was over, he resumed his tours : France, South Africa and Canada were all visited during the immediate post-war years. Regular tours in Great Britain continued to enhance his reputation at home and to add to his enormous circle of friends and acquaintances.

Mark Hambourg's connection with the gramophone industry goes back as far as 1909, when he made his first recording in the original, modest " His Master's Voice " studio in City Road. In his autobiography he tells us that the company had found only one piano whose tone was suitable for reproduction—a terrible old wreck that horrified every pianist who stepped inside the studio. Even when the company moved to its impressive new buildings at Hayes, this ancient piano was taken to continue its senile existence, and it was not until the system of electrical recording was introduced that a more civilized instrument was provided.

Commenting on the number of pianists who get nervous when recording, Hambourg says that the relentless accuracy of the recording machine tends to make one not only feel nervous, but to produce a cold, unimaginative expression that sounds lifeless and unreal when " played-back." Too many pianists, he feels, worry themselves unduly about accuracy when recording, and this stultifies their interpretative powers.

One of Mark Hambourg's anxieties about broadcast music is on account of the power of the engineer at the control board, who has the means to modify or touch-up the artist's work as he thinks fit. He fears that abuse of this power in the future might seriously affect the status of the executant musician.

He is also rather concerned about the type of young conductor one meets to-day who is altogether too impatient to rehearse a concerto properly. Three-quarters of an hour, he declares, should be allowed for the rehearsal of any concerto, if only out of consideration for the soloist. He is inclined to deprecate, too, the modern practice of playing concertos from memory, because he feels that the pianist has to concentrate so intensely upon remembering the entire work that he cannot " let himself go " sufficiently to produce a really brilliant, spontaneous interpretation.

Having travelled all over the world and come into contact with the barbaric music of the eastern and negroid races, Hambourg finds it rather amusing to discover the characteristics of their music emerging in the work of some of our contemporary western composers, and being branded as the last word in modernity! One begins to wonder what really constitutes progress in music.

Dame Myra Hess

WHEN musicians discover that they can draw large audiences in almost any of the more civilized countries, and spend a great deal of their time on tour, they tend to become decidedly cosmopolitan in their outlook, and lose interest in the musical life of their native land. One audience, they feel, is much the same as another, and if the fee is the same there is little to justify the giving of special attention to any particular city. Dame Myra Hess has never adopted this attitude. The musical life of her native London has always been a matter of great concern with her, and in the magnificent series of concerts she has given at the National Gallery throughout the war we have evidence of the great importance she attaches to the provision of regular concerts of a high standard that are within the means of everybody. But of those I shall have more to say in a moment.

Myra Hess was born at Hampstead on February 25th, 1890, the youngest of four children. Her first couple of years at music were much the same as those spent by thousands of other children in this country : she started learning to play the piano at about five years of age, and in due course took the junior examinations held by Trinity College of Music. At the age of seven she became a student at the Guildhall School of Music and came under the influence of Julian Pascal and Orlando Morgan.

A scholarship then took her to the Royal Academy of Music, where she studied the piano as her principal subject under Tobias Matthay, one of the greatest teachers of the pianoforte that this country has yet produced. His deep insight into the psychology as well as the purely physical aspect of playing was probably responsible for Myra Hess's early maturity as a professional pianist. Among her contemporaries at the Academy were such people as Stanley Marchant (now the principal), Eric Coates, W. H. Reed, Irene Scharrer, York Bowen and Arnold Bax. In his autobiography, Sir Arnold Bax, now Master of the King's Music, says that he still remembers Miss Scharrer and Dame Myra as " very small and eternally giggling girls."

Miss Hess made her début at the age of seventeen when she gave a recital at the Aeolian Hall. This brought her an engagement to play the Beethoven G major Concerto with Sir Thomas Beecham, and its outstanding success established her almost immediately. Within a few years she was touring all over Europe.

164

DAME MYRA HESS

Her first appearance in America was at a concert in New York in 1922. Commenting upon her performance, W. J. Henderson, whose death in 1937 robbed America of one of its finest critics, wrote : " She is a great pianist without limitation," and went on to speak of the imagination and delicate sensitivity revealed in the " subtly wrought details of her readings and the singular aptness of her purpose." Since that time she has done a great deal in America, in fact there are few symphony orchestras in the United States with whom she has not played at some time.

Appropriate recognition of her work came in 1936, when King George V made her a Companion of the Order of the British Empire. Five years later she became a Dame Commander of the same Order. Another honour that came to her in 1941 was the Gold Medal awarded by the Royal Philharmonic Society : a distinction conferred only upon the greatest musicians.

Of her tours in France, Holland, Germany and Austria, much could be said, but owing to the very small amount of space available I can add only that her best performances have been of the works of Bach, Scarlatti and Mozart, of which she has made a special study. There are very few pianists of her sex in this country to-day who can equal her in this type of music. The music of Schumann is another of her specialities, and she has taken an active interest in all types of chamber music for many years.

When the Second World War broke out Dame Myra was obliged to abandon an extensive tour of America that had been planned for the 1939-40 season. As my readers are well aware, all music stopped in Great Britain during those dreary first months of the war, and it was a most encouraging stimulus to all music-lovers when she returned to this country and inaugurated that remarkable series of lunch-time concerts at the National Gallery. They were just what everybody wanted, for the black-out made it extremely difficult for thousands of London's suburban residents to go up to town after dark. To give any sort of list of the immense range of works that have been performed at these concerts would be quite impossible here, but mention should, I think, be made of the performance of the complete series of Mozart piano concertos, for which she called in Alec Sherman and his New London Orchestra. One of these special Mozart concerts was patronized by Her Majesty the Queen, who received Dame Myra and Mr. Sherman during the interval and congratulated them upon the excellent work they were doing.

It is noteworthy that up to the autumn of 1944, no less than thirteen hundred concerts had been given at the National Gallery in this series, and although fifteen thousand pounds had been paid out in artists' fees, the sum of ten thousand pounds had been made for the Musicians' Benevolent Fund. The canteen alone contributed a profit of four thousand pounds to the concert fund. Throughout the worst periods of the bombing of London these concerts were continued, though they ran at a loss during the most difficult days. Contributions from music-lovers in America helped to meet the expenses when attendances were small.

The gesture of the Trustees of the National Gallery in making available their premises without charge might well be copied by the governing bodies of art galleries in other parts of the country, for then, many of the smaller orchestras—particularly the chamber music ensembles—could hold frequent concerts without incurring heavy loss. Actually, the National Gallery is not particularly suitable for concerts on account of its acoustic properties, but several of the provincial art galleries would lend themselves well for the purpose of music-making, and then perhaps, the doctrine of the inter-relation of the arts, which has already been mentioned in this book, would become more widely understood.

Eileen Joyce

I HAVE yet to come across another musician with such a remarkable life-story as Eileen Joyce. It reads almost like a fairy tale. In twenty years she has transformed herself from a ragged daughter of a poverty-stricken labourer in the wilds of the Australian bush to one of Britain's finest pianists with an exquisite flat in Mayfair and an engagement book so full that she finds difficulty in visiting all the towns that want to hear her. What rare qualities have led to this amazing accomplishment? I should say: a deep love of music, uncanny skill, inflexible determination, and a propensity for sheer hard work.

She was born in Tasmania just before the outbreak of the Great War—the exact date is unknown, because her parents were so poor that they had to lead a gipsy life and consequently lost count of the days. Her birth took place in a patched old tent somewhere in the middle of a vast forest, and her layette consisted of nothing more than a few tattered garments given by kindly wayfarers who saw that the infant's need was greater than their own. It was in the rainy season, and water dripped dismally from the patches in the canvas. Whenever the howling wind subsided one could hear the mournful whine of the voracious foxes that lurked around every sign of human habitation. Was ever an artist born in so grim an environment?

Her father was of Irish extraction, a labourer whose sole means of subsistence was casual work in timber mills at seven shillings a day, but this did not prevent him from marrying at an early age. Her mother was of Spanish origin.

When Eileen was five or six months old the little family moved to Queenstown, where they found accommodation in a small one-roomed hut with a leaky roof and no windows. Although her father found work loading coal trucks, they were barely able to exist because of the high cost of living. Her mother, under-nourished and rheumatic, went out to earn a few shillings by doing other people's washing, so Eileen was left to crawl about the stony ground upon which the hut stood. At night she slept in a cradle made out of a disused petroleum drum.

It is difficult for us in this country to understand the bitter struggle her father had to keep his family from dying of starvation. After eighteen months of feverish effort to improve their lot, he decided that something drastic would have to be done, so borrowing some money from a friend, he took his wife and children to Western Australia.

They pitched their tent at a place called Mujikine, near the tract of land allotted to Mr. Joyce for him to clear and cultivate, and while the work was in progress they lived on tinned rabbit and boiled wheat. Then an appalling drought dashed their hopes to the ground. Their crops were completely ruined and they almost died of thirst. Eileen can still remember the terrific debilitating heat, the plague of mosquitoes and the horrible sand-flies.

For all that, her father did not give up hope. He borrowed ten shillings, bought an old horse, and travelled every day to the dam nine miles distant to fill two petrol cans with water. On these journeys he would sometimes encounter generous settlers, who, knowing his plight, would give him food to take back to his wife and children.

Eileen's memories of this period of her life are coloured by recollections of the beautiful wild flowers that grew so profusely in that part of Australia —golden wattle and wild orchids, for instance—and the many-hued birds that abounded in the bush. But of the snakes and poisonous lizards she recalls a feeling of perpetual dread : it was dangerous to sit outside the tent after sunset.

One day, somebody gave Eileen a mouth-organ, and she immediately began trying to play the Irish melodies and Spanish folk-songs that her parents sang at their work : she found in herself an indomitable urge to make music. The song of the birds had always moved her profoundly : how grand it was to be able to extemporize on their tunes, and to experiment in crude forms of harmony as well ! Hour after hour she sat improving her skill on the humble instrument, and she devised all manner of accompaniments when her father began to sing.

Just as the Joyce family were beginning to see some signs of progress a fire destroyed their encampment, and having lost everything, they started to walk through the overwhelming heat to Kunnunoppin, eleven miles distant. Mercifully, they were picked up by a cart during the latter stages of the journey. At the settlement, Eileen's uncommon ability to draw forth music from her mouth-organ was the chief subject of local gossip, and the farmers and their womenfolk would gather around her in the evenings to listen.

When Eileen reached her ninth year the family moved again to a settlement near Boulder City and made their home in a two-roomed corrugated-iron shack. Her father found regular work, but they were still very poor, and the youthful mouth-organist became known in the neighbourhood as " Ragged Eily."

Imagine the excitement when Mr. Joyce came home one evening and announced that he had bought an old piano ! This turned out to be a very battered old " cottage " piano, very much out of tune and minus a dozen wires, but to Eileen it was the most wonderful instrument in the world. Her mother had a vague knowledge of the rudiments of music, and the excited little girl needed no persuasion to practise. Within a week she was entertaining the neighbours with *The Campbells are Coming* !

The sisters at a nearby convent then became interested in her and took over the responsibility of her education. Music was one of the subjects of their curriculum, and by the end of the first term Eileen's precocity in the art had made her the school's musical prodigy. Then Percy Grainger, the eminent Australian composer and pianist happened to visit the convent and hear her. He was astonished not only at her technique, but at the remarkable feeling she put into the simple pieces she played, and insisted that she should be sent to Europe and given the chance to study music under a first-rate teacher. When they told him that her parents were penniless he reminded them that he had raised the money for his own musical education by giving concerts. What he had done, she could do.

Eileen listened, her sharp eyes glittering, and became obsessed with this enchanting prospect. With her amazing determination she went to the nearest town and persuaded the management of the theatre to let her appear as a pianist. Her tremendous success enabled her to arrange a tour forthwith, and at the end of this she discovered to her astonishment that she had made the staggering sum of nine hundred pounds by her own effort ! It seemed a vast fortune.

It so happened that another well-known pianist—Backhaus—was touring in Australia, and it was extremely fortunate that out of sheer curiosity he had dropped in at one of her recitals. He sent for her, congratulated her, and asked what plans she was making for her future. As the courageous little girl explained, he nodded with approval, and then told her that she must go to the Leipzig Conservatorium. Before he left her he wrote special letters of introduction on her behalf.

Eileen's memories of her early days at Leipzig are of nothing but intense toil and deep loneliness. Her funds were of course very limited, so there was no question of enjoying the pleasures that go to make up the more glamorous side of the student's life, and, of course, it was necessary to complete her training in the shortest possible time. She was still little more than a child, she had not a single friend in Europe, and to make matters worse, could not speak a word of German.

Then her health broke down, and it seemed impossible to carry on any longer, so she made plans to return to Australia. She was practising a few days later when the eminent teacher Teichmuller happened to pass the door of her apartments. He stood listening for a while, and then entered. " Please continue," he asked, " I am most interested." Miss Joyce concluded the piece and then turned to him, explaining that she was giving up her studies and returning to Australia. " But you have the hands of Paderewski ! " he gasped, " you shall stay and be my pupil, and you shall pay me nothing."

This was the turning point in Eileen Joyce's great struggle. Her spirits revived, and with them her former enthusiasm. With this new impetus she worked an inordinate number of hours each day, until Teichmuller begged her to take her studies more easily.

Two years of hard work, and then he pronounced her ready for the concert platform. He thought she should launch her career in England and gave her various letters of introduction, one of which was to Albert Coates, the eminent conductor, one of his former pupils. It was to Coates that she first played on her arrival in London. Knowing his great interest in Russian music she chose Prokofiev's Third Concerto : a work almost unknown in this country at that time. As she played she watched an expression of satisfaction and delight shaping his features, and it was no surprise to her when during the exciting last movement, he sat down at the second piano and gleefully plunged headlong into the orchestral accompaniment. Curiously enough, not until 1944 did they perform this particular concerto together in public : the occasion then was the great festival of Russian music held at the Albert Hall in the spring of that year.

After the first audition, Albert Coates introduced Eileen Joyce to the late Sir Henry Wood, that persistent sponsor of young talent, who arranged for her to make her début with the same concerto at one of his Promenade Concerts at the Queen's Hall. She was an instantaneous success, and as soon as she got back to her dressing room she received a message from a well-known impresario who wished to present her in a series of provincial concerts.

That was the first of the many tours that have taken her to every town of any size in Great Britain. She then went abroad for a short course of concentrated study with Schnabel, and afterwards made a triumphant tour throughout Australia.

It is interesting, I think, to note how Eileen Joyce came to win the favour of the gramophone lover. During her first few months in this country, when she was quite unknown, she wanted to make a private recording as a " playback " : that is, a record made for study purposes so that she could listen critically to her own playing. This she did, but when she went to collect it and pay the fee she was asked to see the company's recording manager. His affability was a trifle puzzling until he explained that the recording engineer had been so astonished by the skill of the unknown girl pianist that he had taken the record to the manager's office. It had been agreed overnight that instead of Eileen Joyce paying the company, they should pay her, provided that she would make another recording for the reverse side of the disc so that it could be issued for sale to the public.

EILEEN JOYCE

Incidentally, this first record—a study by Liszt and a work by Paul de Schlozer—is still a favourite among her admirers, and one that has been particularly helpful to students of the pianoforte.

In quite a short time she became well-established as a pianist, but that did not mean the end of hard work. During her first few years she memorized more than fifty concertos, not to mention the dozens of recital pieces.

She has never specialized in any particular type of music, not that she disapproves of specialization, but because she loves to play any music that gives her a feeling of deep satisfaction. With the exception of chamber music, she likes to play everything from memory : her ability to memorize is so remarkable that she has no fear whatever of forgetting the music.

During a discussion recently she told me that of all her work she has enjoyed making her recordings more than anything, despite the strenuous nature of these sessions. She finds great joy in the permanence of recorded work : well over fifty records of concertos, solos and chamber music now stand to her credit. I am reminded, by the way, that in her opinion, nothing has yet been invented to surpass fibre needles in the reproduction of piano music, though at the time of writing she has not yet experimented with the new type of needle that rumour tells us has been perfected in America.

Eileen Joyce is extremely interested in the film industry and believes the British films have a brilliant future. Television also appeals to her, and she thinks that it is likely to affect the virtuoso more than any other member of the musical profession when it develops. When people can both hear and see their favourite artists in the comfort of their homes they will not be so willing to endure the discomfort of many of our concert halls. Television would give the listener a much better chance of observing a pianist's hands than he would get by being present in the concert hall.

One of Eileen Joyce's most important tours during the war was when she went with Dr. Malcolm Sargent and the London Philharmonic Orchestra on the tour organized by Jack Hylton in those grim days when it looked as if our great orchestras would have to be disbanded. They played in variety theatres all over England a fine selection of the more popular classics.

She has had some unpleasant experiences, too. At one concert hall not far from London she fell down a flight of stairs behind the stage just as she was going to the platform. Her dress was ruined and she was badly bruised, but after a short rest insisted upon playing the concerto for which she had been billed. At Bournemouth a few years ago she squeezed one of her fingers in a door only four hours before the concert, but played all the same.

Louis Kentner

STRICTLY speaking, Louis Kentner is not an English pianist, but he has worked in this country now for over ten years and has taken his place in the musical life of our people. He applied for naturalization in 1940 but his request was left in abeyance during the war with Germany in common with all other applications by friendly aliens. By the time this book appears in print, however, he will probably have become a British subject.

He was born in the Silesian town of Karvin in July, 1905. His father was a very keen but very bad amateur musician, a great admirer of Puccini's operas. Kentner's earliest memories are of " turning over " for his father as he tried to play such works as *La Tosca*, *Madam Butterfly* and *La Bohème* on the piano. He was about four years old then, and during the ensuing years his chief task was to convince his father that he deserved a good musical education. This was done without difficulty, for his unusual talent emerged quickly, and he was only about seven when he was admitted to the Budapest Academy. At that excellent insitution he came under the influence of such professors as Anton Székely, Leo Weiner and Zoltan Kodály, the distinguished Hungarian composer. His progress may be judged from the fact that he won the Liszt Prize at Budapest and the Chopin Prize at Warsaw. It was in his student days that he first became acquainted with Béla Bartók, one of the greatest of Hungarian composers, whose friendship he enjoyed for many years.

Kodály was the first to recognize the potentialities of Louis Kentner's skill, and urged him to adopt music as his profession. The lad did not require much persuasion, and when he was fifteen he secured his first concert engagement. Within a year he was appearing at some of the most important concerts held in Hungary, Austria, and other central European states. He had by then left the Academy, and it is perhaps significant that from that time he was entirely self-taught.

Louis Kentner then moved to Germany where he spent two years in giving concerts and gaining wider experience. He might have stayed longer and possibly have risen to fame quicker if the obligation to help support his family had not made it necessary to return to Hungary. Nevertheless, he was steadily establishing himself in most of the European countries, including Italy and Spain, and during those years made two visits to London to give recitals under the auspices of a leading firm of pianoforte makers. Although no great attention was at first paid to him over here, he was delighted with everything he saw in England and made up his mind to settle in London when conditions permitted him to leave Hungary. This move was not made until 1935, when he finally made his home in England. Since then he has never wished to live anywhere else in the world ; he believes that London compares favourably with any of the pre-war musical centres abroad, and he has high hopes of its future in the world of culture.

His first few years in this country were not at all easy. He was almost unknown and had to make his way against the competition of the greatest pianists in the world. He began by specializing in the works of Liszt, in fact it was with these that he first drew attention to himself, but when people began to refer to him as " the Liszt pianist " he decided to show the world that he could be equally as successful with the works of such composers as Mozart, Beethoven and Schubert. He does not believe in specializing, for he feels that a good pianist should understand and be thoroughly competent in the works of all the keyboard composers. Moreover, he maintains that to be able to specialize at all, a pianist should be well acquainted with all types of music, for a man who could play nothing but Chopin would not be able to play Chopin with proper understanding.

Kentner's interpretation of the works of modern composers is exceptionally good : his Debussy and other modern French music is excellent, and there are few to compare with him in the performance of Hungarian and Spanish music. Incidentally, he played the first performance of Bartók's Second Pianoforte Concerto under Klemperer. He very much regrets that there are so few *young* Hungarian composers coming to the fore, though he appreciates that the Second World War has probably been responsible for this. On the other hand, he is quite thrilled with the wealth of young creative talent that is now flourishing in England ; he thinks that William Walton, Constant Lambert, Benjamin Britten and Alan Rawsthorne, to mention only a few, are leading in a wonderful renascence of culture, while our older composers, Vaughan Williams and Bax for instance, have taken an important place in the history of music. Apart from its fine quality, their work is very English. There are more promising composers in England to-day, he declares, than in any other country in the world.

Louis Kentner has done a certain amount of composing himself—a set of three Sonatinas was published some time ago by the Oxford University Press and later adopted by various musical academies, including the Royal College of Music, for examination purposes. He is looking forward to the days when he will be able to devote a great deal more time than at present to composition.

When the Second World War was declared, Kentner, deprived of his Hungarian nationality, was one of those " Stateless " individuals, so he joined the Society of Free Hungarians in Britain. Keen to help the Allied war effort, he placed his services at the disposal of E.N.S.A. and made innumerable tours of military camps and factories. He discovered that the enthusiastic young audiences of Service men and women and factory workers were more willing to listen to unusual works than he had expected.

Unlike many of the other musicians with progressive views, he does not favour State subsidies for music, for he would be very sorry to see music getting mixed up with politics. His own early experiences have taught him that the life of the struggling musician is a hard one in this country, yet he feels that it is worth sacrificing a certain amount of security for the sake of independence. He is afraid that if musicians became servants of the State they would come under the control of officials without a sense of true artistry, and their work would be subject to criticisms from people who were their artistic inferiors.

On the teaching of his art, Louis Kentner has some strong views, although he has now become much more tolerant than in his early days of struggle. When I questioned him about technique he declared : " There is no such thing as *technique:* it is all a matter of feeling, rhythmical sense and sound musicianship." He believes that the pianist should subordinate himself completely to the composer whose work he is trying to interpret ; there should be no question of trying to display his own personality at the composer's expense. The pianist's task is to act as the medium between the composer and the audience, and in doing this he should associate himself with the composer's emotions so completely that he and the composer become as it were, indivisible. The pianist does not lose his own personality by doing this : it becomes quite apparent in the degree of his success or failure to fulfil the composer's purpose. Throughout his life, Kentner has been a great admirer of Dohnányi and Rachmaninoff.

Moiseiwitsch

HERE we come to another of the distinguished pianists who are carrying on the great work of Leschetizky. Benno Moiseiwitsch was born in the Russian city of Odessa on February 22nd, 1890. His musical talent was observed by his parents when he was very small, and they took steps to give him a sound musical education. He went to the Imperial Academy of Music at Odessa and became a pupil of Klomoff. At the age of nine he won the Rubinstein Prize.

In 1905 he was sent to Vienna to study with Leschetizky, and spent over three years with him. When he finished his training he came to England and made his first professional appearance in this country at the Town Hall, Reading, on October 1st, 1908. The success of this may be judged from the fact that in little more than a month he was making his London début at the Queen's Hall. This was followed by several seasons of concert work all over England, during which he earned the respect of all the leading critics. They wrote enthusiastically of his deep insight into the works of the great masters and generously praised the technique that Leschetizky had helped him to acquire.

It was not long before reports of this brilliant young Russian pianist spread to the other capitals of Europe, and he then began his continental tours. His first visit to America was in 1919, when he made his initial appearance at the Carnegie Hall, New York. Since then he has made well over a dozen tours through the United States and won the affection of millions of American music-lovers. W. J. Henderson described him as ". . . a pianist of enormous technical skill, and possessed of an affectionate feeling for music of a sentimental import." Another critic, J. G. Huneker, declared : " He is more than a technician, for he has brains and a soul as well as the fleetest of fingers. . . ."

It would be almost impossible to describe in detail all the other tours he has made in different parts of the globe. He has visited the music centres of South Africa twice, made three tours at least to South America, been all through Australia and New Zealand, and even played in China and Japan ! I don't think there is a single country in Europe that he has not visited.

In playing the works of Schumann, Moiseiwitsch has few equals anywhere in the world, and his great technical ability makes him an excellent exponent of Rachmaninoff, Liszt, Brahms, Scarlatti, Debussy, Ravel and

Stravinsky. He is also very interested in Prokofiev, and can interpret the works of this Soviet composer with great sympathy.

Moiseiwitsch is so sound and well-balanced a pianist that no particular quality in his playing stands out strikingly above another. He has great technical skill, as I have already said, yet he never tries to dazzle his listeners with it at the expense of anything else. His superb pianissimos are gently impressive, yet he never exaggerates them for the sake of effect. His fortes and fortissimos are grand and virile, but he never tries to court favour with the type of person who looks upon a concerto as a musical orgy for the destruction of a good instrument. His phrasing is as near perfect as one could wish, but he never does it with that " see-how-clever-I-am " air that one so often meets in the concert hall.

His interpretations are, on the whole, inclined towards boldness, but he is scrupulously careful in following the composer's directions, He gives a colourful performance, but without licence. I like, too, his general demeanour at the piano. His movements are restrained ; there is no fussiness, no affectation. I have often heard him play when he has seemed completely unaware of the presence of an audience. As far as I know he has no fads, and uses none of those little showman's tricks that delight the less intelligent section of the community.

He became a naturalized British subject in 1937, and although he hopes to return to Russia for a while very shortly, I think he will come back and spend the rest of his days in England. He is a most popular member of the Savage Club, that favourite rendezvous of so many of our leading musicians, and is a keen golfer. Although Russia is now very different from the country he knew as a boy, he is deeply interested in its welfare and aspirations, and that reminds me that he has recently given his hundredth recital in support of Mrs. Churchill's Aid to Russia Fund. Altogether, he has raised fifteen thousand pounds, for which Mr. Winston Churchill has thanked him personally. Official recognition came in the 1946 New Year's Honours List, which announced that he had been made a Companion of the Order of the British Empire.

Pouishnoff

THE reader will by now have observed that I am not the sort of person who rhapsodizes indiscriminately over the merits of individual pianists, but I must say that whenever I hear Pouishnoff playing Chopin I find it difficult to restrain myself from the use of superlatives. He seems to understand completely the very soul of Chopin, and unlike so many who attempt to play the immortal works of this composer, he can express what are commonly regarded as the effeminate traits without being saccharine in the process. There are few pianists to whom I listen with as much pleasure and satisfaction.

Leff Pouishnoff, like Moiseiwitsch, was born in Odessa, but a year or so later—on October 11th, 1891. When he was three years old he was given a violin because he always seemed quite enthralled whenever he heard stringed instruments being played. He immediately tried to play it, but was horrified at the distressing sounds he produced. Perseverance seemed to bring no reward, so eventually he smashed the instrument to pieces.

Then he tried the piano. Here, at least, one could pick out little melodies with one finger without causing groans and wails of protest. It was altogether a more docile affair. He also discovered that with a little care one could play two or three notes at once to make most agreeable chords. That was very exciting, and before long he had become completely captivated by the instrument. Every moment he could spare was spent at the keyboard ; he would even get up early so that he could enjoy a session before breakfast. In short, he had " piano-mania."

The next step was to teach himself to play from printed music. Difficult at first, but becoming progressively easier once you got the hang of it. Other people, it seemed, had thought of lots of chords he hadn't discovered. Exploring in the wonderland of music was great fun.

So by the time he was five years old, he could play quite a number of pleasant little pieces, and it was not long before he was able to give two concerts. He was certainly gifted with an uncommon aptitude for music, but his parents disliked the idea of exploiting him as an infant prodigy, and discouraged him from playing in public.

Soon after his ninth birthday, his father died, leaving the family in a precarious position financially. Tempting offers of engagements induced his mother to allow him to return to the concert platform, and within a year he had acquired quite a reputation as a boy pianist. Special arrangements were made so that he could continue his education at a local high school and at the same time give recitals regularly. His best subject at school, by the way, was chemistry ; a science that fascinated him for years.

In due course he proceeded to the St. Petersburg Conservatoire, where to his great delight he was permitted to study under such eminent musicians as Rimsky-Korsakoff, Liadov, Glazunov, Tcherepine and Madame Essipoff. He proved himself to be one of the most brilliant students of the day, and graduated in 1910 with first class honours, winning in addition the Gold Medal, the Rubinstein Prize and a cash award of over a hundred pounds.

With such a fine academic record he could have commanded high fees almost immediately from the impresarios, but he decided to take a holiday and make a musician's pilgrimage through various countries of Europe to study their music and become acquainted with their musicians. This, as one would imagine, broadened his outlook considerably, and gave him experience that proved of the greatest value when he started his concert tours in those countries.

Returning to Russia, he arranged to tour with Leopold Auer, the distinguished Hungarian violinist, giving joint recitals. When these came to an end, he went on another tour alone as a solo pianist, and made such a favourable impression upon the critics that he received many invitations to play in the greatest musical centres of Europe.

He was acquiring an international reputation when the Great War broke out and seriously impeded his progress. His short-sightedness secured exemption from military service, but he was obliged to confine his activities to his native land, so he spent most of his time playing in the military camps. Perhaps the most important feature of his work at that time was the series of concerts he gave to wounded and convalescent men in hospital.

The Revolution was far worse than the war, in fact it almost wrecked his career. The colossal upheaval affected everybody and brought about a tremendous amount of suffering even to those who had little sympathy for the nobility, so it can easily be understood that the people were in no mood for music. They were completely engulfed in the cataclysm. Pouishnoff experienced want and hunger for the first time in his life, yet he carried on, and later in 1919 was rewarded with the offer of a tour in Persia. He was the first prominent European pianist to make a tour in that country.

After this successful venture, he found that life in Russia had become quite intolerable and made plans to escape once and for all. One night he succeeded in slipping across the frontier and evading the guards, and then was able to make his way to Paris. He spent some time there but experienced greater difficulties than he had anticipated : the lack of any sort of regular income was a great handicap.

POUISHNOFF

In 1920 he arrived in London : twenty-nine years of age, with no money, no influence and few friends. Only a very small number of people here had even heard of him, so he had to start from the bottom and build up his career.

His first public performance here was on February 2nd, 1921 ; a recital that brought him the highest praise from our leading critics. Indeed, Ernest Newman said that he was one of twelve living pianists who could be called great. Then followed provincial tours in England and regular visits to most of the principal cities of France, Germany, Holland and Belgium.

One of Pouishnoff's greatest accomplishments, I think, was in the summer of 1926, when he gave a whole week of Chopin recitals—over seventy of the principal piano works of that great composer. This experiment was so widely appreciated that he repeated it during the following year.

By that time he had already made his début in New York. He was in America for the 1924-5 season, and again some twelve months later. Both of these visits were made for the purpose of touring the greater musical centres of the United States. Since then he has been all over the world.

Pouishnoff was one of the first pianists to broadcast, and in 1938 acquired the distinction of being the first to be televised. But the greatest distinction he will ever enjoy rests upon his superb interpretation of Chopin. His technique reveals a profoundly sensitive nature which enables him to make the most subtle gradations of tone. He brings out the wonderful colouring of Chopin with the delicacy of a great painter.

Solomon

THIS exceptionally gifted modern pianist had his first piano lessons when he was about four years of age, but it was not until he was seven that his parents became aware of his uncommon talent and arranged for him to embark upon a course of " serious " study.

Like many of our leading musicians, he is a Jew and is proud of it. He was born in London in 1902, and at the age of eight he made his first public appearance at the Queen's Hall. This was not at a Promenade concert as so many people seem to think, but at a special concert given by the Queen's Hall Orchestra. He played a Mozart Concerto in B-flat and the second movement of the Tschaikovsky Concerto in B-flat minor.

Shortly afterwards he had the honour of playing again in the same hall but this time under the conductorship of Sir Henry Wood, who was most favourably impressed by his performance of the Beethoven Concerto No. 3 and Liszt's *Hungarian Fantasy*. Solomon still recalls the feeling of awe that possessed him on these two memorable occasions, for he was deeply conscious of the great privilege he was enjoying.

There is little evidence to show that he was in any way " spoilt " by his amazingly early successes as a pianist, notwithstanding the number of boxes of chocolates and other tokens of admiration presented to him by friends and various sentimental old ladies. After one of his concerts there appeared on the platform a very fine tricycle that had been sent by one of his admirers. As soon as he saw it he forgot all about the applause which demanded a bow of acknowledgement: he immediately jumped on it and proudly rode off the platform, much to the delight of both audience and orchestra.

Solomon made his first tour when he was nine and played in all the larger towns of Great Britain with the London orchestras, the Hallé, Liverpool and Scottish Orchestras. Among the many famous conductors he played under were Weingartner, Nikisch, Sir Hamilton Harty and Sir Landon Ronald.

Because of the many tours he made in his childhood, his general education was somewhat erratic, though it was in no way neglected. Looking back over those early days, Solomon now realizes how much he owes to the encouragement and good advice of his father, a great lover of music, who with various interested friends, made it possible for him to study and to keep up with the incessant demand for concerts. During the early part of the

Great War, for instance, he appeared at ten Promenade concerts in one season, and played a different concerto at each.

When he was about fourteen he retired for a period of four or five years to devote himself to extensive study, first under Dr. Rumschisky of the Leschetizky school, and later in Paris. He considers that Rumschisky was one of the greatest teachers of the piano the world has ever known, and he remembers him with a sense of deep gratitude.

Solomon resumed his public engagements in October 1921 with a recital at the Wigmore Hall, London. Since then he has travelled in America, France, Italy, Germany and Holland, and has given recitals in every town of any size in Great Britain. In 1939 he journeyed to America to play for precisely thirty-five minutes! This was when he performed the Piano Concerto by Arthur Bliss which was commissioned by the British Council for the New York World Fair. Sir Adrian Boult conducted on this occasion.

One of the happiest tours he has ever made was when in October, 1943, he went to the Middle East and gave twenty-eight concerts in twenty-five days to the men and women of the forces in North Africa, Egypt, Palestine, Malta and Gibraltar. His programmes were made up largely of classics and modern works for the piano, and the audiences, packed almost to suffocation point, applauded with an enthusiasm that surpassed anything he had ever known before.

All the travelling on this tour was done by air : it was certainly a novelty to be playing in Cairo one evening and to be performing at Gibraltar, two thousand miles distant, on the next! He discovered that a night spent in an aeroplane was considerably more peaceful than some he spent in London during the war ; in fact, in making the journey to Gibraltar he was able to sleep quite soundly, and felt none the worse for his experience on the following day. " I had a sense of being completely exhilarated by those journeys in the air," he told me, " I was in splendid form the whole time, though of course the excitement might have had something to do with it."

One of his greatest joys during his tour of the Middle East came from playing with the Palestine Symphony Orchestra, which he found to be a really marvellous ensemble.

Solomon has given a great many concerts to factory workers and members of the Forces in this country under the auspices of E.N.S.A. When he goes to play for the men and women of the Services he is sometimes amused to find an officer waiting to see him before the concert to explain rather apologetically that " of course " the audience could not be expected to appreciate " highbrow " music, and to express a hope that he would overlook any lack of attention on their part. He has never yet found an audience of Service men and women lacking in appreciation : his greatest difficulty has always been to persuade them to let him go at the end of the recital ! " The response I get from the Services is really wonderful: it is profoundly gratifying to play for them." It was this that made him offer to accompany the allied troops in their invasion of Western Europe. He went over soon after the first landings were made, and spent many weeks in playing to men enjoying a short respite from the front lines.

In March, 1944, he played in the great concert held to celebrate the seventy-fifth birthday of the late Sir Henry Wood at the Albert Hall before the Queen, the two Princesses and a vast audience. During the interval, Solomon was presented to Her Majesty with Sir Henry Wood, Sir Adrian Boult and Basil Cameron, the conductors. The Queen expressed her appreciation of Solomon's performance and said that she remembered attending some of the concerts he gave as a small boy wearing a white lace collar!

When I discussed musical problems with him recently, Solomon expressed some concern about the standard of orchestral playing in this country, which owing to the fact that our orchestras are being lamentably overworked, is tending to deteriorate. The fault lies not in any lack of ability on the part of the instrumentalists, which he considers to be equal to any in the world, but in their exhausting activity. The majority are now playing, rehearsing and travelling for anything up to sixteen hours a day, and their fatigue is too often reflected in their performances. It seems such a pity that now the public are demanding first-class music they should be offered second-rate performances merely because the instrumentalists are either weary or have had insufficient rehearsal.

Solomon feels that the only solution to this problem is the provision of State grants to the orchestras so that they would not be obliged to overwork themselves in order to pay their way. For this reason, he would like to see a Ministry of Fine Arts set up, with the musical side of it entirely in the hands of responsible, knowledgeable musicians.

Such a ministry could then offer State grants to young musicians struggling for recognition. Solomon would like to see every young music student—composer or executant—given a grant as soon as he can prove that he possesses outstanding ability, so that he can be free to give himself wholly to his work without being tormented by the anxiety of having to earn money by the prostitution of his art in the field of what is commonly called "swing." It should of course be understood that grants could be given only to those who amply justify assistance, and they should be continued only as long as the recipient provides evidence of diligent work. Under no circumstances should such grants be acquired too easily. Solomon has found that success cannot be achieved without really hard work, and would deplore any system of grants that gave the impression that a musician's life is an easy one.

SOLOMON

His own success he attributes to innumerable hours of dogged practice and to acute listening. His advice to young pianists is : " Work hard and develop sensitive ears. Be certain that the sounds you produce are those you really want." When the cost of making private gramophone records comes down again, Solomon thinks it would be advisable for piano teachers occasionally to make records of their pupils' work, so that they can be played back to the students afterwards. The pupils would get many surprises, and the majority would be of an unpleasant variety.

For all piano students Solomon recommends " a good grounding in the classics, particularly Bach and Chopin, before any attempt is made to play modern music."

Solomon is a bachelor. His recreations are driving his car in the country, golf, cards and reading. He thinks that golf is an excellent game, but knows that he will never make a good player. When I asked him what his handicap was he replied : " The clubs and the ball." At bridge and poker he is rather better.

He reads an amazing variety of books, fiction and otherwise : in fact he can find something of interest in almost any book unless it is an extremely indigestible technical work. The use of that adjective reminds me that he never takes a meal before a concert because he finds that " nerves " and food do not make a happy combination. But, he assures me, he makes up for it afterwards.

So many people are curious about Solomon's name that I had better explain that he *does* possess another name, but never uses it. Throughout his career he has always refused to acquaint people with his surname, and therefore I see no reason for offending him by divulging it here.

BIBLIOGRAPHY

The following are the principal works consulted in the preparation of this volume, and are commended to those who wish to make a further study of the subject. To the authors and publishers, as well as to all others who have helped him in collecting the material for this book, the author is deeply grateful.

J. S. Bach. J. A. P. SPITTA (Novello).
J. S. Bach. ALBERT SCHWEITZER (Black).
Bach. C. S. TERRY (Oxford University Press).
Bach. C. H. H. PARRY (Putnam).
J. S. Bach. J. N. FORKEL (Constable).
Dr. John Bull. HENRY LEIGH (Joseph).
Ferruccio Busoni. E. J. DENT (Oxford University Press).
Chopin. H. C. HADDEN (Dent).
Frederic Chopin. M. KARASOWSKI (Reeves).
Chopin. BASIL MAINE (Duckworth).
Chopin. W. MURDOCH (Murray).
Frederick Chopin : Man and Musician. F. NIECKS (Novello).
Chopin : Man of Solitude. GUY DE POURTALÈS (Butterworth).
From Piano to Forte. M. HAMBOURG (Cassell).
Theodor Leschetizky. A. HULLAH (Lane).
Liszt. F. CORDER (Kegan Paul).
Franz Liszt and his Music. A. HERVEY (Lane).
Liszt. RALPH HILL (Duckworth).
Franz Liszt. J. GIBBONS HUNEKER (Chapman & Hall).
The Man Liszt. E. NEWMAN (Cassell).
Liszt. SACHEVERELL SITWELL (Faber).
Mozart. E. BLOM (Dent).
Mozart. ANNETTE KOLB (Gollancz).
Mozart. MARCIA DAVENPORT (Heinemann).
Mozart. F. GEHRING (Sampson Low).
Life of Mozart. E. HOLMES (Dent).
Life of Mozart. OTTO JAHN (Novello).
Mozart : the Man and his Works. W. J. TURNER (Gollancz).
Mozart. J. E. TALBOT (Duckworth).
Mozart. V. WILDER (Reeves).
Ignaz Jan Paderewski. E. A. BAUGHAN (Lane).
Paderewski. ROM LANDAU (Nicholson & Watson).
Paderewski : the Story of a Modern Immortal. C. PHILLIPS (Macmillan).
The Paderewski Memoirs. I. J. PADEREWSKI and MARY LAWTON (Collins).
Recollections : Rachmaninov. OSKAR VON REISEMANN (Allen & Unwin).
Autobiography. ANTON RUBINSTEIN. (Sampson Low).
Anton Rubinstein. A. MACARTHUR (Black).
A Background for Domenico Scarlatti. SACHEVERELL SITWELL (Faber).
Clara Schumann. B. LITZMANN (Macmillan).

051660